The *Eucharistic Epiclesis*

A Detailed History from the Patristic to the Modern Era

Second Edition

D1566729

John H. McKenna, CM

HillenbrandBooks

Chicago / Mundelein, Illinois

In accordance with c. 827, permission to publish is granted on October 21, 2008 by the Very Reverend John F. Canary, Vicar General of the Archdiocese of Chicago. Permission to publish is an official declaration of ecclesiastical authority that the material is free from doctrinal and moral error. No implication is contained therein that those who have granted it agree with the content, opinions, or statements expressed in the work; nor do they assume any legal responsibility associated with publication.

Originally published as part of the Alcuin Club Collection No. 57, as *Eucharist and the Holy Spirit: The Eucharistic Epiclesis and Twentieth Century Theology (1900–1966)*. Published by Mayhew-McCrimmon for the Alcuin Club. First Edition Copyright © 1975 by John H. McKenna. All rights reserved. Used with permission.

Chapter 9, "The Epiclesis Revisited" is a revised version of an article originally published in *Ephemerides Liturgicae* 99 (Nos. 4–5, 1985) 314–336. Used with permission.

THE EUCHARISTIC EPICLESIS: A DETAILED HISTORY FROM THE PATRISTIC TO THE MODERN ERA, SECOND EDITION © 2009 Archdiocese of Chicago: Liturgy Training Publications, 3949 South Racine Avenue, Chicago IL 60609; 1-800-933-1800, fax 1-800-933-7094, e-mail orders@ltp.org. All rights reserved. See our Web site at www.LTP.org.

Hillenbrand Books is an imprint of Liturgy Training Publications (LTP) and the Liturgical Institute at the University of Saint Mary of the Lake (USML). The imprint is focused on contemporary and classical theological thought concerning the liturgy of the Catholic Church. Available at bookstores everywhere, through LTP by calling 1-800-933-1800, or visiting www.LTP. org. Further information about the **Hillenbrand Books** publishing program is available from the University of Saint Mary of the Lake/Mundelein Seminary, 1000 East Maple Avenue, Mundelein, IL 60060 (847-837-4542), on the web at www.usml.edu/liturgicalinstitute, or e-mail litinst@usml.edu.

Cover photo © The Crosiers/Gene Plaisted, osc

Printed in the United States of America.

Library of Congress Control Number: 2008936780

ISBN 978-1-59525-025-4

HEE

To

my mother and father

who showed me God's love

long before I could think of the how and why of it.

Contents

Abbreviations

AAS	*Acta Apostolicae Sedis* (Rome, 1909 ff.).
ALW	*Archiv für Liturgiewissenschaft* (formerly *JLW*) (Regensburg, 1950 ff.).
BLE	*Bulletin de littérature ecclésiastique* (Toulouse, 1899 ff.).
BTAM	*Bulletin de Théologie Ancienne et Médiévale* (Louvain, 1929 ff.).
CCL	*Corpus Christianorum* (series Latina) (Turnhout, 1953 ff.).
CL	*Collectio Lacensis: Acta et Decreta sacrorum conciliorum recentiorum*, edited by the Jesuits of Maria Laach, 7 vols. (Freiburg i. Br., 1870—1890).
CSEL	*Corpus scriptorium ecclesiasticorum latinorum* (Vienna, 1866 ff.).
DACL	F. Cabrol, H. Leclercq (and H. Marrou) (eds.), *Dictionnaire d'archéologie chrétienne et de liturgie*, 30 vols. (Paris, 1907—1953).
DS	H. Denziger-A. Schönmetzer (eds.), *Enchiridion Symbolorum* (Freiburg i. Br., 1953).
DT	*Divus Thomas.* Commentarium de Philosophia et Theologia. (Piacenza, 1880 ff.).
DThC	A. Vacant, E. Mangenot, and E. Amann (eds.), *Dictionnaire de théologie catholique*, 15 vols. + Tables générales (Paris, 1930 ff.).
ECQ	*The Eastern Churches Quarterly* (Ramsgate, 1936 ff.).
EL	*Ephemerides Liturgicae* (Rome, 1887 ff.).
EO	*Echos d'Orient* (Paris, 1897 ff.).
ERE	J. Hastings (ed.), *Encyclopaedia of Religion and Ethics*, 12 vols. + one Index vol. (Edinburgh, 1908–1926, reprint 1925–40).
ETL	*Epherimerides Theologicae Lovanienses* (Bruges, 1924 ff.).
FC	J. Deferrari, *et al.* (eds.), *The Fathers of the Church* (New York, 1947–60, Washington, 1961–).

GCS   *Die griechischen christlichen Schriftsteller der ersten drei Jahrhunderte*
          (Leipzig, 1897 ff.).

HTR   *The Harvard Theological Review* (Cambridge, Mass., 1908 ff.).

JLW   *Jahrbuch für Liturgiewissenschaft,* 15 vols. (Münster, 1921–41—
          now *ALW).*

JTS   *The Journal of Theological Studies* (London, 1899 ff.).

LThK   J. Höfer and K. Rahner (eds.), *Lexikon für Theologie and Kirche,*
          10 vols. + Register (Freiburg i. Br., 1957–1965).

LW   L. Brinkhoff *et al.* (eds.), *Liturgisch Woordenboek,* 2 vols.
          (Roermond en Maaseik, 1958–68).

MANSI   J. D. Mansi (ed.), *Sacrorum conciliorum nova et amplissima collectio,*
          31 vols. (Florence-Venice, 1757–98); reprint and continuation
          edited by L. Petit and J. B. Martin, 60 vols. (Paris 1899–1927).

MD   *La Maison Dieu* (Paris, 1945 ff.).

MELV   J. Quasten (ed.), *Monumenta eucharistica et liturgica vetustissima*
          (= *Florilegium Patristicum* 7) (Bonn, 1935–37).

MSR   *Mélanges de science religieuse* (Lille, 1944 ff.).

OC   *Oriens Christianus* (Leipzig) (Wiesbaden, 1901 ff.).

O.Chr.P. *Orientalia Christiana Periodica* (Rome, 1935 ff.).

Or.Chr.A. *Orientalia Christiana (Analecta)* (Rome, 1923–24 = *Orientalia
          Christiana;* 1935 ff. = *Orientalia Christiana Analecta).*

OS   *L'Orient syrien* (Paris, 1956 ff.).

PE   Anton Hänggi-Irmgard Pahl (eds.), *Prex Eucharistica*
          (Fribourg, 1968).

PG   J. P. Migne (ed.), *Patrologia Graeca,* 161 vols. (Paris, 1857–66).

PL   J. P. Migne (ed.), *Patrologia Latina,* 217 vols. + four Register
          vols. (Paris, 1844–64).

QLP   *Questions liturgiques et paroissiales* (Louvain, 1921 ff.).

RAC   Theodor Klauser (ed.), *Reallexikon für Antike und Christentum*
           (Stuttgart, 1941 [1950] ff.).

REM   *Revue des études byzantines* (Paris, 1946 ff.).

RSPT   *Revue des sciences philosophiques et théologiques* (Paris, 1907 ff.).

RTAM   *Recherches de théologie ancienne et médiévale* (Louvain, 1929 ff.).

SC   H. de Lubac and J. Daniélou (eds.), *Sources chrétiennes*
           (Paris, 1941 ff.).

SE   *Sacris Erudiri.* Jaarboek voor Godsdienstwetenschapen
           (Bruges, 1948 ff.).

SH   E. Schillebeeckx, *De sacramentele Heilseconomie* (Antwerp, 1952).

ST   Thomas Aquinas, *Summa Theologiae.* Editio Piana (Ottawa,
           1953).

SVNC   A. Mai, *Scriptorum veterum nova collection e vaticanis codicibus
           edita,* 10 vols. (Rome, 1825—38).

TPQS   *Theologisch-praktische Quartalschrift* (Linz on D., 1848 ff.).

TQS   *Theologische Quartalschrift* (Tübingen, 1929 ff.).

TWNT   G. Kittel-G. Friedrich (eds.), *Theologisches Wörterbuch zum
           Neuen Testament* (Stuttgart, 1933 ff.).

ZKT   *Zeitschrift für Katholische Theologie* (Innsbruck) (Wien, 1877 ff.).

Glossary of Technical Terms

We have decided that it would be helpful to the reader to provide a brief, *preliminary* glossary of terminology that occurs often in the course of the following chapters. Our use, however, of terms such as "consecratory epiclesis," "consecration," and "real presence" in the sense given below merely reflects current usage. It is not intended as a judgment on our part of the theological correctness or desirability of such expressions. We shall attempt to deal with that aspect in Part III.

eucharistic prayer—anaphora—canon: We have used these terms interchangeably to indicate that part of the eucharistic celebration which extends from the opening dialogue (of the *Sursum Corda*) to the great doxology preceding the Our Father.

logos epiclesis: An epiclesis or invocation that appeals for the Logos.

spirit epiclesis: An epiclesis that appeals for the Holy Spirit.

epiclesis of sanctification: An epiclesis that appeals for the sanctification of the bread and wine and/or the faithful.

consecratory epiclesis: An epiclesis that appeals for the transformation of the bread and wine into Christ's body and blood.

epiclesis proper or epiclesis in the strict sense: An epiclesis that appeals for the *Holy Spirit* (occasionally, the Logos) to transform or sanctify the bread and wine and/or to sanctify the faithful who partake of these gifts.

Epiclesis: We have adopted this form to indicate the notion, closely associated with the name of Odo Casel, of the whole anaphora as an epiclesis. For a more detailed examination of Casel's terminology, cf. chapter 4, n. 31.

consecration: The transformation of the bread and wine into the body and blood of Christ.

real presence: The presence of Christ in the bread and wine after the "consecration."

paschal mystery: The death, Resurrection, and Ascension of Christ seen as his "passover" through death to a new life with the Father in the Holy Spirit. Pentecost forms the seal and crown of this mystery which is a theological unity.

hylomorphism (hylomorphic theory): The word comes from the Greek *hylē* (matter) and *morphē* (form) and is used to describe the Aristotelian-Scholastic teaching that all natural or physical bodies are composed of two essential principles, one of which is indeterminate, passive, purely potential (matter) and the other determining, actualizing (form). Scholastic and Roman Catholic theologians have often used this theory to explain such things as the relationship of body and soul, the relationship of words and elements in the sacraments, etc.

transubstantiation: Literally, the change or conversion of one substance into another. In Scholastic circles, it is the explanation of Christ's presence in the Eucharist by the substance of Christ's body and blood replacing the substance of the bread and wine. According to this view, the appearances or "accidents" of bread and wine remain and are supported by the substance of Christ's body and blood.

Introduction to the First Edition

In an excellent study of the Holy Spirit and the Eucharist, J.M. Tillard in 1968 remarked that the epiclesis question is a very secondary one which often tends to stifle theological reflection and make us myopic in regard to the Holy Spirit and the Eucharist.[1] On the other hand, Edmund Bishop, one of the greatest liturgical scholars living at the turn of the twentieth century, insisted that the epiclesis lay at the heart of matters liturgical.[2] More recently Lukas Vischer proclaimed the epiclesis question to be of key importance to the ecumenical dialogue on the Eucharist[3] and Orthodox theologian Paul Evdokimov cited the question of the epiclesis as methodologically even more important than that of the *filioque* in this same ecumenical dialogue.[4] What is the basis of what at first glance appears to be a flat contradiction between Tillard's view and that of the others? Who is right? Hopefully the following study will shed some light on the significance of the eucharistic epiclesis and thereby provide an answer to these questions.

The primary aim of this study is to examine what twentieth-century writers have had to say about the eucharistic epiclesis. By so doing we hope to arrive at a better understanding of the theology of the epiclesis. The main interest within the primary target range is, then, theological. A healthy theology must rest on solid historical and liturgical foundations. An attempt has therefore been made to take into account and to respect the data of historical studies and liturgical texts. The author approaches the epiclesis, however, not as an historian but as a theologian and has tried to heed Dom Bernard Botte's rather pointed reminder "Que chacun fasse son métier, et les vaches seront bien gardées."[5]

In the attempt, therefore, to blend the theological with the historical and liturgical data we have relied to a great extent on the

---

1. Tillard, "L'Eucharistie et le Saint-Esprit," 387, 379, 364.

2. Cf. Bishop, "Notes . . . VIII," 39 Abercrombie, 252, 378–79.

3. Vischer, "Epiklese, Zeichen der Einheit, der Erneuerung und des Aufbruchs," 302–312.

4. Evdokimov, "Eucharistie . . . ," 62 n. 33.

5. Botte, "A propos de la 'Tradition Apostolique,'" 186.

findings of experts, e.g., in textual and historical studies. This approach seems both justifiable and necessary. Nevertheless, it goes without saying that, in disputed points and in areas basic to the theological conclusions of twentieth-century writers as well as to our own theological conclusions, we have had recourse to the texts themselves.

Some temporal limitation was obviously necessary to make a study of the eucharistic epiclesis workable. The year 1900 was set as the early limit because important text studies that appeared around this time led to a number of significant insights in regard to the epiclesis question. The identification and dating of *The Apostolic Tradition* of Hippolytus and the discovery of the Dêr Balyzeh fragments are two cases in point. Moreover, after this date the liturgical and ecumenical movements bore increasing fruit and created an atmosphere which has had considerable consequences for the study of the epiclesis question. At the same time, the "older mentality" in regard to the epiclesis question is still visible. This enables one to see where one is coming from as well as where one hopes to go on this question.

In choosing 1966 as a final date, we sought to avoid entering into a "new era" of theological speculation on the eucharistic epiclesis. This era opened with the introduction of epiclesis into the new eucharistic prayers of the Roman Catholic tradition, a fact which has given rise to a new speculation and an ever increasing bibliography on these eucharistic prayers and their epiclesis. Although we shall at times refer to works outside this period, the main object of our study remains the works written within these limits.

We have limited ourselves here to twentieth-century works appearing in Latin, German, French, or English. Schillebeeckx's *Da sacramentele Heilseconomie* (Antwerp, 1952) forms an important exception to this rule. It does so because it contains a number of sections important for the epiclesis question and because, through the courtesy of Herr Hugo Zulauf, it was possible to obtain an unpublished German translation of these sections.

We have tried to cover all the works in the period under consideration that deal directly with the eucharistic epiclesis and to make a fairly comprehensive coverage of Roman Catholic works on the Eucharist in so far as they touch upon the eucharistic epiclesis. In addition, an attempt to examine the major works on the Eucharist in the Anglican, Calvinist, Lutheran and Orthodox traditions, in so far as these touch upon our theme, seemed indispensable, we were forced to rely on those familiar with these traditions in forming a bibliography. In this connection thanks are due to Fr. Louis Weil, an Anglican liturgist who was a teacher at Nashotah House Seminary, Nashotah, Wisconsin; Abbot Laurentius Klein, who was one of the moving forces behind the Anglican Institute at Sankt Matthias Abbey, Trier, and also was very engaged in ecumenical work in Jerusalem, Fr. Max Thurian of Taizé, Prof. J. J. von Allmen, Rev. Reinhard Groscurth, and Prof. Nikos Nissiotis of the World Council of Churches Secretariat on Faith and Order and the World Council of Churches Ecumenical Institute respectively, and especially Fr. Boris Bobrinskoy, St. Serge Institute for Orthodox Theology, Paris, for his continuing assistance and encouragement. The responsibility for any shortcomings in the treatment of these traditions remains, of course, the author's.

The first part of this study puts the twentieth-century writings on the eucharistic epiclesis into perspective by presenting the liturgical data and historical background that form the historical heritage of these writings. The appearance of a collection of texts selected from ancient liturgies and published in A. Hänggi and I. Pahl (eds.), *Prex Eucharistica* (Fribourg, 1968) has simplified the task of presenting the liturgical data (Chapter 1). In most cases we have followed the judgment expressed in this work for the selection of texts. Next comes a brief history of the epiclesis question, especially of its entanglement with the "moment of consecration" problem, an entanglement continuing into the twentieth century (Chapter 2).

Part II contains a systematic presentation of twentieth-century writings on the eucharistic epiclesis. After a brief treatment of the twentieth-century terminology in regard to the epiclesis (Chapter 3), Part II outlines the various reconstructions of the history of the eucharistic epiclesis that twentieth-century writers have suggested (Chapter 4) and then sketches the various theological explanations which they have proposed, (Chapter 5). After that, twentieth-century treatments of the epiclesis in relation to the "substance of the sacrament," to the praying, believing assembly and to the Holy Spirit are dealt with (Chapter 6).

The Part III of this study attempts to form a synthesis and to come to grips with some of the more important problems connected with the epiclesis question. This involves once again having to deal with the "moment of consecration," a problem which has plagued the epiclesis question for centuries (Chapter 7). To end the study an attempt is made to put into proper perspective some of the problems which have cropped up in conjunction with the relation of the epiclesis to the praying, believing assembly and to the Holy Spirit (Chapter 8).

A special word of thanks is due to Prof. Wilhelm Breuning of formerly of Bonn University and Prof. Balthasar Fischer, former Director of the Liturgical Institute in Trier, who have provided not only the scholarly guidance necessary for this work but also friendships which were among its richest rewards. Hopefully, the study which follows will shed some light on the apparent contradiction between the views of Tillard and Bishop, Vischer and Evdokimov as to the value of examining the epiclesis question. It is hoped, too, this study will reflect the sharing of insights made possible by an atmosphere of increasing ecumenism and, in some small way, will also reflect the fruit of such a sharing.

Introduction to the Second Edition

The first edition of *Eucharist and the Holy Spirit* was published in 1975 for the Alcuin Club (UK) as part of their highly-regarded Alcuin Club Collections series. It was very well received at the time. I was asked by Hillenbrand Books to revise and update the work, and knowing that some development has continued on the history and significance of the epiclesis, I am pleased to make this revised edition available to a new audience. Some of the issues that I treated in the first edition continue to be debated today on both the popular and scholarly levels.[1] As with the first edition, the primary aim of this study is to examine what twentieth-century writers have had to say about the eucharistic epiclesis. By so doing, we hope to arrive at a better understanding of the theology of the epiclesis.

By examining the theology of the epiclesis, I expect the reader to come away from this book with a new appreciation of the profound activity of the Holy Spirit in the Holy Sacrifice of the Eucharist.

Perhaps the most dramatic development since the publication of the first edition is an agreement ratified by the Vatican that acknowledges the ancient eucharistic prayer of Addai and Mari as valid and legitimate, despite the absence of an explicit institution narrative.[2] This fact would seem to support my findings that the moment of consecration was not an issue of concern for the early Christian writers (Chapter 2), that the "substance of the sacrament" was not a specific form but gestures and words that the Church's faith at a given time judged suitable (Chapter 6). I include a rather extensive treatment of the "moment of consecration" discussion (Chapter 7).

---

1. See, for instance, Mark Plaiss, "This, Too, Is My Body: When Does the Consecration Happen?" *Commonweal* 133/10 (May 19, 2006) and Paul Bradshaw, *The Search of the Origins of Christian Worship*, Second Edition (Oxford: University Press 2002), 131, who suggests that Louis Ligier's position on the origin of the institution narrative may be biased by the debate over the moment of consecration or the consecratory force of the institution narrative.

2. See Robert Taft, "Mass without the Consecration? The Historic Agreement between the Catholic Church and the Assyrian Church of the East Promulgated 26 October 2001," *Worship* 77 (Nov. 2003) 482–509. Taft, in an article that deserves more recognition, notes that there is a scholarly consensus that the prayer did not contain an explicit institution narrative.

I have updated and expanded footnotes, for instance, in regard to the ever-current topic of the force of the institution narrative. I have added recent English texts and commentaries on the early eucharistic prayers and included recent debate on such key texts as the *Apostolic Tradition* in the new Chapter 9. I have also provided charts and commentaries on the content and positioning of the invocation of the Holy Spirit (epiclesis) in modern Catholic and Protestant eucharistic prayers.

It has been a labor of love. In the midst of the complexity of issues, I have rediscovered the beauty of the Eucharist that, like a beautiful diamond, has many facets. I hope my readers will discover the many facets, too.

Part I

The Historical Heritage

Chapter 1

The Epiclesis in Early Liturgical Texts

The data of the early liturgical texts form a necessary basis of interpretation for scholars in search of a theology of the epiclesis. It is, moreover, necessary to approach these texts with an open mind. As long as one comes to them persuaded that one knows what a proper eucharistic epiclesis is or what it should be, one runs the risk of forcing the data into molds of one's own making.[1]

It is, however, easier to denounce the fallacy than to avoid it. The fragmentary nature of the documents makes it extremely difficult, if not impossible, to form a solid, purely objective, genetic study or reconstruction of the primitive forms of the eucharistic prayer. As Bouyer puts it, "There are too many gaps, and the worst thing is that the further back we go, the more numerous and the wider they are, so that we cannot avoid hypotheses or mere guesses."[2]

As true as this may be, the theologian still has the task of trying to control these "hypotheses" and "guesses" on the basis of the available liturgical texts. The purpose of this chapter is to examine a number of the most important texts that twentieth-century scholars used, or failed to use, in forming their theories about the eucharistic epiclesis. Only by viewing them against the background of the available textual evidence will the theologian, in our opinion, be in a position to judge the success or lack of success, the probability or improbability of these theories.

Therefore, after a brief sketch of possible forerunners of the developed epiclesis, we shall examine the more developed epiclesis as

---

1. Cf. Bouyer, "The Different Forms . . . ," 158.
2. Ibid.

found in the early anaphoras. We shall seek to situate the epiclesis by giving the structure and some general characteristics of the liturgical "family" or type to which the anaphora belongs and the context of the epiclesis within each anaphora. Then we shall present the text of the epiclesis and a brief analysis of the text, noting: the addressee, the person or thing called *for* (Logos, Spirit, etc.), the verb used to describe the *coming*, the verb used to describe the *effect* of the coming and the presence or absence of an appeal related to those partaking in the Eucharist.

In this way we hope to provide a partial basis for judging the relative merits of some of the theories put forward on the eucharistic epiclesis.

Possible Forerunners of the Developed Epiclesis

It is interesting to note that specific New Testament texts have received relatively little attention as possible bases of the developed epiclesis. Hebrews 9:14, ". . . how much more effectively the blood of Christ, who through the eternal Spirit offered himself (διὰ πνεύ ματος αἰωνίου ἑαυτὸν προσήνεγκεν) unblemished to God . . ."; John 15–17 (the farewell discourse) and Luke 1:35 (cf. Matthew 1:18, 20), "The Holy Spirit will come upon you (πνεῦμα ἅγιον ἐπελεύ σεται ἐπί σέ) and the power of the Most High will overshadow you; and for that reason the holy child to be born will be called 'Son of God'"; as well as John 6:63, "The spirit alone gives life (τὸ πνεῦμά ἐστιν τὸ ζωοποιῦν)"[3] have come under consideration in this regard.

The expression *Maranatha* from 1 Corinthians 16:22[4] has drawn a good bit of attention to itself. Some authors would see in this expression a "*Christus-epiklese*" and an ancestor of the developed epiclesis.[5]

---

3. Cf., for instance, Salaville, "Les fondements scripturaires . . . ," 5–14 and the same author's "L'épiclèse eucharistique," 222–24. Brunner, "Zur Lehre vom Gottesdienst . . . ," 354 n. 370. For Hebrews 9:14, we have used the New American Bible Translation. Elsewhere, unless otherwise indicated, we shall use the New English Bible translation.

4. Cf. also Apocalypse 22:17, 20 and Didache 10:6.

5. Cf. Stählin, "Der Herr ist Geist," 51, 54 and in the same work Ritter, "Bemerkungen zur eucharistischen Epiklese," 167. Cf. also Goldammer, 15; Betz, *Die Eucharistie . . . ,* 334, says of this expression in Didache 10:6 that it is at least the starting point for a fully developed epiclesis.

The Scriptures have also been brought to bear on the question of the primitive meaning of the word *epiclesis,* but we shall go into that question in more detail in Part Two of this volume.[6]

Another area which has rightly received more attention recently in connection with the epiclesis is the Jewish *berakoth* formulas. A number of studies have traced the broad lines of the *berakah* and have pointed out how the *berakah-anamnesis* often unfolds into supplication or prayer.[7] The opening addresses of the Pauline epistles have been proposed as illustrations of this movement.[8]

Noteworthy in this context are also the general attempts to link the Jewish concept of the divine *Shekinah,* or the divine presence, with the epiclesis. Oesterly, for instance, contends "The conception of the *Shekinah,* familiar as it was to all Jews, would have been the obvious one to suggest a prayer for the sanctification of the worshippers, gathered together in the name of God, by means of the descent of the Divine Spirit upon them."[9] Thus he concludes ". . . It may be reasonably maintained that from the beginning what was later known as the *Epiclesis* was in its essence a prayer for the Divine Presence among the worshippers during their most solemn act of worship."[10]

Perhaps even more significant than these general probes are recent attempts to trace in detail the link between the elements of the

---

Ligier, *Magnae* . . . , 155–57, 162 also includes further bibliography and Dinesen, 75–76 n. 28, cites several other authors who hold that *Maranatha* was a forerunner of the epiclesis. Dinesen himself (76–80) opposes this view.

6. For now the reader may refer to O. Casel, *Das christliche Opfermysterium,* 499–504 and K. L. Schmidt, ἐπικαλέω TWNT 3 (1938), 498–501 as examples.

7. Cf., for instance, J. P. Audet, "Esquisse historique de genre litteraire de la 'bénédiction' juive et de l' 'eucharistie' chrétienne," Revue Biblique 15 (1958), 380–81 and the same author's "Literary Forms and Contents of a Normal 'Eucharistia' in the First Century," in The Gospels Reconsidered (Oxford, 1960) 35, and "Genre litteraire et formes culturelles de l'Eucharistie. 'Nova et vetera,'" EL 80 (1966), 358, 368, 383–84. Cf. R. Ledogar, Acknowledgment (Rome, 1968), 165–67 and the same author's "The Eucharistic Prayer . . . ," 582–86, 596 for some necessary precisions on Audet's thought as expressed in these articles. For more recent treatments, see John H. McKenna, "From 'Berakah' to 'Eucharistia' to Thomas Talley and Beyond," Proceedings of the North American Academy of Liturgy 1995 87–99 and Bradshaw, The Search . . . , 23–46, 118–143.

8. Cf. Bouyer, *Eucharistie* (Paris, 1966[1]), 110–116 (106–113). We shall give in parentheses the page numbers of the English translation based on the *second* French edition (1968) which has appeared under the title *Eucharist* (Notre Dame, 1968). In general we have followed the spelling of this English edition for the transliteration of Hebrew terms.

9. Oesterley, 228–29; cf. 223–28.

10. Ibid., 217–218; cf. 219. Cf. also Kretschmar, 188 n. 6; Dix, *The Shape* . . . , 182–85 and Ligier, *Magnae* . . . , 155.

berakoth and those of the anaphora, including the epiclesis. Especially interesting is the claim that among the meal *berakoth* (*berakoth ha-mazon*) the supplication (*berakah rahem*) together with its embolism (the *ya'aleh we-yabho*) formed the basic model for the Christian eucharistic epiclesis.

The text referred to reads:

> Have mercy, Yahweh, our God, on your people Israel, on your city Jerusalem, on Zion, the dwelling place of your glory, on the kingdom of the house of David your servant, and on the great and holy house upon which your name is invoked. Feed us, nourish us, sustain us, provide for us, relieve us speedily from our anxieties, and let us not stand in need of the gifts of mortals, for their gifts are small and their reproach is great, for we have trusted in your holy, great and fearful name. And may Elijah and the Messiah, the son of David, come in our life-time, and restore the kingdom of the house of David to its place, and reign over us, you alone, and save us for your name's sake. And bring us up in it and gladden us in it and comfort us in Zion your city.

And on special feasts the following is added here:

> Our God, and the God of our fathers, may our memorial and the memorial of our fathers and the memorial of the Messiah, the son of David, your servant, and the memorial of your holy city Jerusalem and the memorial of your people, the whole house of Israel, arise and come (ya'aley we-yabho), come to pass, be seen and accepted and heard, be remembered and be mentioned before you for deliverance, for good, for living kindness and for mercy on this Passover feast. Remember us on this day, Yahweh, our God, for good and visit us on this day for blessing and save us on this day unto life. And by a word of salvation and mercy, spare, favor us and show us mercy, for our eyes look to you, for you are a gracious and merciful God and King.

> Blessed be you, Yahweh, who rebuild Jerusalem. Amen.[11]

The early Christians, according to one theory, adapted this form to fit the memorial, eschatological character of the Eucharist.[12]

According to this same hypothesis another *berakah* text, the *berakah Avodah* from the so-called eighteen blessings (the *Shemoneh*

---

11. PE, 11–12, 27. Cf. also 51. The English translation is adapted from D. Hedegard, *Seder R. Amram Gaon* I (Lund, 1951) 147 ff. For more recent translations of Jewish prayers see Jasper-Cumings, 7–12.

12. Cf. Ligier, "De la Cène . . . ," 36, 42–44.

Esreh) also eventually came to play a role in the formation of the epiclesis. One version of this prayer reads:

> Be favorable, Yahweh, our God, to your people Israel (cf. Psalm 149:4), heed their prayer and restore the service to the Holy of Holies of your house, and readily accept in love and favor the fiery offerings of Israel and their prayer, and may the service of your people Israel ever be acceptable to you, and let our eyes behold you returning to Zion.[13]

In the course of time, the Christians coupled the contents of this prayer, with its sacrificial theme, to the supplication stemming from the paschal meal *berakoth*. With the adoption of this sacrificial element the primitive significance of the epiclesis thus underwent a transformation.[14]

L. Ligier, one of the most articulate proponents of this hypothesis, hastens to add, however, that the Church never lost sight of the basic signification of this prayer, the restoration and gathering together of the people of God around the *Shekinah* or divine presence.[15]

Precisely because the relationship between elements of the Jewish *berakoth* and the developed epiclesis is such a fascinating possibility, a certain reserve seems in order here. Parallels do not necessarily mean dependence, and a detailed hypothesis in this area is difficult to control on the basis of the data now available to us.[16] Further in-depth studies of these texts in relation to the epiclesis would be most welcome.

A similar reserve seems called for when treating possible forerunners to the developed epiclesis as they appear in *Didache* 9:4 (cf. 10:5), "Just as this bread which we break, once scattered over the hills has been gathered and made one, so may your Church too be assembled from the ends of the earth into your kingdom;" and 10:6,

---

13 PE, 50–51 (the English translation adapted from Hedegard, 96–97).

14. Cf. Ligier, "De la Cène . . . ," 36, 44–45.

15. Ibid., 46.

16. Ligier's theory on the relationship between *berakah* and epiclesis is rather close to that of L. Bouyer in *Eucharisite* 175–76 (176–77), 183–84 (183–84), 300–304 (310–314) and in "The Different Forms . . . ," 164–69. We shall see Bouyer's hypothesis in more detail later on in our study. For the moment, however, it would be well to note the words of caution that experts like Botte and Jungmann offer in regard to Bouyer's thesis. Botte, reviewing the first edition of *Eucharistie* in QLP 48 (1967), 173, remarks that it is very difficult to control a detailed hypothesis such as Bouyer's with the data now available to us. Jungmann reviewing *Eucharistie* in ZKT 89 (1967), esp. 460, 466, offers a similar critique.

"May grace ['the Lord' in the Coptic version] come and this world pass away. . . . Maranatha!"[17] A number of recent writers have allowed us to glimpse the promise that a study of the *Didache* in conjunction with the epiclesis holds out for us.[18] The texts are indeed striking but the complexity of the question is likewise imposing.[19]

The same may be said for certain passages of the Apocryphal Acts of the Apostles which could serve as possible forerunners of the developed epiclesis.[20] Here, however, even more caution is necessary in handling such texts in conjunction with the epiclesis because they seem at times to approach pagan magical notions more than the other texts to which we have been referring.[21]

THE EPICLESIS IN THE EARLY ANAPHORAS

Having glanced briefly at the possible forerunners of the developed epiclesis, we are now ready to turn our gaze toward the main object of this chapter, namely, the epiclesis in the early liturgical texts. Once again, no attempt is made here to settle the many thorny textual problems associated with these texts. It is rather a question of trying, on the basis of good texts, to set the stage for a balanced judgment on the worth of the various twentieth-century interpretations regarding the eucharistic epiclesis.

The Apostolic Tradition

The eucharistic prayer of *The Apostolic Tradition*, in the last century generally attributed to Hippolytus of Rome and dated around 215 AD, provides the matter for our first inquiry.

Following a brief introductory dialogue the anaphora takes up the theme of thanks. It thanks God (the Father) through Jesus Christ,

17. Cf. PE, 66–68.

18. Cf., for instance, A. Kavanagh, "Thoughts on the Roman Anaphora," 8, and Bouyer, *Eucharistie*, 119–121 (116–19), 200–203 (210–204), 206 (208). Cf. also Gamber, 379–81 and J. Godart, "Aux origins de la celebration eucharistique," QLP 46 (1965), 114–15, 120–21.

19. For instance, the question of the eucharistic or non-eucharistic character of Chapters 9 and 10 has proved to be a thorny one. Cf. PE, 66–67 and Audet, *La Didachè* 372–433 as well as Clerici, 1-2 and J. Betz, "Die Eucharistie in der Didache," ALW 11 (1969), 10–39. Cf. Bradshaw, *Eucharistic Origins*, 24–42.

20. PE, 76–77. Cf., for instance, Lietzmann, 244; Rauschen, 113 n. 1; R. M. Wooley, *The Liturgy of the Primitive Church* (Cambridge, 1910), 93 f. and Gamber, 377–79.

21. Cf. Laager, 588 and Lietzmann, 244.

his "Child" ("puerum"), through whom he has created the world and whom the Father has sent to be born of a virgin and to redeem mankind through his suffering. This thanksgiving leads up to the institution narrative with its command to "do it in memory of me." Then follows the epiclesis, tightly woven into the text of the anamnesis that precedes it and the doxology that follows it.

In general we shall follow the texts selected by *Prex Eucharistica*. Here, by way of exception, we have chosen as our basic text Botte's juxtaposition of his Latin reconstruction and Duensing's edition of the Ethiopian version. The Latin version is, moreover, practically identical with that offered by *Prex Eucharistica*.[22] The English translation of Botte's text,[23] with the epiclesis proper in italics, reads as follows:

Latin	*Ethiopian*
Mindful therefore of his death and resurrection, we offer this bread and wine to you, thankful that you have judged us worthy to stand in your presence and serve you.	Mindful therefore of his death and resurrection, we offer this bread and wine to you, thankful that you have judged us worthy to stand in your presence and serve you.
And we pray that you send your Holy Spirit upon the offering of your holy Church: gathering together in unity all those who partake of these holy mysteries so that they may be filled with the Holy Spirit unto the strengthening of the faith in truth. Thus may we praise and glorify you through your child Jesus Christ, through whom be glory and honor to you Father and Son with your Holy Spirit in your holy Church now and forever. Amen.	*And we pray that you send your Holy Spirit upon the offering of your holy Church: joining together all those who partake of this holy mystery so that they may be filled with the Holy Spirit unto the strengthening of the faith in truth.* Thus may they praise and glorify you through your Son Jesus Christ, through whom be glory and honor to you in your holy Church now and always and for all eternity. Amen.

The context makes it clear that the addressee in this epiclesis is God, the Father. The prayer asks the Father to *send* ("mittas") his *Holy Spirit* upon the oblation of the Church. This explicit mention of the Holy Spirit does not, however, entirely exclude the possibility that for Hippolytus the term "Holy Spirit" referred to the Logos, the Second Person of the Trinity.[24] The effect on the "oblation" of this

---

22. PE, 81. Cf. also Jasper-Cuming, 31–38.

23. Botte, *La Tradition Apostolique* . . . , 16. Cf. also Dix, *The Treatise* . . . 9.

24. Cf. Dix, Ibid., 78–79. Cf. also Dölger, I, 73–79, 81; Bishop, "The Moment . . . ," 158–63; Frere, *The Primitive*. . . , 19 and the same author's *The Anaphora*, 43–44.

sending of the Holy Spirit is not specified. The effect desired for those taking part, on the other hand, comes through more clearly. The prayer asks that those partaking be gathered together into one and that they be filled with the Holy Spirit for the confirmation of their faith in truth so that they might in turn praise and glorify God.[25]

There does seem to be general agreement that the epiclesis in the *Apostolic Tradition* is not "consecratory," at least not clearly so.[26] There is also general agreement that the epiclesis has the communicants and in particular their unity in view.[27] Some see this plea for unity as reflecting the *Didache* and the Jewish liturgical tradition.[28]

The Testament of Our Lord

We have chosen to treat the *Testamentum Domini* or *The Testament of Our Lord* here because of its relationship to Hippolytus in the epiclesis

---

25. We should note that there were some who questioned the authenticity of the epiclesis in the *Apostolic Tradition*. Dix, *The Treatise* . . . , 75–79, E. C. Ratcliff, "The Sanctus and the Pattern of the Early Anaphora," *Journal of Ecclesiastical History* I (1950) 29–36, 125–34 and Bouyer, *Eucharistie*, 158–81 (158–82), esp. 170–77 (170–77) have all questioned Hippolytus's authorship of this epiclesis. If they could come up with convincing arguments against the authenticity it would make a significant difference in tracing the epiclesis. Botte, on the other hand, in "L'épiclèse dans l'anaphore d'Hippolyte," 241–51 and "A propos . . . ," 183–86 makes a case for the authenticity of the epiclesis in the *Apostolic Tradition*. Cf. also Frere, *The Primitive* . . . 17; Chadwick in Dix, *The Treatise* . . . , k-m and C. C. Richardson, "The So-Called Epiclesis . . . ," 101–108; Botte, "Les plus anciennes . . . ," 344–45 even suggests that Hippolytus's epiclesis served as the basis for the later oriental epicleses. More recently a growing number of scholars, while not in the majority, have again challenged Hippolytus's authorship.

Among them are Bradshaw, *Eucharistic Origins*, 19–20, 48–50, 135–38 and *The Search* . . . , 80–83; McGowan, 28–29, and John Baldovin, 520–42 who shows good balance in concluding: "There is a very real possibility that the *Apostolic Tradition* describes liturgies that never existed. A fortiori, great caution must be employed in appealing to this document to justify contemporary rites. (I do not object to someone wanting to use the anaphora contained in the ordination rite for a bishop, for example, as the basis of a contemporary prayer . . . . But I do question the unjustifiable reason for using this prayer, namely the assumption that it was *the* eucharistic prayer of the early-third-century Church at Rome) . . . . Many doubts have been expressed here, and many questions left open. Even if the liturgies described in the so-called *Apostolic Tradition* never existed in practice, they have had a major impact on the subsequent history of liturgical practice especially and perhaps even ironically in the West. The document addressed in this study has shaped the contemporary liturgies of initiation, ordination, and Eucharist. Of this there can be no doubt at all"(542).

26. Cf., for instance, Botte, "L'Epiclèse de l'Anaphore d'Hippolyte," 251; Lietzmann, 80; Connolly, "The Eucharistic Prayer of Hippolytus," 367. for a somewhat different view, cf. C. Vagaggini, *The Canon* . . . , 91 n. 7.

27. Botte, Ibid.; Lietzmann, Ibid., 81; Connolly, Ibid.

28. Cf. Chadwick in Dix, *The Treatise* . . . , l-m and Lietzmann, 81 who also notes the parallels in the liturgies of Serapion and Basil.

question. Some authors, as we have seen, challenge the authenticity of the epiclesis in Hippolytus. The basis of their argument is the absence of an epiclesis in the text of *The Testament of Our Lord*.[29]

Botte contends, however, that *Testamentum Domini* does in fact have a vestige of an epiclesis. He claims, moreover, that the Syriac translator of the *Testamentum Domini* misunderstood the Greek original, and he attempts to reconstruct the original Greek passage on the basis of the Syriac translation which has come down to us.[30] He comes up with a reconstruction which differs greatly from the translations of the Syriac that Rahmani and Cooper and MacLean have given us. Botte's reasoning seems sound and, while remaining aware of the hypothetical nature of his reconstruction, we shall use the *Prex Eucharistica* text that takes this reconstruction into account.[31]

Following an introductory dialogue the anaphora takes up the theme of thanksgiving to the Father, portrayed by a number of laudatory attributes, especially for having sent his Son as savior. A number of attributes of the Son are then listed before the thanksgiving theme turns again to the Father's goodness in sending his Son to become man and to save, through his passion, those who hope in God. The frequent use of attributes to portray Father and Son and the appearance of petitions in the course of the thanks theme are striking features of this thanksgiving prayer.[32]

The mention of Christ's passion paves the way for the introduction of the institution narrative. Then comes the anamnesis followed by the epiclesis proper. On the basis of Botte's reconstruction the text reads:

> We give you thanks, eternal Trinity, Lord Jesus Christ, Lord Father, from whom every creature and every nature trembles fleeing into itself; Lord, send the Holy Spirit upon this drink and this your holy food, cause it to be

---

29. Cf. Dix, *The Treatise* . . . , 75 ff. and, more recently, Bouyer, *Eucharistie*, 170–77 (170–77).

30. Cf. Botte, "A propos . . . ," 184 and especially the same author's "L'Epiclèse de l'Anaphore d'Hippolyte," 245–47. Cf. also Frere, *The Primitive* . . . , 17.

31. Botte, "L'Epiclèse de l'Anaphore d'Hippolyte," 245–47. Cf. also Bouyer, *Eucharisite*, 170–75 (170–76) where Bouyer outlines Botte's reasoning only to disagree with it. In the second edition of this work, p. 186 (176 n. 56). Cf. also Jasper-Cuming, 138–41 and Bradshaw, *The Search* . . . , especially 86–91, 94–95. Bouyer provides an additional note containing a reference to Botte's response to Bouyer's criticism. Bouyer himself, however, reaffirms his earlier stand.

32. PE, 219–20.

for us not judgment, disgrace or perdition but rather health and strength of our spirit.[33]

At this point, a number of intercessions intervene only to be followed by a passage strikingly similar to the conclusion of Hippolytus's epiclesis.

> Grant then, God, that all who in partaking receive from these your holy mysteries may be united to you, so that they may be filled with the Holy Spirit unto the strengthening of the faith in truth, so that they may always render doxology to you and to your beloved Son, Jesus Christ, through whom glory and direction be to you with your Holy Spirit forever and ever. Amen.[34]

The addressee in the text chosen is the Father[35] and the Holy Spirit is the person called for.[36] The epiclesis asks the Father to send ("mitte") the Holy Spirit upon the bread and wine so that they become a means not of spiritual harm but of benefit to those partaking. In addition, if one includes the passage following the intercessions, the epiclesis asks that God unite those partaking to himself so that they may be filled with the Holy Spirit for the confirmation of their faith in truth so that, in turn, they may glorify the Trinity.

The Apostolic Constitutions

The Apostolic Constitutions, which seem to date from around the end of the fourth century, and the eighth chapter of which contains an anaphora often referred to as the "Clementine Liturgy,"[37] forms the next object of consideration. It is treated here because of its close relationship to the anaphora of Hippolytus of which it seems to be an

---

33. PE, 221.

34. PE, 222. Cf. Cooper and MacLean, 73–75.

35. Cf. Botte, "L'Epiclèse de l'Anaphore d'Hippolyte," 247 who notes that on the basis of a reconstruction other than his own the Holy Spirit could be considered the addressee. On the other hand, Cooper and MacLean, 174 and Richardson, "A Note on the Epicleses . . . ," 358 in following their respective reconstructions of the text in question, see the whole Trinity as the addressee.

36. In the text offered by Cooper and MacLean this would of course not be the case and they (176) see the epiclesis from *The Testament of Our Lord* as deliberately omitting a reference to the Holy Spirit—a reference which they contend was contained in its predecessors.

37. Cf., for instance, Dinesen, 64; LEW xxix ff.; P. Drews, *Untersuchungen über die sogenannten clementinische Liturgie* (Tübingen, 1906); R. H. Cresswell, *The Liturgy of the Eighth Book of "The Apostolic Consitutions,"* (London, 1924²). Cf. Jasper-Cuming, 100–113.

amplification. In fact, the first part of the anaphora from *The Apostolic Constitutions* is so long that it has raised doubts that this part, at least, was ever intended for actual use in the liturgy.[38]

After an introductory dialogue comes a long hymn of praise to the Father for creating, through his only begotten Son, the angels, the visible world and man. This section then goes on to depict the fall of man and to praise the Father for the events subsequent to the fall, his promise of a resurrection for man, the flood, his treatment of the patriarchs, the events of the Exodus, and the entry into the promised land. A mention of the angels leads into a form of *Sanctus*. The hymn then picks up the theme of praise to the Father, this time for what he has done in the Son, depicting the Incarnation, Christ's earthly life, his passion, death, Resurrection, and Ascension.

This long hymn of praise has prepared the way for the assembly's present eucharistic celebration in fulfillment of the command Christ gave on the night he was betrayed. The institution narrative recounts this command and serves as the basis for the anamnesis proper and the epiclesis.[39] The epiclesis in turn sets the stage for a long series of intercessions followed by the doxology which concludes the anaphora.[40]

The text of the epiclesis itself reads as follows:

> And we beg you to look favorably on these gifts set before you—you, O God, who needs nothing—and be pleased with them in honor of your Christ. And send down your Holy Spirit upon this sacrifice, witness of the sufferings of the Lord Jesus, so that he may show this bread [to be] the body of your Christ and this cup [to be] the blood of your Christ; so that those sharing in it may be strengthened in godliness, experience forgiveness of sins, be delivered from the devil and his deceit, be filled with the Holy Spirit, become worthy of your Christ, [and] receive eternal life through your being reconciled with them, Almighty Lord.[41]

---

38. Cf. PE, 82–83. Bouyer, *Eucharistie* 245–46 (250–51) argues, on the other hand, that it was actually used in the liturgy.

39. A number of authors make a point of the fact that in *The Apostolic Constitutions* and other anaphoras the institution narrative serves as the basis of the epiclesis. *Because* Christ has commanded us to do this as a memorial of him, we now pray the epiclesis asking for the realization here and now of the command and promise made once and for all at the Last Supper. Cf., for instance, Chavasse, 201 and Dinesen, 98–101.

40. Cf. PE, 83–95.

41. PE, 92.

The addressee has been throughout and remains God, the Father. The assembly prays that he look graciously upon the gifts and that he send (καταπέμψῃς) his Holy Spirit upon the sacrifice (ἐπί τὴν Θυσίαν). Why? So that the Holy Spirit may show or declare (ἀποφαίνω) the bread and wine (to be) the body and blood of Christ. Finally, all this is done so that it may benefit the communicants by bringing them a strengthening in piety, forgiveness of sins, a greater fullness of the Holy Spirit, eternal life, etc.[42]

The signification of the word ἀποφαίνω is important. We shall return to it later in conjunction with some of the theories on the development of the epiclesis. Suffice it to note here that the ordinary lexicographical meaning of the root word is "to show forth, to declare" although it can sometimes be found with the meaning "to render, make, produce."[43]

The Alexandrian Type Anaphora

Having examined the epiclesis of *The Apostolic Tradition* and two others closely related to it, namely, those in the anaphoras of *The Testament of Our Lord* and of *The Apostolic Constitutions*, we now turn to the Alexandrian family of anaphoras. In general the arrangement of its prayers distinguishes this type from the other oriental families of anaphoras. In the Alexandrian type we find the following order: Introductory Dialogue—Praise and Thanks—Intercessions— Introduction to *Sanctus* and the *Sanctus* itself—Epiclesis I—Institution Narrative—Anamnesis—Epiclesis II—Doxology.[44]

Among the characteristic features of this family one may note the position of the intercessions before the *Sanctus*, the introduction of the institution narrative by a causative ὅτι or γάρ, an anamnesis

---

42. We cannot, therefore, share Bouyer's view in *Eucharistie* 260 (267), 277 (286), 303 (313) that here and in the anaphora of the Twelve Apostles the epiclesis asks that the Holy Spirit produce in those partaking all the effects of the mystery and *thereby* "manifest" the bread and wine to be the body and blood of Christ. The texts which he uses (Brightman, 21 and A. Raes, *Anaphorae syriacae* [Rome, 1940], 1/2, 212 ff. respectively) seem to us to indicate that the request is for the Holy Spirit "to manifest" the bread and wine as the body and blood of Christ *in order that* ('ίνα, "ut") the effects of the mystery may be realized in those partaking.

43. Cf. Lampe, 218, Arndt-Gingrich, 101 and Liddell-Scott, 225. Cf. also, Atchley, *On the Epiclesis . . .* , 114–15 and Casel (Review of Atchley's *On the Epiclesis . . .*), 445.

44. Cf. PE, 101.

which speaks of the offering in the past tense and finally the presence of an epiclesis prayer (I) immediately after the *Sanctus*.[45]

The texts of this family which most interest us, namely, the Greek anaphora of Saint Mark, the Dêr Balyzeh fragment and the anaphora from the Euchologium of Serapion stem from the Greek Church in Egypt.

The Greek Anaphora of Saint Mark

Following an introductory dialogue which is almost identical with that of Hippolytus, the anaphora of Saint Mark takes up the theme of thanks and praise to the Father for all the wonderful things that he has done through Christ, his Son and our Savior. The creation of heaven and earth and man, the goodness shown to man despite his fall all receive mention and lead up to the statement that the thankful assembly now wishes, through Christ and with the Holy Spirit, to join its worship to the "pure sacrifice" being offered to God's name throughout the ends of the earth.[46] Then comes the long list of intercessions, with its diptychs for the dead and its commemoration of those offering their gifts together with an appeal for the acceptance of these offerings.[47] A return to the theme of praise—praising God above all things— leads to a mention of the angels which in turn leads to the *Sanctus*. [48]

This brings us to epiclesis (I) which uses the note of "fullness" as a springboard for its appeal that God fill the present sacrifice through the coming of his Holy Spirit. The text based on the twelfth century *Codex Rossanensis* reads as follows:

> For as heaven and earth are truly filled with your glory through the appearance of the Lord and God and of our Savior Jesus Christ, fill also, O God, this sacrifice with your blessing through the visitation of your most Holy Spirit.[49]

45. Ibid.

46. Cf. PE, 102. Bouyer, *Eucharistie*, 193 (193) sees this as a "pre-epiclesis." Cf. Jasper-Cuming, 52–56.

47. PE, 102–108. Bouyer, Ibid., sees this latter as the starting point of epiclesis (I).

48. PE, 110.

49. PE, 112. The fragment of the anaphora of Saint Mark in the Strasbourg Papyrus (4–5th cent.) (cf. PE, 116–18) does not contain this passage and the Manchester Papyrus (6th cent.) (cf. PE 120) from the John Rylands Library is practically identical with the text we have cited, the main difference being the absence of ἐπιφανείας and ἐπιφοιτησέως in the Manchester manuscript.

From the context it seems clear that the Father is the addressee of this epiclesis as he has been for the eucharistic prayer as a whole. The appeal is for the Father to fill (πλήρωσον) this sacrifice with his blessing (εὐλογίας) through the Holy Spirit or, in the case of the *Codex Rossanensis*, through the visitation or intervention (ἐπιφοιτή σεως) of the Holy Spirit.

After the epiclesis (I) the characteristic ὅτι introduces the institution narrative followed by the anamnesis proper and epiclesis (II) which closes with the final doxology. The text of the epiclesis and its accompanying doxology runs:

> And we pray and call upon you, good lover of mankind to send from your holy heaven, from your prepared dwelling place, from your unlimited presence, the Paraclete himself, the Spirit of truth, the Holy One, the Lord, the life-giver . . . *Look upon us and send your Holy Spirit upon these loaves and these chalices so that he may sanctify and perfect them, as the almighty God, and make this bread the body [and] this cup the blood of the new covenant of our Lord, God, Savior and sovereign King, Jesus Christ . . . so that they may become, for all those who partake of them, [a source of] faith, self-restraint, healing, good judgment, holiness, renewal of soul, body and spirit, communion in the blessedness of eternal life and immortality, glorification of your most holy name and the forgiveness of sins* so that in this, as in all things, your most holy, precious and glorious name be glorified and praised and sanctified together with Jesus Christ and the Holy Spirit.[50]

Once again the context indicates the Father as the addressee who is asked "to look upon us" and send forth (ἐξαπόστειλον) his Holy Spirit upon the bread and wine. The purpose of the Spirit's coming shows up more clearly here than in epiclesis (I). He is to sanctify (ἁγιάση) and perfect (τελειώση) the bread and wine and to make (ποιήση) them the body and blood of Christ. This is to be done so that all those who partake of this transformed bread and wine may attain to various virtues, remission of sin, communion in eternal life, etc. These effects in the communicants are once again related, as was the case in *The Apostolic Tradition* and *Testamentum Domini*, to the further purpose of giving glory to God's name. Thus, once again, the epiclesis concludes by flowing into the doxology at the end of the anaphora.

50. PE, 114.

The Fragment of Dêr Balyzeh

The anaphora from the sixth/seventh century Dêr Balyzeh papyrus shows some similarities with that of the liturgy of Saint Mark.[51] Unfortunately, the Dêr Balyzeh text is fragmentary at a point important for our study.

The fragment starts with the concluding formulas of the intercessions such as we have seen in the liturgy of Saint Mark, namely, the petition against unbelievers and for the faithful. The praise of God above all things leads to the mention of the angels which in turn leads to the *Sanctus*. A fully developed epiclesis (I) follows. The text reads:

> Fill us also with your glory and deign to send your Holy Spirit on these creatures and make the bread the body of the Lord and our Savior, Jesus Christ, and the cup the blood of the new covenant of our Lord and God and Savior, Jesus Christ. And just as this bread was scattered on the mountains and hills and in the valleys and was mixed together to become one body . . . as this wine, come forth from the holy vine of David, and this water from the spotless lamb were together and became one mystery, so too gather together the catholic Church of Jesus Christ.[52]

As in the liturgy of Saint Mark, there is an appeal to the Father, at least so it would seem from the context, to "fill" (πλή ρωσον). This time, however, the object of this "filling" is not the sacrifice, as was the case in Mark, but "us" (ἡμᾶς)—"fill us also with your glory." In addition, the Father is called upon to send down (κατ απ́ έμψαι) the Holy Spirit and to make (ποίησ̂ ον) the bread and wine into the body and blood of Christ. As in Hippolytus and Botte's reconstruction of *The Testament of Our Lord*, the theme of unity crops up. This time, however, it is in terms reminiscent of Didache 9:4, one of the possible forerunners of the developed epiclesis.[53] It is also

---

51. Cf. PE, 124–25 and Bouyer, *Eucharistie* 119–200 (200–201). Cf. also Jasper-Cuming, 79–81.

52. PE, 126. Cf. L. Th. Lefort, "Coptica Lovaniensia," *Museon* 53 (1940), 22–24 for a similar epiclesis before the institution narrative. Cf. Jasper-Cuming, 81.

53. Cf. Kavanagh, "Thoughts on the Roman Anaphora," 7–8 and the same author's "Thoughts on the New Eucharistic Prayers," 10–11. Cf. also Clerici, 106–108.

possible to see a reference to the "communicants" here[54] or even in the terse, "fill *us* also with your glory."[55]

After epiclesis (I) the causative γάρ introduces the institution narrative. A concise anamnesis type statement, this time directed to Christ, follows: "We announce your death, we proclaim your resurrection *and we pray* . . . καί δεόμεθα." The fragment tantalizingly breaks off here at what seems to have been the beginning of epiclesis (II) only to pick up with the words, ". . . grant us, your servants, the power of the Holy Spirit, the strengthening and increase of faith, the hope of the everlasting life to come through our Lord Jesus Christ, with whom to you, Father, be the glory, with the Holy Spirit, forever. Amen."[56]

One can conjecture that a full blown epiclesis (II) once stood here.[57] One can also conjecture that, in view of the completeness of epiclesis (I) before the institution narrative, the most one could expect here would be an appeal to accept the sacrifice and/or to make it fruitful for those partaking.[58] Unfortunately, the fragmentary nature of our present data permits no more than mere conjecture.[59]

The Anaphora of Sarapion

The last of the three Greek-Egyptian texts to occupy our interest is the anaphora generally attributed to Sarapion, bishop of Thmuis. This anaphora has generally been dated around 350 AD and considered to reflect the Alexandrian tradition at that time.[60] This view has, however,

---

54. Cf. Kavanagh, "Thoughts on the New Eucharistic Prayers," 11.

55. Dinesen, 56. In this context it would be well to recall what E. Bishop, "Notes and Studies: Liturgical Comments and Memoranda VIII–IX," 28–32, 61 had to say in conjunction with the Euchology of Serapion. "As already explained 'the Church' in the mind of the writer in Serapion appears from the tenor of the prayer (for the communicants) not the Catholic church diffused throughout the world, but 'the Church,' the congregation, the people in assembly here present" (61 footnote 1).

Vagaggini, *The Canon* . . . , 69 maintains, on the other hand, that epiclesis (1) in the Dêr Balyzeh fragment has no reference to the communicants or to "a fruitful communion," as he puts it. This position has earned for him the accusation of Kavanagh, ibid., that Vagaggini's oversight stems from ". . . the bias of looking for 'communion' material only after the anamnesis."

56. Cf. PE, 127.

57. Cf. Salaville, "Le nouveau fragment . . . ," 333–34.

58. Cf. P. de Puniet, "A propos de la nouvelle anaphore égyptienne," EO 13 (1910), 72–76, esp. 74–75.

59. Cf. Bouyer, *Eucharistie* 201–202 (202–203).

60. Cf. Ibid., 201–207 (203–209) represents this view. Cf. also Jasper-Cuming, 74–79 and Maxwell Johnson, 73–107.

come under fire from a number of directions. In 1946 Capelle challenged the supposition that the Logos epiclesis, as well as other prayers in Serapion's anaphora, really was typical of the Alexandrian liturgy around 350.[61] Botte has gone one step further. He not only contends that the Logos epiclesis does not represent the Alexandrian tradition but also that the redactor of the text, as we now have it, was not Sarapion but rather an arianizing Pneumatomachian who deliberately tried to relegate the Holy Spirit to the shadows. Maxwell Johnson, on the other hand, rejects these theories.[62] It is not our function here to settle this question. The closely reasoned studies of Capelle and Botte should, however, caution against giving too much weight to traits peculiar to the anaphora bearing Serapion's name.

The text begins with a hymn of praise to the Father, the source of life, light, grace, and truth, as he is known and made known by his only begotten Son, the Logos. Whereas a long series of intercessions came next in the Marcan liturgy, here there is a short prayer asking for light to know and help to proclaim God and his mysteries. Then follows, as it did in the liturgy of Saint Mark and in the Dêr Balyzeh papyrus, the return to the praise of God above all things and the mention of the angels leading up to the *Sanctus*.[63] Epiclesis (I) again arises out of the *Sanctus* theme of "fullness." The text reads:

> . . . Heaven is filled and the earth is filled with your magnificent glory, Lord of Powers. Fill also this sacrifice with your power and participation. For it is to you that we have offered this living sacrifice, this unbloody offering.[64]

We have already examined the possible signification of πλή ρωσον in conjunction with epiclesis (I) in the liturgy of Saint Mark. Here, however, the Father, who once again seems to be the addressee, is asked to fill the sacrifice (τὴν θυσίαν) not with his Holy Spirit but with his power (δυνάμεως) and his "participation" (μεταλήψεως). The lexicographical comment on this last word leaves it still somewhat

---

61. Capelle, "L'Anaphore . . . ," 425–43, esp. 439, 443. The author rightly makes the point (439) that the question here is not whether a Logos epiclesis existed in the ancient Church but rather whether the Alexandrian tradition had such an epiclesis at the time of Serapion and Athanasius. His answer is a decisive, "No" (443).

62. Botte, "L'Eucologe . . . ," 50–56.

63. PE, 128, 130.

64. PE, 130.

nebulous.[65] Lietzmann, on the other hand, sees the entire sentence as, ". . . a pithy expression for 'give us the possibility of tasting you, that is, through the full indwelling and operation of your δύναμις."[66] The sentence, "For it is to you that we *have offered* (προσηνέγκαμεν) this living sacrifice, this unbloody offering," seems almost to have been tacked on here as an added incentive for God to hear the prayer.

The next two sentences, which also seem to have been inserted somewhat awkwardly, speak of having offered the bread as a symbol (ὁμοίωμα)[67] of Christ's body. The causative ὅτι then introduces the first part of the institution words, the part referring to the bread. A somewhat terse anamnesis and a prayer for unity, reminiscent of Didache 9:4 and epiclesis (I) of the Dêr Balyzeh fragment, interrupts the institution narrative at this point: "For this reason, we, too, celebrating the symbol (ὁμοίωμα) of his death, have offered (προσηνέγκαμεν) this bread and pray (παρακαλοῦμεν), through this sacrifice be reconciled with us all (καταλλάγηθι) and be merciful (ἱλάσθητι). . . And just as this bread which once was scattered over the hills and brought together as one, do you also bring together your holy Church . . . and make her the one living and catholic Church." Next comes the other half of the institution words, the part referring to the cup. This concludes with a sentence like the one which follows the first half of the institution words: "For this reason we have offered the cup, symbol (ὁμοίωμα) of the blood."[68]

The epiclesis (II) leads into a short series of intercessions which in turn issue in a sort of doxology concluding the anaphora. The text of epiclesis (II) reads:

> May your holy Word, O God of truth, come upon this bread, so that the bread may become the body of the Word, and upon this cup, so that the cup may become the blood of truth. And cause all those who partake of this life-giving remedy to receive healing for all diseases, strength for

---

65. Cf. Liddell-Scott, 1113 and Arndt-Gingrich, 512.

66. Lietzmann, 74.

67. On the meaning of ὁμοίωμα cf. Betz, 180–81 as well as Liddell-Scott, 1225; Lampe, 956; Arndt-Gingrich, 570

Cf. also, O. Kuss, *Der Römerbrief* (Regensburg, 1957), 300–304, esp. 301–302 for use of the word in Pauline thought.

68. PE, 130.

all their accomplishments and virtues, and not judgment, reproof and disgrace, O God of truth.[69]

The Father has been the addressee throughout the anaphora and remains so here. He is asked that his Logos may come (ἐπιδη–μησάτω) upon the bread and the cup so that they may become (γέ νηται) the body of the Logos and the "blood of truth." The Father is also asked to see to it (ποίησον) that all those who partake of this life-giving remedy (κοινωνοῦντες) receive from it healing and strength for all progress and virtue rather than condemnation, confusion or shame. By far the most striking aspect of this epiclesis (II) is the fact that it calls for the *Logos* to come upon the gifts. Whatever may be the value of this text as a witness to a widespread tradition, it is in fact the only example to date of a clear-cut, developed eucharistic epiclesis in the Eastern tradition calling for the Logos.

The Antiochene Type Anaphora

The Antiochene family or type, which includes versions from the Byzantine and Syro-Antiochene Churches as well as versions from the Maronite, Armenian, and Egyptian Churches, also has its own characteristic arrangement: Introductory Dialogue—Praise and Thanks—Introduction to the *Sanctus* and the *Sanctus* itself—Prayer of Thanks—Praise after the *Sanctus*—Institution Narrative—Anamnesis—Epiclesis—Intercessions—Doxology.[70]

Among the other characteristic traits of this Antiochene type is the fact that the *Sanctus* seems to interrupt the flow of the prayers of praise and thanks which come before and after it. These two prayers taken together generally praise God for the creation of the universe, and especially of man, and for the redemption of man made possible by the Incarnation. Another interesting trait of the Antiochene family is the anamnesis. The Syro-Antiochene version always directs it to Christ and protracts the events of his life to include his second "awesome" coming, at which point the people break in with "Have mercy on us." With the exception of the liturgy of Saint James and a few others, the Syro-Antiochene version also omits mention of the act of

---

69. Ibid.
70. Cf. PE, 204.

offering whereas the Byzantine version adds a mention of active offering and a gesture to express it.[71]

The influence of the Antiochene type, which originated in the vicinity of Antioch or, in the case of the anaphora of Saint James, in Jerusalem, at least by the fourth century, has been widespread. From this type we have selected three anaphoras of the Byzantine Church, viz., those from the liturgy of Saint John Chrysostom, the liturgy of Saint Basil (together with its Alexandrian version) and the Greek liturgy of Saint James. We have also selected two examples of this type which have come down to us from the Syro-Antiochene Church, namely, the Syriac liturgy of Saint James and the anaphora of the Twelve Apostles.

The Anaphora of Saint John Chrysostom

The so-called liturgy of Saint John Chrysostom[72] begins with an introductory dialogue bearing Pauline characteristics.[73] Then comes a hymn of praise and thanks directed to the Father together with his Son and Holy Spirit. This hymn or prayer acknowledges the fact that God created "us" (ἡμᾶς), raised us up after the fall, and refuses to desert us until he has led us into heaven and his future kingdom. An introduction to the *Sanctus* interrupts this movement to thank God for the present service (λειτουργίας) and leads into the *Sanctus* itself.[74]

The prayer after the *Sanctus* takes up once again the interrupted theme of praise and thanks by thanking God (the Father) for having loved the world so much that he gave his only begotten Son to bring everlasting life to those who believe in him. This readies the scene for the institution narrative which characteristically adheres rather closely to New Testament texts, without however containing the command "Do this in my memory." Then a short anamnesis, which

---

71. Cf. PE, 205.

72. On the question of the authenticity of this liturgy and its relationship with the anaphora of the Twelve Apostles see, Raes, "L'Authenticié . . . ," 5–16. Raes concludes that Chrysostom was the author of none of the prayers of the anaphora (14-15). Bouyer, *Eucharistie*, 273–74 (282) sees Chrysostom as the reviser of a number of the prayers in question and Robert Taft, "Saint John Chrysostom and the Byzantine Anaphora that Bears His Name," in Bradshaw, *Essays . . . ,* 195–226 argues that Chrysostom probably introduced the anaphora into Constantinople in 398. Cf. also Jasper-Cuming, 129–134.

73. PE, 224 and cf. also Bouyer, Ibid., 277 (286).

74. PE, 224.

includes a mention of Christ's second coming, leads to the epiclesis which in turn flows into the intercessions with their concluding doxology.[75] The epiclesis text reads:

> We also offer you this spiritual and unbloody worship and we call upon you and pray and beseech you to send your Holy Spirit upon us and upon these gifts set before you, and to make this bread the precious body of your Christ, changing it by your Holy Spirit. Amen. And that which is in this cup, the precious blood of your Christ, changing it by your Holy Spirit. Amen. [We ask this] so that it may become for those receiving [a source of] soberness of soul, forgiveness of sins, communion of your Holy Spirit, the fullness of the Kingdom, easy approach to you and not judgment or punishment.[76]

Following the remark that we are offering a spiritual (λογικὴν) and unbloody worship, the Father is asked to send down (κατάπεμψον) the Holy Spirit upon us (ἐφ ἡμᾶς) and upon the gifts and to make (ποίησον) the bread and wine the body and blood of Christ, changing (μεταβαλών) them by his Holy Spirit. It is interesting to note that, in this version it is the Father who both sends the Spirit and makes the bread and wine into the body and blood through the Spirit. Finally, this is done so that they may be for those receiving them a means to sobriety, remission of sins, communion (κοινωνίαν) of the Holy Spirit, the fullness of the kingdom and easy approach to God rather than a means of judgment and condemnation.

The Anaphora of Saint Basil

The longer, Byzantine version of the liturgy of Saint Basil opens with a dialogue such as that just seen in the so-called Chrysostom liturgy. In its general lines the hymn of praise and thanks which follows lauds the Father for having given us knowledge of his truth and of himself through Jesus Christ who also manifested the Holy Spirit to us. The fact that the Father is praised by the angels is noted, and that leads to the *Sanctus*. The theme of thanks picks up again with saving history and its motive—the creation of man, his fall, the continued goodness of God in sending the prophets and, "when the fullness of time came," his own Son to take flesh from a virgin.[77]

---

75. PE, 224–28 and 204. Cf. also, Bouyer, *Eucharisitie*, 279 (288).
76. PE, 226.
77. PE, 230–34. Cf. also Jasper-Cuming, 114–133 and Stuckwisch, 109–130.

The mention of Christ's saving Passion, death, Resurrection, and Ascension leads up to the memorial which he has left us and "which we have here presented according to his orders." The institution narrative follows with its account of how Jesus took bread and having presented it (αναδείξας) to the Father and having given thanks and blessed it (ἐλθεῖν ἐρ ἡμᾶς), gave it, etc. The anamnesis, with its mention of Christ's "awesome" (φοβερᾶς) second coming, serves as a bridge between the institution narrative and the epiclesis. The intercessions flow from the final words of the epiclesis and conclude with a doxology.[78]

The text of the epiclesis reads:

> Therefore, Holy Lord, we, sinners and your unworthy servants . . . offering the images of the holy body and blood of your Christ, pray and call upon you, O Holy of Holies, that through your good pleasure the Holy Spirit might come upon us and upon these gifts which we offer and bless them and sanctify them and make this bread the precious body of the Lord and God and our Savior, Jesus Christ. Amen. And this cup the precious blood of the Lord and God and our Savior, Jesus Christ. Amen . . . And all of us who partake of the one bread and cup unite us with one another in the communion of the one, Holy Spirit and see to it that none of us partakes of the holy body and blood of your Christ unto judgment and punishment, but rather that we find mercy and grace with all the saints who have been pleasing to you from the beginning . . .[79]

The addressee was, and remains, once again the Father. After speaking of the unworthiness "of your servants" and mentioning the offering of the images (προθέντες τὰ ἀντίτυπα) of Christ's body and blood the epiclesis makes its appeal.[80] The Father is asked that the Holy Spirit might come (ἐλθεῖν) upon us (ἐλθεῖν ἐρ ἡμᾶς) and upon the gifts to bless them (εὐλογῆσαι), to sanctify (ἀγιάσαι) and to show forth or present and/or make (ἀναδεῖξαι)[81] the bread and wine

---

78. PE, 234–42.

79. PE, 236, 238.

80. Cf. Lampe, 159 on the meaning of this word in Basil. Cf. also Liddell-Scott, 165 and Arndt-Gingrich, 75.

81. The lexicon usually gives "show forth," "lift up to display" as the meaning of this word (cf. Liddell-Scott, 103 and Lampe, 101). The list of authors, however, who sees here the meaning of "to make," "to consecrate" is impressive. Cf. Moreau, 59 n. 1 who supports his stand with quotes from Basil and Chrysostom and who cites Salaville, Renaudot, and LeBrun as holding the same. Cf. also Botte, (Review of Jugie's *De forma* . . .) 246; Kern, 173–74; Jugie "De

(as) the body and blood of Christ. [82] All this is asked for so that those partaking of the one bread and one chalice may be united with one another in the communion (κοινωνίαν)[83] of the one Spirit and that their partaking will not lead to judgment and condemnation but to mercy and union with the saints in heaven.

For the Alexandrian version of the epiclesis in the liturgy of Saint Basil we have selected, by way of exception, the text offered by Doresse-Lanne instead of that of Renaudot as contained in *Prex Eucharistica*.[84] It seems likely that the Doresse-Lanne text reflects the simpler, more primitive version better than Renaudot's text. Doresse-Lanne offer the following version of the Coptic:

> We sinners, unworthy and wretched, adore you and beseech you, our God, that, through your good pleasure, your Holy Spirit descend upon us and upon these gifts which we offer and that he sanctify them and they be presented as the holy of holies. Make us worthy of sharing in the holy of holies as a means to sanctification of soul and body, so that we may be made one body and one spirit and may find a place with all the saints who have pleased you from the beginning.[85]

It is unnecessary to delay for long on this text. The term "to bless" (εὐλογῆσαι) is absent, in contrast to the Byzantine version. The most striking difference lies, however, in the absence of the mention of the bread and wine (becoming) the body and blood of Christ. The epiclesis simply asks that the Holy Spirit come upon us and upon the gifts and sanctify them and present them as the holies of holies ("ostendantur sancta sanctorum" δ ἀναδεῖξαι ἅγια ἁγίων).[86] The

---

epiclesi . . . Basilium Magnum," 205–207; Peterson, 320–26; and recently Bouyer, *Eucharistie* 289–90 (299).

82. As the text now stands it is the Spirit who not only comes but also blesses, sanctifies and presents. Cf. in this regard, M. Gelsinger, "The Epiklesis in the Liturgy of Saint Basil," ECQ 10 (1953/54), 243–48.

83. Cf. Bobrinskoy, "Liturgie et ecclésiologie trinitaire de saint Basile," 18-21 for some enlightening observations on this term in the thought of Basil.

84. Cf. PE, 352.

85. Doresse-Lanne, 20–22.

86. Raes, "un nouveau document . . . ," 406–407 sees the absence of an explicit demand that the bread and wine become the body and blood of Christ as an indication that we have here a more primitive epiclesis than that of the Byzantine version. He adds, however, that this does not mean that the appeal that the Holy Spirit "consecrate" the gifts was not very ancient but rather that the need to *express* the transforming action of the Holy Spirit was felt only later. Cf., moreover, what has been said above (n. 81) in regard to the meaning of ἀναδεῖξαι.

petition for the communicants has an appeal for sanctification of soul and body, for unity and for eternal life with the saints but no mention of judgment and condemnation.

The Greek Anaphora of Saint James

Following an introductory dialogue similar to those of the Basil and Chrysostom liturgies, the Greek liturgy of Saint James[87] sounds the praises of the Father for the wonders of creation. Mention of the angels once again leads to the *Sanctus*. The idea of holiness serves as the springboard for the post-*Sanctus* portion of praise that mentions the Son and the Holy Spirit for the first time. Here God is praised for the fact that he not only created man but rather than abandon him after the fall continued to assist him even to the point of sending the only begotten Son to be born of a virgin. Mention of Christ's life among men does not include the Passion, Resurrection, etc., before the institution narrative, as was so often the case in the other anaphoras we have examined. Here the institution narrative, with its account of how our Lord presented (ἀναδείξας) the bread, giving thanks, blessing, and sanctifying it, and how he did the same with the wine filling it with the Holy Spirit (πλήσας πνεύματος ἁγίου) serves as a prelude to the mention of the Passion, Death, Resurrection, Ascension, and Second Coming in the anamnesis. The anamnesis, besides being somewhat less tightly interwoven with the institution narrative than in other anaphoras we have seen, also contains a relatively long plea for mercy and forgiveness.[88]

The epiclesis, starting off on this same note, leads into an extremely elaborate series of intercessions which ultimately conclude in a final doxology. The text of the epiclesis runs:

> Have mercy on us, O God, Father, Almighty One. Have mercy on us, God our Saviour. Have mercy on us, O God, according to your great mercy and send your all-Holy Spirit upon us, and upon these holy gifts which we offer. [He is] the Lord and Life-giver, enthroned with you, God and Father, and with your only begotten Son . . . Send your all-Holy Spirit

87. For a brief background on this anaphora, cf. B.-Ch. Mercier, "La Liturgie de saint Jacques," *Patrologia Orientalis* 26 (1946), 123–25 who gives the fourth or fifth century as the probable date of the original text. Cf. also Bouyer, *Eucharistie* 261–62 (268–69) and Jasper-Cuming, 88–99. Cf. also Witvliet, 153–72.

88. PE, 244–48.

himself, O Lord, upon us and upon these holy gifts which we offer, so that by visiting them by his holy, good and splendid presence he may sanctify them and make the bread the holy body of Christ. Amen. [We ask this] so that they may become for all those who receive them [a source of] forgiveness of sins and eternal life, holiness of souls and bodies, the fruit of good works, strength for your holy, catholic and apostolic Church which you have founded on the rock of faith so that the gates of hell may not prevail against her, preserving her from all heresy and from the scandals of evildoers, and from enemies rising up and rebelling in her until the end of time.[89]

Once again the Father is the addressee. An encomium of the Holy Spirit follows an initial appeal that the Father send (ἐξαπό στειλον) his Spirit "upon us" and upon the gifts. After the encomium the Father is once again asked to send down (κατάπεμψον) the Holy Spirit upon both people and gifts so that by visiting (ἐπιφοιτῆσαν) them with his presence (παρουσιά) the Spirit may sanctify (ἁγιάση) the bread and wine and make (ποιήση) them the body and blood of Christ. This is asked for so that they may become (γένωνται) for all those who receive them a means of forgiveness of sins, eternal life, health of body and soul, fruitfullness in good works and the strengthening (στηριγμὸν) of the Church against everything threatening her.

The Syriac Anaphora of Saint James

The Syriac liturgy of Saint James has basically the same structure as the Greek version just examined. The text of the Syriac epiclesis, which Botte[90] sees as representing the primitive form of James, reads:

Have mercy on us, God, Father Almighty, and send, upon us and upon these gifts which we offer, your Holy Spirit, the Lord and Life-giver, enthroned by you, God the Father and the Son . . . So that descending he may make the bread truly the life-giving body, the salutary body, . . . the body of the Lord and God and our Savior, Jesus Christ, for the forgiveness of sins and life eternal for those partaking. And may he make the mixture which is in this cup the blood of the New Covenant, the salutary blood, the life-giving blood, . . . the blood of the Lord and God and our Savior, Jesus Christ, for the forgiveness of sins and eternal life for those partaking. So that they might become for all those receiving them [a source of] holiness

---

89. PE, 250.

90. Botte, "L'épiclèse dans les liturgies syriennes orientales," 56.

of souls and bodies, the accomplishment of good works, the strengthening
of your holy Church which you have founded upon the rock of faith
(and the gates of hell will not prevail against her), delivering her from all
heresies and from the scandals of evildoers until the end of time. Amen.[91]

The content of this version though arranged somewhat
differently is virtually the same as that of the longer Greek version.
The Father is called upon to send ("mitte") his Holy Spirit upon us
and upon the gifts so that the Spirit in coming down ("illabens")
makes ("faciat") the bread and wine into the "vivifying . . . salutary . . .
heavenly . . . liberating" body and blood of Christ. This is sought so
that those partaking may receive forgiveness of their sins, eternal life,
holiness of body and soul, fruitfulness in good works, and so that the
Church may be strengthened against all opposition.

The Anaphora of the Twelve Apostles

The similarities between the anaphora of the Twelve Apostles and
the Greek version of the liturgy of Saint John Chrysostom are striking
enough to argue to a common source. Rather than repeat much of
what has already been said in regard to the Chrysostom liturgy,
we simply refer the reader to the excellent comparative study which
A. Raes has made of these two anaphoras.[92]

Among the differences that Raes notes is the presence in the
Twelve Apostles, or more astonishingly, the absence in the Chrysostom
liturgy, of our Lord's command to repeat as a memorial what he has
just accomplished. The anamnesis in the anaphora of the Twelve
Apostles does not mention the burial of Christ nor does it make
explicit the offering of the gifts by the faithful, being content simply to
make a general reference to the faithful offering thanks.[93] Perhaps even
more striking is the fact that the anamnesis is directed to Christ.

The Syriac epiclesis reads as follows:

Indeed, then, prostrate before you, we beseech you, Almighty Lord and
God of the holy powers, to send your Holy Spirit upon these oblations
which are offered, and show this bread [to be] the venerable body of our
Lord Jesus Christ and this chalice the blood of our Lord Jesus Christ so

---

91. PE, 271–72.
92. Raes, "L'Authenticité . . . ," 5–16. Cf. also Jasper-Cuming, 124–28.
93. Ibid., 13–14. Cf. PE, 266–67.

that they may be, for all those partaking of them, [a means of] life and resurrection, and forgiveness of sins and health of soul and body, enlightenment of mind, justification before the awesome tribunal (βῆμα) of Christ; and let none of your people be lost, Lord, but make all of us worthy who serve you peacefully and who minister before you all the days of our life, so that through your grace and mercy and love of mankind, we may now enjoy your heavenly, immortal and life-giving mysteries. Amen.[94]

Once again it seems to be the Father who is beseeched that he send ("mittas") his Spirit upon the offerings ("oblationes") and that he show ("ostendas") the bread and wine to be the body and blood of our Lord Jesus Christ. This is asked so that [95] those who partake may obtain life and resurrection, forgiveness of their sins, health of soul and body, enlightenment of their understanding ("mentis") and justification ("apologia") before the awesome tribunal of Christ. The epiclesis closes with an appeal that none of the people go astray but that God make them worthy to serve him and enjoy heavenly, immortal and life-giving mysteries. A group of intercessions followed by a doxology round out the anaphora.[96]

The East Syrian Type Anaphora

The last type of Eastern anaphora to be considered is that of the East Syrian family. Here, too, one finds a characteristic arrangement: Dialogue—Praise and Thanksgiving—Introduction to the *Sanctus* and the *Sanctus* itself—Post-*Sanctus* Prayer of Praise, Thanks—Institution Narrative—Anamnesis—Intercessions—Epiclesis—Doxology.[97]

Besides its arrangement this family shows a number of other characteristic features. The epiclesis comes immediately before the doxology that concluded the eucharistic prayer. Generally, the intercessions immediately precede the epiclesis. The anamnesis is lacking in some documents. In its place one finds a prayer by which the assembly offers the sacrifice to God reconciling us with himself.[98] There are not

---

94. PE, 267.

95. Here, as in *The Apostolic Constitutions,* the action upon the gifts seems to us to be in view of the communicants and not vice versa as Bouyer, *Eucharistie* 277 (286) seems to indicate.

96. PE, 267–68.

97. PE, 374.

98. Ibid.

many anaphoras of this type but the ones we have are ancient and of great importance for the history of the eucharistic prayer in general, and for the epiclesis in particular.

The Anaphora of the Apostles Addai and Mari

C. Vagaggini in his study of the Roman Canon and liturgical reform has indicated the late date of the manuscripts for this anaphora and the difficulty in determining its primitive content and order. On the basis of these factors he contends that it would be foolish to take Addai and Mari as an example of the East Syrian tradition.[99] Nevertheless, it seems to be the most primitive anaphora of this type to come down to us, dating originally from the fourth or fifth century.[100] It is also the anaphora from this family that one most frequently encounters in conjunction with epiclesis studies. We have therefore decided to take the anaphora of Addai and Mari as the basic text and to compare its epiclesis with those of two other East Syrian anaphoras, the anaphora bearing the name of Theodore of Mopsuestia (sixth century) and that bearing the name of Nestorius (sixth/seventh century).[101]

Following an introductory dialogue which speaks of the God of Abraham, Isaac, and Israel, the prayer of praise begins,[102] praising the name of the Trinity for creating the world as well as those dwelling in it and for the compassion and grace shown mankind. Mention is then made of the angels who praise the name of God and this leads to the *Sanctus*. After the *Sanctus* the theme of thanks comes to the foreground—thanks to the Lord for having clothed himself with humanity, for having restored, forgiven and exalted mankind and for having granted victory to frail nature. In the text of Addai and Mari one next encounters the intercessions. The anaphoras of Theodore and

---

99. Vagaggini, *The Canon* . . . , 59.

100. Botte "L'Anaphore Chaldéene . . . ," 266, 276 writing in 1949 placed the origin of Addai and Mari in Edessa in the third century. In "Problèmes . . . ," 90, written in 1965, he states, however, that this anaphora could date back to the *fourth* century. Raes, "Liturgie: Orientalische Liturgien (Einzeltypen)," LThK 6 (1961²), 1089–90, thinks that the anaphora of Addai and Mari was probably redacted in the fifth century. Cf. also Jasper-Cuming, 39–44, 135–37 and Wilson, 19–37.

101. Cf. Botte, "L'épiclèse . . . syriennes orientales," 49–50 on the dating of these.

102. We are omitting the Cushara, the prayers, often of a penitential nature, which the priest says quietly at various points in the anaphora although these prayers are contained in the text presented by *Prex Eucharistica*. These have little bearing on our study and are obviously later interpolations.

of Nestorius, on the other hand, more characteristically have the intercessions immediately preceding the epiclesis.[103]

Another striking feature of the anaphora of Addai and Mari is the absence of an institution narrative. This has given rise to much debate but the problem does not directly concern us here.[104] The next thing is an anamnesis that asks that the assembly, gathered together to commemorate and celebrate the Passion, death, burial, and Resurrection of Christ, have a place in God's blessings.[105]

The epiclesis comes next. Botte has made easier a comparison of the epiclesis in Addai and Mari with those of the anaphoras of Theodore and of Nestorius by juxtaposing the three texts.[106]

---

103. PE, 375–80, 384–85, 392–95. Macomber, 361–67.

104. Cf. Botte, "L'Anaphore Chaldéene . . . ," 269–75; Macomber, 367 n. 7 and 371 n. 2. Cf. also A. Raes, "Le Récit de l'institution eucharistique dans l'anaphore chaldéene et malabare des Apôtres," OCP 10 (1944), 216–26.

105. PE, 380.

106. The question whether or not this epiclesis is a later interpolation has also been the occasion of much writing. Cf., for instance, Ratcliff, 29 and Botte, "Problèmes . . . ," 99–100, 105–106.

Addai & Mari

And may your Holy Spirit come and rest upon this offering of your servants and bless and sanctify it so that it might be for us, Lord, [a means to] pardon for offenses and forgiveness of sins and a great hope in the resurrection of the dead and new life in the kingdom of heaven with all those who have been pleasing before you.

Theodore

And may the grace of your Holy Spirit come upon us and upon this offering and may he dwell in, and descend upon, this bread and this chalice and bless and sanctify and sign them in the name of the Father and the Son and the Holy Spirit and, by the power of your name, may this bread become the body of o. Lord Jesus Christ and this cup the precious blood of o. Lord Jesus Christ and may it become for whoever eats this bread and drinks this cup [a means to] pardon for offenses and forgiveness of sins and a great hope in the resurrection of the dead and health of soul and body and a life and glory which is forever. Also make us all worthy, through the grace of Jesus Christ o. Lord, so that we may rejoice in the kingdom of heaven, in future blessings which do not pass away, with all those who have been pleasing to you and have lived according to your precepts.

Nestorius

And may the grace of your Holy Spirit come and rest upon this offering which we offer in your presence and bless and sanctify it and make this bread and this cup the body and blood of o. Lord Jesus Christ. Transforming and sanctifying them by the operation of the Holy Spirit, so that the reception of these glorious and holy mysteries might be [a means to] eternal life and resurrection from the dead, purification of mind and body, enlightened understanding, confidence before you and the eternal salvation about which Jesus Christ o. Lord, spoke to us . . . so that we may rejoice with the saints who have pleased you from the beginning.[107]

It is not immediately clear in the anaphora of Addai and Mari whether the addressee, "Domine," is the Father or Christ or simply "God" without any further Trinitarian precision.[108] The appeal is for the Holy Spirit to come ("veniat") and rest ("quiescat") upon the offering and to bless ("benedicat") and sanctify ("sanctificet") it. This is asked so that it might be "for us" a means to pardon for offenses, forgiveness of sins, hope of resurrection, and new life in heaven with the saints.

The Anaphora of Theodore

In the anaphora of Theodore it is asked that the grace of the Holy Spirit ("gratia Spiritus sancti") come ("veniat") "upon us" and dwell in ("habitat") and descend upon ("illabitur") the gifts. In addition to blessing and sanctifying, the Spirit is to sign ("obsignet") the gifts in the name of the Trinity and thus the bread and wine are to become ("fiat") the body and blood of Christ by the power of "your" name. Here we see a greater determination of the Spirit's sanctifying activity than in Addai and Mari. In addition to the benefits asked for in Addai and Mari, it is asked here that those who communicate may receive health of body and soul.

The Anaphora of Nestorius

In the so-called Nestorius anaphora, it is again the grace of the Holy Spirit that is called for upon the gifts to bless, sanctify and make ("faciat") them into the body and blood, the Father transforming ("transmutante") them by the operation of the Spirit. This is asked so that those partaking may receive eternal life, resurrection from the dead, purification of mind and body, enlightened understanding, confidence in approaching God, and eternal salvation with the saints.[109]

---

107. Botte, "L'épiclèse . . . syriennes orientales," 51–52. Both Botte and Ratcliff, 25, have based their studies of Addai and Mari on the sixteenth-century Latin manuscripts of the Urmi missal. In 1966 Macomber, 335–71 published tenth/eleventh century manuscripts of this anaphora. The Latin translation Macomber offers of the epiclesis is virtually identical with that of Botte and PE, 380. Botte, however, drops the last sentence beginning with "Et propter universam . . ." since he thinks it originally belonged to the anamnesis.

108. Ratcliff, 30–32 sees indications that in its original form this East-Syrian eucharistic prayer was addressed to Christ. Botte, "L'Anaphore Chaldéene . . . ," 265–66 thinks that the first part of Addai and Mari is addressed to "God" and not to Christ.

109. Cf. PE, 395–96. The text there also speaks of unity.

Later Western Tradition

The Roman Canon

The Roman canon presents some special difficulties. In conjunction
with the epiclesis question some see this canon as containing a number
of epiclesis type prayers, including the *Te igitur* and the *Hanc igitur*.[110]
Generally, however, the lion's share of attention goes to the prayers
Quam oblationem and *Supplices*. Even here the answers to the question
whether or not either or both of these prayers is an epiclesis range
from categorical affirmatives to equally categorical negatives.[111] To
some extent this question is one of terminology, and we shall treat that
in Part II. For the moment, however, we shall simply present the texts
in their context and leave the decision whether or not they could be an
epiclesis or epicleses until later.

   The Roman canon begins with a Preface introduced by a
dialogue such as that in the *Apostolic Tradition* of Hippolytus. This
Preface is variable and usually concentrates on praising God for one
aspect of the work of redemption, singing the praise of the saints or
imploring divine help.[112] Next comes the *Sanctus* followed not by
continuing thanksgiving as we have often seen with the Eastern
anaphoras but rather by a series of supplications. The *Te igitur* appeals
for the acceptance of the gifts offered first of all for the Church, and
its pope. The *Memento* that follows is a remembrance of different
classes of the living and leads into the *Communicantes*, a commemoration of the saints.[113]

---

110. Cf. Lietzmann, 117–122, esp. 121; Vagaggini, *The Canon* . . . ,98; Moreau, 60 n. 4; Betz,
181 n. 146; also Bouyer, *Eucharistie*, 145 (144), 213 (215), 232 (237) and the critique by Jungmann
(Review of Bouyer's *Eucharistie*), 465 of Bouyer's position. Cf. also Jasper-Cuming, 159–67.

111. Among those affirming *Quam oblationem* and/or *Supplices* as an epiclesis are M. de la
Taille II, 169–71; L. Duchesne, *Christian Worship* trans. by M. L. McClure (London, 1920⁵),
181–82; R. Woolley, 117–18; Cabrol, "Anamnèse," 1885; Cabasilas, 76–79; Betz, 181 n. 146;
Vurmester, 286, 295–96; Jungmann, *Liturgien der christlichen Frühzeit*, 76, 207 ff. and *Missarum
Sollemnia* II, 238 ff., 292–93. Cf. also, Cagin, *L'Eucharistia*, 53 ff.

   O. Casel, *Das christliche Opfermysterium*, 547 and (Review of Lietzmann's *Messe und
Herrenmahl*), 211–12 is an instance of a categorical negative on this question. Cf. Drews, 13–14,
19–22, 24, 26. A number of authors show more reserve or adopt somewhat of a middle position.
Among these we might note: Botte, *Le Canon* . . . , 60–61, 66–67; Bishop, "The Moment of
Consecration," 131–36; Atchley, *On the Epiclesis* . . . , 180; SH, 325–27.

112. Cf. PE 438–47.

113. PE, 427–31. Cf. Jungmann, *Missarum Sollemnia* II, 185–225; Botte, *Le Canon* . . . ,
52–57 and L. Eizenhöfer, "Te igitur und Communicantes im römischen Mess-Kanons," SE 8
(1956), 14–75.

The *Hanc igitur*, which at first glance appears to be another petition for acceptance of the offerings[114] but which closer examination shows to be a further determining of the intention of the present celebration,[115] leads up to the *Quam oblationem*. The *Quam oblationem* usually runs as follows:

> We beseech you, O God, be pleased to make this offering blessed, approved, perfect, spiritual and acceptable so that it becomes for us the body and blood of your beloved Son, our Lord and God, Jesus Christ.[116]

The Father is here, as throughout the canon, the addressee. Besides being asked to make the offering blessed, approved, spiritual,[117] and acceptable, the Father is asked in this prayer to see to it that this offering becomes for us ("fiat nobis") the body and blood of Christ. The institution narrative follows, then an anamnesis which mentions the Passion, Resurrection, and Ascension, and the offering the faithful make upon recalling these events.[118] The *Supra quae*, with its mention of Abel, Abraham, and Melchisedech, then asks God to regard and accept the present sacrifice. Next comes the *Supplices* which reads:

> We humbly beseech you, Almighty God, command that these [offerings] be carried by the hand of your angel to your heavenly altar, in the sight of your divine majesty, so that as often as we receive the body and blood of your Son by partaking of this altar below, we may be filled with every heavenly blessing and grace . . .[119]

Once again the addressee is the Father who is beseeched to have the present sacrifice carried to his heavenly altar by his "angel." This is asked so that those partaking from the altar may be filled with every heavenly blessing and grace. A *Memento* for the dead, an appeal to give "your servants" a share in the company of the saints (*Nobis quoque*), and a prayer for the blessing of material things or the first fruits lead up to the doxology which closes the canon.[120]

---

114. Cf. Bouyer, *Eucharistie* 145 (144). This is one point on which Jungmann (Review of Bouyer's *Eucharistie*), 465 criticizes Bouyer.

115. Jungmann, *Missarum Sollemnia* II, 225–34. Cf. PE, 431.

116. PE, 433. Cf. 421 for a similar version cited from *De Sacramentis* IV, 5, 21.

117. Cf. Casel, "Ein orentalisches Kultwort . . . ," 1–19 and "Die λογικὴ θυσία . . . ," 37–47. Cf. also, B. Botte-C. Mohrmann, *L'Ordinaire de la Messe* (Paris, 1953), 117–22 and Lebau, 115 ff.

118. PE, 433–34.

119. PE, 435.

120. PE, 435–38.

Gallican and Mozarabic Liturgies

The difficulties one runs into when trying to bring the Roman canon to bear on the epiclesis question seem minor compared to those one has to face in dealing with the Gallican and Mozarabic liturgies. The number alone of *Post Secreta* and *Post Pridie*[121] prayers would make an effort to apply their contents to the epiclesis question a study in itself. In 1924, for instance, J. A. Robinson was able to report:

> I have examined 225 forms of the *Post Pridie* prayer, and find that in 39 only is sanctification asked for through the Holy Spirit. In 29 it is asked direct from Christ; in one from the Holy Trinity; in six by means of an angel: usually the petition is simply addressed to God. In only six instances is there a request that the Holy Spirit may be sent for the purpose of effecting the change of the elements into the Body and Blood of Christ. These sixth- and seventh-century witnesses are evidence of Eastern influence, and are but the exceptions that prove the rule for the West.[122]

This quote not only gives one some idea of the vast numbers of forms involved but also indicates two other difficulties which the data poses in regard to the epiclesis question, namely, the dating of the Eastern influence and the apparent absence of any consistent form in these prayers.

As for dating the Eastern influence, Bouyer has recently tried to argue that the fluidity of the Gallican and Mozarabic prayer formularies reflect the state of affairs in Syria in the fourth century. He thus claims that the primary layer of the Gallican and Mozarabic prayer formularies reveals an early—mid-fourth century—Syrian influence. This would be before the wild improvisation which later characterized these Western liturgies.[123] Bouyer's position, however, is far from being a universally accepted one.[124]

---

121. The terns *Post Mysterium* and *Post Secreta* in the Gallican liturgies and *Post Pridie* in the Mozarabic liturgy designate a variable prayer that follows the institution narrative. Its theme may be either a commemoration of our Lord (an anamnesis of sorts) and/or a petition for the offerings. J. A. Robinson, 94.

122. J. A. Robinson, 94.

123. Bouyer, *Eucharistie*, 309–18 (320–29).

124. Cf. Jungmann (Review of Bouyer's *Eucharistie*), 463–64. Cf. also, Casel, "Neue Beiträge . . . ," 177–78 n. 9 and (Review of Lietzmann's *Messe* . . .), 211; Porter, 186–94; Gamber, 381–82 and Abercrombie, 395–96.

The other difficulty that the *Post Secreta* and *Post Pridie* prayers bring with them is their bewildering diversity. Some are addressed to the Son, some to the Father. Some waver between Christ and the Holy Spirit. Some appeal for the Son, while others ask for the Holy Spirit and still others for an impersonal force. The absence of any consistent pattern has often led to the conclusion that the Gallican and Mozarabic epiclesis-type prayers are the product of a lost sense of the real meaning of an epiclesis.[125]

As a result of the difficulties in evaluating those prayers some authors simply reject them as a basis for certain epiclesis theories.[126] Others merely attempt to fit them into general categories and to give some examples without being able to provide any common theological thread.[127]

We, too, shall have to content ourselves with offering some examples of the *Post Secreta* and *Post Pridie*. We have selected these particular ones not because they are necessarily typical of the Gallican and Mozarabic tradition but rather because they at times serve as support for, or at least illustrations of, some of the theories on the epiclesis which we shall see later. Of the five prayers which make up the Gallican and Mozarabic anaphoras or canons only two remain more or less invariable. The anaphora begins with a form of preface (*illation, contestation*) followed by the first invariable, the *Sanctus*. Then comes the *Post Sanctus* which picks up the theme of holiness. The next invariable, the institution narrative, and then the *Post Secreta* or *Post Pridie* round out the anaphora. Characteristic of both these types is a freedom of improvisation which at times verges on license.[128]

The first example comes from the Gallican liturgy:

O God of Abraham, God of Isaac, God of Jacob, God and Father of our Lord Jesus Christ: graciously benevolent from your heavens, bestow your most kind love on this sacrifice of ours. May the fullness of your majesty, divinity, love, power and glory descend O Lord, upon this bread and upon this cup and let it become for us a legitimate eucharist through

---

125. Cf. Dinesen, 79; W. C. Bishop, *The Mozarabic and Ambrosian Rites* (London, 1924), 47–54; Lietzmann, 98–99. Cf., however, Casel (Review of Lietzmann's *Messe* . . .), 211 for some reservations on the implications of Lietzmann's view. Cf. also Porter, 187–94.

126. Cf., for instance, Dinesen, 79.

127. Cf., for example, Lietzmann, 93–113 and Atchley, *On the Epiclesis* . . . , 148–67.

128. Cf. PE, 461, 494–95.

the transformation of the body and blood of the Lord; so that whoever
and as often as we taste of this bread and this cup, we may receive for
ourselves protection of the faith, purity of love, peaceful hope of resurrection and of everlasting immortality in your name and that of your Son and
Holy Spirit, communion with all the saints, forgiveness of all our faults.
We believe that you will grant these things to us when we ask them with
a firm faith . . .[129]

We have chosen this example primarily because of its use of the
phrase "*legitima eucharistia*." It is sometimes used, as here, in conjunction with the transformation into the body and blood of Christ. At
other times it appears as the principal effect desired and has given rise
to interesting opinions.[130]

The second example reads:

Behold we dare to approach your eucharist and to call on your name.
Come, therefore, communicate with us. Come, perfect heart. Come, communion of man . . . Come, communicate with us in your eucharist, which
we celebrate in your name and in your love, we who are gathered together
in your name. To you is every honour and glory forever . . .[131]

We have chosen this not only because it is an example of a
Logos epiclesis but because it also shows definite affinity to the possible
epiclesis-forerunner in the apocryphal Acts of Thomas and perhaps to
Didache 10:6, another possible forerunner of the developed epiclesis.[132]

The third choice comes from the Mozarabic liturgy and reads:

. . . because of this, therefore, we your servants ask that you sanctify this
offering by the commingling of your Holy Spirit and that you form ("conformes") it through the full transfiguration of the body and blood of our
Lord; [we ask this] so that through the sacrifice, by which we recall that we
are redeemed, we may merit to be cleansed from the filth of crimes; and do
not reject us from your care, we who are pierced through with misfortune;
you are the physician, we are the sick; you are mercy, we are in need of
mercy; therefore, because we do not hide our wounds from you, heal us
through these sacrifices by which you are pleased. Grant this, Unbegotten

---

129. PE, 480–81.

130. Cf. PE, 492, 493, 505. Cf. also Frere, *The Anaphora*, 114–115; Porter, 187, 189; and
Havet, 70, 83–84.
For the lexicographical meaning of the word, cf. Blaise, 491.

131. PE, 491.

132. Gamber, 377–81.

Father, through your Only Begotten, our Lord Jesus Christ, through whom you create all these good things for us, your unworthy servants . . .[133]

The primary object of interest in this passage lies in the word "*conformes.*" The "*confomatio sacramenti*" of which Isidore of Seville speaks has raised the question of whether he is speaking of the transformation of the bread and wine into the body and blood of Christ or of some further sanctification in view of the communicants.[134] Along the same lines the following prayer has been appealed to as proof that a further sanctification of the already transformed gifts is meant:[135]

This is the holy and salutary sacrifice, God and Father, by which the world was reconciled to you: this is that body which hung on the cross; this is also the blood which flowed from the holy side. We thank you then for your love, because you have redeemed us by the death of your Son and have saved us by his resurrection; in an attitude of dependence we beseech you, O God of love, that, sprinkling this offering with the benediction of your Holy Spirit, you bring sanctification to the hearts of those receiving it; purified by it from the stain of our sins, we shall rejoice fully on this day of the Lord's resurrection. Amen.[136]

The final example is a type which serves as support for those who claim that the primitive epiclesis, in the Mozarabic as well as elsewhere, was a Prayer to God that he bless or sanctify the eucharistic oblation to the spiritual benefit of the offerers and communicants.[137] The text reads:

Make our fast acceptable you, Almighty God, and sanctify this sacrifice offered by us: through it is granted, to all those receiving from it, forgiveness of sins and through it is given to all the faithful in common the fullness of your grace.[138]

---

133. PE, 500.

134. Blaise, 197, for instance, sees the phrase as referring to the transformation of bread and wine into the body and blood of Christ. Cf. Brightman (Correspondence: Invocation in the Holy Spirit, 39). Cf., on the other hand, Havet, 63–65, and the authors he cites there.

135. Geiselmann, 194–95; SH, 320–21, 327; and Havet, 66–72, esp. 68. Cf. also, Cagin, *L'Eucharistia*, 51.

136. PE, 507.

137. Porter, 193–94. Brinktrine, "Zur Entstehung . . . ," 306–17, esp. 314.

138. M. Férotin, *Le Liber Mozarabicus et les Manuscripts Mozarabes (Monumenta Ecclesiae Liturgica* VI) (Paris, 1912), 215–216, n. 507.

As unsatisfying as such a scanty sampling of the Gallican and Mozarabic texts may be, it will have to suffice. Even this small sample should, however, give one an inkling of the variety and at times the state of confusion often found in the *Post Secreta* and *Post Pridie* of these liturgies. It should also make one circumspect in regard to historical or theological theories that appeal to these prayers for their main support.

SUMMARY

At this point it might be helpful to summarize what we have seen in the texts of the early Christian anaphoras. The following table should supply an overall view of the findings thus far.

Table 1.1 The Epiclesis in the Ancient Anaphoras

Anaphora	After instit. narrative	Father as Addressee	asked	For Holy Spirit	upon us	upon elements
Apost. Trad.	x	x	mittas	x	—	oblationem s. ecclesiae
Test of O. Lord[1]	x	x	mitte	x	—	potum, escam
Ap. Const.	x	x	καταπέμψῃς	x	—	θυσίαν
Alexandrian Type						
Gr. Mark (I)	before	x	πλήρωσον	your blessing through the visitation of H. Spirit		θυσίαν
(II)	x	x	ἐπιδέφ ἡμιᾶς ἐξαπόστειλον	x	—	ἄρτους, ποτήρια
Der Balyzeh (I)	before	x	πλήρωσον ἡθᾶς-χαταλπέμψαι	x	—	χτίσματα
(II)	x	x(?)		(?)	(?)	(?)
Serapion (I)	before	x	πλήρωσον	your power & participation Logos	—	Θυσίαν
(II)	x	x	ἐπιδημησάτω		—	ἄρτον, ποτήριον
Antiochean Type[2]						
Chrysostom	x x		κατάπεμψον	x	x	προκείμενα δῶρα
Basil (Byz.)	x	x	ἐλθεῖν	x	x	
Basil (Alex.)	x	x	descendat	x	x	dona proposita
Gr. James	x	x	ἐξαπόστειλον κατάπεμψον	x	x	προχείμενα ἀγία δῶρα
Syr. James	x	x	mitte	x	x	oblationes propositae
Twelve Ap.	x	x	mittas	x	—	oblationes propositae
East Syrian Type						
Addai-Mari	x	x(?)	veniat quiescat	x	—	oblationem
Theodore	x	x	veniat illabitur inhabitat	grace of H. Sp.	x	panem, calicem
Nestorius	x	x	veniat quiescat	grace of H. Sp.	—	oblationem
Later W. Tradition						
Roman Canon Quam "oblationem"	before	x	facere benedictam, ascriptam, ratam rationabilem, acceptabilemque	—	—	—
"Supplices"	x	x	jube haec perferri in conspectu tuae	—	—	—

Gallican-Mozarabic   (the number and variety of the *post-secreta* and *post-pridie* prayers seem to preclude presenting any as really "typical")

1. acc. To Botte's reconstruction
2. To this group belong Testament of Our Lord, Apost. Const. as well.

So that bread, wine Body, Blood	So that partakers benefit			other benefits
	unity	forgiveness	resurr. &/or eternal life (eschatological)	
	x	—	—	filled w. H. Spirit, confirm in faith
	—	x	x	confirm in faith, spiritual health strength, not judgment & condemnation
ἵνα ἄποφήιη	—	x	x	fullness of H. Spirit defense against Satan/ reconciliation
	—	—	—	—
ἵνα ἁγιαση τελειώση, ποιήση	—	x	x·	various virtues, renewal of body & soul & spirit
καί ποιησον	x(?)	—		
(?)	(?)	(?)	(?)	power of H. Sp. strengthening, increasing, of faith, hope, eternal life
	—		—	—
ἵνα γένηται	—	—	—	healing, strength, not condemnation
καὶ ποιήσον μεταβαλών	x	x	—	sobriety, fullness of kingdom, not condemnation (eschat.?)
καί ευλογη ἁγιασαι ἀναδείξαι	x	—	x	
et sanctificet et ostendantur[3]	x	—	x	sanctification of soul and body
ἵνα ἁγιάσῃ ποιήση	—	x	x	health of body & soul, good works, strength of Church against threats
ut faciat	—	x	x	"same as preceding"
et ostendas	—	x	x	health of soul & body, enlightened understanding
et benedicat sanctificet[4]	—	x	x	—
et benedicat et sanctificet et obsignet in nomine Patris, Filii, Sp. Sancti et fiat	—	x	x	health of body & soul
et benedicat, sanctificet, et faciat transmutante	—	—	x	purification of mind and body, enlightened understanding
et fiat nobis	—	—	—	
—	—	—	—	filled with every heavenly grace and blessing

---

3. No mention made of body and blood.

4. There is no institution narrative in the present text.

Chapter 2

The Epiclesis and the Moment of Consecration Question: A Brief History

In Chapter 1 we examined the liturgical data of the early anaphoras. In that chapter, we were dealing with one component of the historical heritage with which the student of the epiclesis must work. In this chapter, we will focus on another component of this heritage: the history of the epiclesis prior to the modern period and, especially, the entanglement of the epiclesis with the "moment of consecration" question during the twentieth century. The issue became whether the institution narrative or the epiclesis was consecratory. This chapter lays no claim to being an exhaustive or even a detailed historical study. For a more complete picture of the historical background of the eucharistic epiclesis, works such as those of Atchley, Salaville, Cabrol, and Schillebeeckx are indispensable.[1]

THE EPICLESIS IN PATRISTIC WRITINGS

Odo Casel once asserted that the solution to the epiclesis question lay not in rational arguments ("Verstandesgründe") but rather in a proper understanding of the Fathers of the Church.[2] Besides seeming to set up a false dichotomy, such a statement could mislead one into minimizing the difficulty of the patristic texts in question. The writings of the Fathers must indeed form part of the basis for an intelligent interpre-

---

1. Atchley, *On the Epiclesis* . . . ; Salaville, "Epiclèse eucharistique," 194–300; Cabrol, "Epiclèse," 142–84; SH, 307–54. Cf. also Smit, 95–136 for a good summary of the problem.

2. Casel, *Das christliche Opfermysterium*, 536.

tation of the eucharistic epiclesis. Even a passing acquaintance with the pertinent texts and the interpretations given them shows, however, that they are not only most crucial, they are also most controversial.

We have selected some of the patristic texts that seem pivotal in forming an interpretation of the epiclesis. Any attempt to be selective, of course, runs the risk of being arbitrary. We have generally tried, however, to choose those texts that seem to have had the greatest impact on the interpretation of the epiclesis in the twentieth century.

The questions of greatest concern here are: did the Fathers consider the epiclesis to be "consecratory" and, if so, in what sense? In trying to answer these questions we have had, of necessity, to turn for help to twentieth-century writers, and this may at first glance seem to be anticipating the main body of this study. This chapter, however, shall limit itself to presenting the pertinent patristic texts, calling on twentieth-century writers only in so far as they can help us to understand these texts. Only in Part II of this study shall we examine and attempt to evaluate the theories these writers have evolved in regard to the development and, especially, the theology of the eucharistic epiclesis.

Justin Martyr (d. c. 165)

The first object for consideration is Justin Martyr and his *I Apology*, a work which dates from around 150–55. This work is particularly important. If it can shed some light on the eucharistic epiclesis, we will be able to reach all the way back to the middle of the second century for a basis of interpretation. This text is significant for another reason. It gives one a foretaste of the headaches in store for the historians (and the theologians relying on them) in their efforts to decipher some of the patristic texts.

In describing the Eucharist of the newly baptized, Justin draws upon the parallel between the Incarnation and the Eucharist to make the point that it is no longer "ordinary" bread and wine that is involved but the body and blood of Christ. The text reads:

> And this food is called by us the Eucharist. Of which no one is allowed to partake but he who believes that the things which we teach are true, and who has been washed in the bath for the forgiveness of sins and to regeneration, and who so lives as Christ has directed. For not as ordinary bread and ordinary drink do we receive these, but in like manner as by the word

of God Jesus Christ our Saviour was made flesh and had both flesh and blood for our salvation, so also the food, which is *blessed by the prayer of the Word* which proceeded from him and from which our flesh and blood by transmutation are nourished, is, we are taught, the flesh and blood of that Jesus who was made flesh. For the apostles in the memoirs which they composed and which are called gospels have declared that they were commanded to do as follows: that Jesus took bread and gave thanks and said, "this do in remembrance of me, this is my body," and in like manner he gave thanks and said "this is my blood" and gave it to them alone.[3]

The italicized phrase is the key one. That the bread and wine become "euchatistized" (δί εὐχῆς λόγου) is clear. Precisely what Justin means by this latter phrase is not so clear. The lexicographical meaning of the words εὐχή and λόγος hardly suffice to clear up the doubt.[4] There are no less than five possibilities of translating or interpreting this phrase.

It could refer to a Logos epiclesis, a prayer *for* the Logos. It could refer to a prayer from the personal Word, the Logos. One could translate this same phrase as "the prayer (made up) of words (stemming) from him (Christ)" or "the word of prayer (coming) from him (Christ)," e.g., the institution narrative or the entire eucharistic prayer including the institution narrative. Finally, one might see this phrase as simply referring to a general sort or type of prayer ("eine Art des Gebetes").[5]

The three possibilities which are of the greatest interest are that of the Logos epiclesis, that of the institution narrative alone and that of the entire eucharistic prayer including the institution narrative.

The first possibility is that Justin is speaking of a Logos epiclesis. Supporters of this view appeal to the passage's parallel with the Incarnation and to its grammatical reconstruction. In addition, they argue that second-century theology tended to attribute to the Logos what post-Nicene theology would later attribute to the Holy Spirit, and they point to fourth-century echoes of a Logos epiclesis to bolster this argument.[6]

---

3. PE, 70 = MELV, 17–18. English version from Quasten, I, 216. Cf. also Jasper-Cuming, 25–30 and Bradshaw, *Eucharistic Origins*, 61–77.

4. Cf. Liddell-Scott, 739, 1057–59 and Lampe, 580–84, 807.

5. Cf. Betz, *Die Eucharistie . . .* , 270 n. 32 and Perler, 300.

6. Cf. Dölger I, 73–79; II, 497–502; MELV, 62–63 n. 5; Betz, ibid., 270. Cf. Perler, 296–303, 308–309, 313 for critique of this position.

It is also possible to take the position that the phrase δί εὐχῆς λόγου in Justin refers to the institution narrative pure and simple. This position presumes that the words, "This is my body . . . This is my blood," which follow shortly upon the aforementioned phrase are synonymous with it. The sureness, however, with which some propose this interpretation is at times remarkable.[7] It is all the more surprising in view of at least the possibility that Justin intended the words, "This is my body, etc." not as a commentary on the phrase δί εὐχῆς λόγου but rather as a proof that the bread and wine had indeed become the body and blood of Christ.[8]

Finally, it is possible to argue that the Fathers did not try to isolate particular prayers within the anaphora or to underline a precise "moment of consecration," and to claim that Justin is referring to the whole eucharistic prayer with the institution narrative as its center.[9]

It is difficult to come up with a clear-cut judgment in favor of any one of these interpretations. If one were to judge by the weight of authority alone, the position claiming that Justin is referring to a Logos epiclesis would appear at first glance to have the upper hand. The list of those favoring this theory is impressive.[10]

The other theories in regard to Justin's δί εὐχῆς λόγου also have noteworthy proponents, however, and it is difficult to consider the arguments offered in favor of any of the theories as absolutely conclusive. Atchley may be a bit strong when he maintains that in the case of Justin: "His witness is therefore of no avail either for or against a Pneuma-epiclesis: nor indeed for any detail of the content of the

---

7. Cf. Altaner-Stuiber, 70, for instance, and L. Baurain, "L'épiclèse," *Revue Augustinienne* 1 (1902), 462–64. Cf. also, Renz, 163; Struckmann, 61; Jugie, *De forma . . .* , 104–106 lists Justin as "most probably" witnessing to the institution narrative as the "form" of the Eucharist; Batiffol, "Nouvelles Etudes . . . ," (1), 525 and the same author's *L'eucharistie*, 181–82.

8. Cf., for instance, Quasten's translation of this text in his *Patrology* I, 216. Cf. also Perler, 302.

9. Cf. Casel, "Die Eucharistielehre des hl. Justinus Martyr," 332–41. Cf. also, Varaine, *L'épiclèse. . . ,* 19; H. Elfers, *Die Kirchenordnung Hippolytus von Rom* (Paderborn, 1938), 245 and Casel's review of this work in ALW 2 (1952), 125; Salaville, "La liturgie décrite . . . ," 224; Rauschen, 121–22 (at least at the time this was published); and perhaps Kretschmar, 190.

10. Besides Dölger and Betz, whom we have already cited as holding this position, the list includes, Cabrol, "Epiclèse," 143; Lietzmann, 77 n. 1; Stählin, 40–41; Betz also lists Pascher, *Eucharistia* (1953²), 115–116 but although Pascher uses the translation, "Gebet um den Logos," he hastens to add that it is unclear whether Justin is referring here to the whole eucharistic prayer or a part of it; Jungmann, *Missarum Sollemnia* II, 239 n. 24, states: "Die Stelle dürfte eine Logosepiklese besagen." In PE, 69, however, he seems to prefer the interpretation that it is the institution narrative within the framework of the entire eucharistic prayer to which Justin is referring.

form of consecration, to use later phraseology."[11] Nevertheless, given the sketchiness of the sources, it would seem that Justin taken alone is less than crystal clear. Consequently, the foundation he provides for a theological or historical position on the eucharistic epiclesis would seem correspondingly less than unshakeable.

We have lingered on this passage from Justin in the hope of indicating the complexity of the epiclesis question. The patristic texts which must necessarily form a partial basis for attempts to explain the epiclesis often do not allow a simple interpretation. It is true that not all of the patristic texts are as obscure as that of Justin. Nevertheless, one's experience with his δί εὐχῆς λόγου τοῦ παρ᾽ αὐτοῦ should make one wary of categorical interpretations of the pertinent passages from other Fathers.

Irenaeus

With this caution in mind, let us examine Irenaeus of Lyon and relevant passages from his *Adversus Haereses*, composed around 180–185. Irenaeus is important because of his reputation as a theologian and because it takes us back once again into the second century.

Irenaeus argues from the real presence of the body and blood of Christ in the Eucharist to the reality of the bodily resurrection:

> When, therefore, the mingled cup and the manufactured bread receives the Word of God (ἐπιδέχεται τὸν λόγον τοῦ θεοῦ) and the Eucharist becomes the blood and body of Christ, from which things the substance of our flesh is increased and supported, how can they affirm that the flesh in incapable of receiving the gift of God, which is life eternal, which is nourished from the body and blood of the Lord and is a member of him? . . . that flesh which is nourished by the cup which is his blood and receives increase from the bread which is his body. And just as a cutting from the vine planted in the ground fructifies in its season, or, as a grain of wheat falling into the earth and becoming decomposed rises with manifold increase by the Spirit of God, and becomes the Eucharist, which is the body and blood of Christ, so also our bodies, being nourished by it, and deposited in the earth, and suffering decomposition there, shall rise at their appointed time . . . For as bread from the earth, receiving the invocation of God (προσλαβόμενος τὴν ἐπίκλησιν τοῦ θεοῦ) is no longer common

---

11. Atchley, *On the Epiclesis . . .* , 27. See also the same author's "The Epiclesis: A Criticism," 31.

bread but a Eucharist composed of two things, both an earthly and a heavenly one, so also our bodies, partaking of the Eucharist, are no longer corruptible, having the hope of eternal resurrection . . .[12]

This, then, is the context of Irenaeus's statements on the epiclesis. De Jong[13] has obligingly provided us with a juxtaposition of the pertinent passages:

1. *IV, 18, 5*	2. *V, 2, 2*	3. *V, 2, 3:*
. . . bread from the earth, receiving the invocation of God is no longer common bread but a Eucharist composed of two things, both an earthly and a heavenly one.	. . . the manufactured bread receives the Word of God and the Eucharist becomes the body of Christ.	. . . a cutting from the vine . . ., a grain of wheat . . . receiving the Word of God becomes the Eucharist . . . which indeed is the body and blood of Christ.

At first glance the case of Irenaeus seems open to a fairly simple interpretation. Few will challenge the fact that Irenaeus sees an "epiclesis" as playing a key role in transforming the bread and wine into the body and blood of Christ.[14] It is when one asks the meaning of the term "epiclesis" for Irenaeus, however, that the battle is joined. One could, for instance, maintain that Irenaeus like Justin witnesses to a Logos epiclesis.[15] It also seems possible, however unlikely, to include Irenaeus with those clearly teaching that the institution narrative is the "form" of the Eucharist.[16] Some authors maintain that Irenaeus understands the whole anaphora or eucharistic prayer under the term "epiclesis."[17] This last group appeals to Irenaeus's sneering reference to the Gnostic Marcus, "pretending to consecrate cups mixed with wine,

12. Quasten, Patrology I, 304–305.

13. De Jong, "Der Ursprüngliche Sinn . . . ," 37. Cf. Harvey, 204–208, 319–20, 322–23 and A. Rousseau, *Irénée de Lyon: Contre les Hérésies (Livre IV)* (= SC 100) (Paris, 1965), 610–11 for a more recent edition of IV, 18, 5.

14. Atchley, *On the Epiclesis* . . . , 29–30 even sees these passages as proving that this "epiclesis," whatever it was, was in Irenaeus' day consecratory and therefore offers, "no support for the theory that the invocation originally was on those about to communicate." Cf. MacLean, 408.

15. Cf. for instance, Betz, *Die Eucharistie* . . . , 334 and Buchwald, 29–32.

16. Jugie, *De forma* . . . , 92–94 and the same author's "La forme . . . d'après Saint Irénée," 231–32. Cf. also Struckmann, 87.

17. Casel, "Die Eucharistielehre . . . ," 336 n. 1; Salaville, "Epiclèse eucharistique," 233 holds that it was not an epiclesis in the strict sense, *at least not exclusively,* but rather the whole anaphora. Cf. also Gretschmar, 189; Rauschen, 121–22; and Varaine, *L'épiclèse* . . . , 22. Jugie, "La forme . . . ," 224–26 agrees that the term "epiclesis" as used in Irenaus's reference to the

and spinning out *at great length* the logos of the invocation (τὸν λόγο
ν τῆς ἐπικλήσεως), he makes them appear purple and red . . ."[18]
This passage indicates, they claim, that for Irenaeus the term "epiclesis"
meant more than a short formulary.[19]

Once again, then, the text seems to admit of more than one
interpretation. In this situation certain authors suggest that we simply
agree that Irenaeus regarded an "epiclesis" as "consecratory" and admit
that the exact nature of this "epiclesis" remains obscure.[20]

The limitations of time and space involved in this brief
historical sketch forbid an individual treatment of Cyprian and
Firmilian, Clement of Alexandria and Origen, Athanasius and the
Cappadocians. The reader is referred to more detailed historical
studies for this purpose.[21]

One point, however, deserves at least a passing reference. This
is the running battle which centered around the Cappadocians' silence
in regard to an epiclesis of the Holy Spirit. Some authors maintain
that if there had been a Spirit epiclesis at the time, the same Fathers
who appealed to the baptismal formula in the Pneumatomachian
controversy (literally "Opponents of the Spirit," a fourth-century
Christian heresy that denied the full personality and divinity of the
Holy Spirit) would also have appealed to the eucharistic epiclesis to
vindicate the Holy Spirit's divine status. Moreover, the fact that these
authors find, with the exception of Cyril, consistent reference to a
Logos epiclesis from Justin to Gregory of Nyssa leads them to question the general existence of a Spirit epiclesis during this same period.[22]

Gnostic Marcus is used in a sense corresponding to the whole anaphora but insists (231–32) that
in IV, 18, 5 Irenaeus uses the term "epiclesis" to refer to the institution narrative.

18. *Adversus Haereses* I, 13, 2 (= Harvey, I, 115–16).

19. Cf. Lampe, 526 and Kretschmar, 189 n.1.

20. Perler, 313–14; cf. also Connolly, "The Meaning . . . ," 340. Also Atchley, *On the Epiclesis* . . . , 29 and MacLean, 408.

21. In addition to the works we have already mentioned in footnote 1, the reader might
profitably consult the following studies: Betz, *Die Eucharistie* . . . , 334–335; Bishop, "The
Moment of Consecration," 155–57; Strawlwy, esp. 44, 110; Connolly, "On the meaning of
'Epiclesis,'" 28–43; Varaine, *L'épiclèse* . . . , 23–36, 38–40 and his summarizing article with the
same title, 119–31, esp. 123–24; Casel, *Das christliche Opfermysterium*, 536–38 and the same
author's (Review of Frere's *The Anaphora*), esp. 162; Perler, 314–15; G. A. Michell, "Firmilian
and Eucharistic Consecration," JTS n.s. 5 (1954), 215–20; Jugie, *De forma* . . . , 96–98, 106 and
the same author's "De epiclesi eucharistica secundum Basilium magnum," 202–207; Renz,
345–51; B. Bobrinskoy, "Liturgic et ecclésiologie . . . ," 1–32; Havet, 80–89.

22. Cf. Bishop, "The Moment . . . ," 140–43 and Dix, "The Origins . . . ," 197–98.

This argument from silence is, however, not without its opponents. They contend that the argument from silence works just as well against those holding for a Logos epiclesis during this period. If there had been a Logos epiclesis why did the Fathers not appeal to it to defend the Godhead of Christ when *that* was under attack? Moreover, there were in fact those who appealed to the operation of the Holy Spirit in the Eucharist, for instance, Ambrose and, later on, Isidore of Pelusium. The main reason for the Cappadocians' failure to cite the Spirit epiclesis against the Pneumatomachians is to be found in the nature of the attack brought to bear against the divinity of the Holy Spirit. The Pneumatomachians, continuing this objection, viewed the sending, the temporal mission of the Holy Spirit, as evidence of his inferiority. They also claimed the orthodox doctrine was not scriptural. To counter these claims, the Fathers would hardly have been well advised to appeal to an epiclesis which was not biblical and which spoke of the sending of the Holy Spirit. With the Matthaean baptismal formula these problems did not present themselves. It was biblical and it put the Holy Spirit on equal footing with the Father and the Son.[23]

Cyril of Jerusalem (d.c. 386)

The next patristic text which seems pivotal is from the *Mystagogical Catecheses* of Cyril of Jerusalem.[24] The importance of this text lies in the fact that it is one of the most ancient and most complete witnesses to a so-called consecratory Spirit epiclesis in the strict sense.[25]

Already in the first of the *Mystagogical Catecheses* Cyril makes it clear that it is the "epiclesis" which effects the change of the bread and wine into the body and blood of Christ. There he tells his hearers: "The bread and wine of the Eucharist before the holy invocation of

---

23. Atchley, *On the Epiclesis . . .*, 62–63 or perhaps even more clearly expressed in his "The Epiclesis: A Criticism," 33–34. Cf. also, Tyrer, *The Eucharistic Epiclesis*, 66–68 and MacLean, 412. Dix, "The Epiclesis: Some considerations," 292 was to keep the argument alive by rejecting Atchley's claim that the Fathers hesitated to use references to a "mission" of the Holy Spirit, as not reflecting the data.

24. Although the dating and authenticity of this work will quite naturally play a role in the interpretation of the text, we cannot enter into the dispute revolving around these two points. For the present we shall presume that these writings reflect Cyril's thought and we shall try to point out where differences in dating might most affect the interpretation of pertinent passages. Cf. Quasten, *Patrology* III, 362–66; Altaner-Stuiber, 312–13 and, for a detailed summary of the dispute over the work's authenticity, Piédagnel-Paris, 18–40.

25. Cabrol, "Epiclèse," 148.

the Adorable Trinity (ἐπικλήσεως τῆς προσκυνητῆς τράδος) was simply bread and wine, while after the invocation (ἐπικλήσεως) the bread becomes the body of Christ and the wine the blood of Christ" (I, 7, 5).[26] In the fifth *Catechesis* Cyril explains the liturgy of the Mass and in treating the anaphora provides us with an idea of the epiclesis in its context. The text runs:

> (4) Then the celebrant cries: "lift up your hearts." For truly it is right in that most awful hour to have one's heart on high with God, not below, occupied with earth and the things of earth. In effect, then, the bishop commands everyone to banish worldly thoughts and workaday cares and to have their hearts in heaven with the good God.
>
> Assenting, you answer, "We have them lifted up to the Lord." Let no one present be so disposed that while his lips form the words, "We have them lifted up to the Lord," in his mind his attention is engaged by worldly thoughts. At all times we should commemorate God, but at least, if this is not possible to human weakness, we must aspire to it in that hour.
>
> (5) Then the priest says: "Let us give thanks [make eucharist] to the Lord." Indeed we ought to give thanks to the Lord for calling us, when we were unworthy, to so great a grace, for reconciling us when we were enemies, and for vouchsafing to us the spirit of adoption.
>
> Then you say: "It is meet and just." In giving thanks we do indeed a meet thing and a just; but He did, not a just thing, but one that went beyond justice, in deigning to bestow on us such marvelous blessings.
>
> (6) After that we commemorate the heavens, the earth and the sea; the sun and moon, the stars, the whole rational and irrational creation, both visible and invisible: Angels and Archangels; Virtues, Dominions, Principalities, Powers, Thrones and the many-faced Cherubim: equivalently saying with David, "O magnify ye the Lord with me." We commemorate also the Seraphim whom Isaiah in the Holy Spirit saw encircling the throne of God, "with two wings veiling their faces and with twain their feet, while with twain they did fly," as they chanted: "Holy, Holy, Holy, Lord of Hosts." It is to mingle our voices in the hymns of the heavenly armies that we recite this doxology which descends to us from the Seraphim.
>
> (7) *Next, after sanctifying ourselves by these spiritual songs, we implore the merciful God to send forth His Holy Spirit upon the offering to make the bread*

---

26. Cf. Piédagnel-Paris, 94 for the Greek text.

*the Body of Christ and the wine the Blood of Christ. For whatever the Holy
Spirit touches is hallowed and changed.*

(8) Next when the spiritual sacrifice, the bloodless worship, has been completed, over that sacrifice of propitiation we beseech God for the public peace of the Churches, for the good estate of the world, for the Emperors, for the armed forces and our allies, for those in sickness, for the distressed: for all, in a word, who need help, we all pray and offer this sacrifice.

(9) Then we commemorate also those who have fallen asleep: first of all, the patriarchs, prophets, apostles, and martyrs, that God through their intercessory prayers may accept our supplication. Next we pray also for the holy Fathers and Bishops who have fallen asleep, and generally for all who have gone before us, believing that this will be of the greatest benefit to the souls of those on whose behalf our supplication is offered in the presence of the holy, the most dread Sacrifice.[27]

I have italicized the passage that is most pertinent. In itself the text seems quite clear. There are some authors who, while acknowledging that Cyril appears to witness to a "consecratory" Spirit epiclesis, see this passage as contradicting "Catholic doctrine," i.e., the view that the institution narrative alone is "consecratory." They try to work out of the difficulty by suggesting that the phrase "epiclesis of the Holy Spirit" is synonymous with the phrase "epiclesis of the adorable Trinity" found in *Mystagogical Catecheses* I, 7, 5. This latter phrase, they contend, refers to the whole eucharistic prayer including the institution narrative.[28]

Another possible interpretation is that "Spirit" here was understood as referring to the Logos. Thus we have no basic difference in content between the epiclesis now in question and the Logos of the epiclesis. The difference would, then, lie solely in the terminology employed.[29] The opinion, however, which asserts that Cyril is referring to a prayer for the descent of the Holy Spirit, the Third Person of the Trinity, and that Cyril sees this prayer as "consecratory," seems truer to the text.[30]

---

27. PE, 206 = Piédagnel-Paris, 150–58 and cf. also 154 of the latter for text of III, 3, 5 where Cyril uses similar terminology in drawing the parallel between the effects of the eucharistic epiclesis and the epiclesis over the chrism. English version from FC, LXIV, 193–97.

28. Cf. Jugie, *De forma* . . . , 111–14 and Salaville, "Epiclèse eucharistique," 238–39.

29. Cf. Betz, *Die Eucharistie* . . . , 340–41.

30. Cf. Dix, *The Shape* . . . , 198–99; Atchley, *On the Epiclesis* . . . , 52; Cabrol, "Epiclèse," 148; Bishop, "The Moment . . . ," 142; Schmidt-Lauber, 158; MacLean, 408; Varaine,

In dealing with Cyril's reference to an epiclesis the answers to two questions seem to be crucial for reconstructing the history and trying to determine a theology of the epiclesis. Was Cyril an innovator? In *Mystagogical Catecheses* V has he left behind a description of the *complete* anaphora as he knew it? A number of authors have taken the stand that Cyril was indeed an innovator and therefore cannot be considered typical of his day in a number of areas, the epiclesis included.[31]

Atchley, on the other hand, rejects the implication that Cyril might have introduced the invocation of the Holy Spirit or even that he was an innovator. Working from a date of 347–348 for the *Mystagogical Catecheses*, he reasons that Cyril was only a "junior presbyter" at the time and therefore in no position to be an innovator. Even if he was inclined to innovate he would be unlikely to introduce novelties into a set of addresses to the newly baptized. Finally, in three discourses he shows himself to be a strict traditionalist, appealing to the Scriptures and received traditions as the basis for what he says. "It may safely be concluded, therefore, that the epiclesis given by him was not new in his days but, at any rate in his opinion, was of long standing and traditional."[32]

The answer given the question whether or not Cyril was an innovator is important in tracing the historical development of the eucharistic epiclesis. The question whether or not in describing the anaphora in general, and the epiclesis in particular, he gave their content in its entirety, has far-reaching theological implications. One can argue that, as improbable as it might seem to some, we have to take the text at its face value. Proponents of this view contend that Cyril is giving the anaphora as he knew it, i.e., without an institution narrative, without an *anamnesis* clause, and with a consecratory Spirit epiclesis as the only possible candidate for the later title of "moment of consecration."[33] This could be theologically significant since it could be taken as a confirmation of a point of view which runs consistently through Atchley's study

---

L'épiclèse . . . , 38 and Brunner, "Zur Lehre . .," 349. Cf. also, Casel, "Neue Beiträge . . . ," 171 and Piédagnel-Paris, 95 n. 2.

31. Cf. Bishop, "Notes and Studies: Liturgical Comments and Memoranda VII-IX," 38, 43, 57, 59 and "The Moment . . . ," 142 and Dix, *The Shape* . . . , 199–200, 202, 280–81.

32. Atchley, *On the Epiclesis* . . . , 51.

33. Cf. Dix, *The Shape* . . . , 197–98, 200. Atchley, *On the Epiclesis* . . . , 52 would tend to agree with Dix at least insofar as the epiclesis is concerned.

of the epiclesis: "It is to be noted that there is no mention of the Holy Spirit on the communicants, but only on the elements."[34]

The contention, however, that Cyril has provided the entire content of the eucharistic prayer as he knew it poses some thorny problems. In a section which he acknowledges as the most speculative of his whole book, Dix attempts to explain the absence of the words of institution. In addition, he tries to cope with the unusual lack of any mention of actually receiving Communion. His explanations of the absence of both these elements appear somewhat strained and hardly satisfactory.[35] Thus we would tend to go along with the interpretation which holds that Cyril is not attempting to give a detailed commentary on each element in the anaphora.[36] While this view does not necessarily rule out the claim that the epiclesis as Cyril knew it did not contain a reference to the communicants, it does point up the fact that such a claim rests on evidence that is far from incontrovertible.

John Chrysostom (d. 407)

We now turn to John Chrysostom. The fiery Antiochene is especially important because of all the Eastern Fathers Chrysostom is one of the most explicit in regard both to the intervention of the Holy Spirit and to the effect of the institution narrative in the Eucharist.[37] Moreover, his teaching in these two areas will play a key role in the debates and in the final declaration by the Greeks at the Council of Florence. This council, as will be seen below, was pivotal in the history of the epiclesis question.

As is to be expected, Chrysostom's importance leads to a series of claims and counterclaims about the meaning of his texts—texts which do indeed seem at times to be ambivalent. He seems to refer the transformation of the offerings sometimes to the Holy Spirit called down by the epiclesis and sometimes to the words of institution.

On the one hand, there are texts in which he speaks of the priest raising his hands toward heaven and calling upon the Holy

---

34. Atchley, ibid., 53. Cf. Also footnote 1, 53–54.

35. Dix, *The Shape* . . . , 200–203.

36. Cabrol, "Epiclèse," 148; Piédagnel-Paris, 55–56 n. 2; Wooley, 111; Salaville, "Epiclèse eucharistique," 238–39. Cf. also LEW, 469 and Merk, "Die Epiklese: Ein neuer Lösungsversuch," 107–108.

37. Salaville, "Epiclèse . . . ," 236.

Spirit to come and "touch" or "take hold of" the offerings. When the Spirit comes and gives his grace then the sacrifice takes place, the bread becomes the "heavenly bread."[38]

On the other hand, there are texts—and these have received the lion's share of attention in the dispute over the epiclesis—in which Chrysostom seems to indicate clearly that it is the words of institution which are responsible for the transformation of the offerings. Perhaps the most famous of these texts are two Maundy Thursday instructions dealing with the institution of the Lord's Supper and the treason of Judas. In the course of these instructions, which are entitled *Homilia* 1 and 2 *De proditione Judae* and which are almost identical recensions of the same work, Chrysostom compares the power contained in the words, "Increase and multiply . . ." with that contained in the words, "This is my body . . ." The texts reads as follows:

> It is not man who causes what is present to become the Body and Blood of Christ, but Christ Himself who was crucified for us. The priest is the representative when he pronounces those words, but the power and the grace are those of the Lord. "This is my Body," he says. This word changes (μεταρρυθμίζει) the things that lie before us; and as that sentence "increase and multiply," once spoken, extends through all time and gives to our nature the power to reproduce itself; even so that saying "This is my Body," once uttered, does at every table in the Churches from that time to the present day, and even till Christ's coming, make the sacrifice complete.[39]

These words have unleashed a series of interpretations, the nuances of which are enough to send the head of the eager student spinning. Some maintain that the homilies *De proditione Judae* make the case rather clear-cut. They see Chrysostom among those Fathers who clearly teach that the institution narrative is the "form" of the Eucharist. The only way to avoid open contradiction in the writings of Chrysostom, they suggest, is to regard the references which he some-times makes to the action of the Holy Spirit in the Eucharist as references to a petition for the sanctification of the faithful rather than

---

38. *In coemeterii appellationem et in crucem Domini* . . . (PG 49:397–98); *In Joannem:* Homilia 45, 2 (PG 59:253); *De sacerdotio:* liber 3 (PG 48:642) and liber 6 (PG 48:681).

39. PG, 49:380, 389. Cf. also *In epistolam primam ad Timotheum:* Cap. 1, Homilia 2 (PG 62:612). English version from Quasten, III, 481.

for the transformation of the gifts.[40] Others, while seeking to show that Chrysostom attributed the consecration to the words of institution and that such a position is not an isolated phenomenon in the East, are equally strong in insisting that Chrysostom also held for the intervention of the Holy Spirit in "transubstantiation."[41]

It is possible, however, to take quite a different tack. One can argue that it is wrong to maintain that Chrysostom would be contradicting himself if he said at one time that the institution narrative was essential and another time that the epiclesis was essential. Chrysostom did indeed stress the role of the institution narrative, claims to the contrary notwithstanding,[42] but always in a context of the whole eucharistic prayer as "consecratory." In this context Chrysostom would have seen no contradiction in also maintaining that the epiclesis was essential for realizing the Eucharist.[43]

From the Orthodox viewpoint comes still another possibility. This view insists that there were not two currents of thought among the Fathers—one favorable to the institution narrative as "form" and the other favorable to the epiclesis.[44] It takes Latin historians to task for citing only those texts of Chrysostom which appear favorable to the institution narrative as alone consecratory. Further, it contends that Chrysostom stands with the other Greek Fathers of his day who neither attributed "preponderant importance" to the words of institution nor considered them as a "unique, consecratory formula." For John Chrysostom, with all his references to the words of institution, the epiclesis is indispensable for the realization of the Eucharist.[45]

To round out the picture on John Chrysostom, one should mention a further interpretation or nuance espoused by a number of scholars. This view maintains that the great Antiochene orator was not

---

40. Cf. Jugie, *De forma* . . . , 98–100 and *Theologia Dogmatica* . . . III, 261 and Brinktrine, "De epiclesi eucharistia," 15–16. Cf. also Quasten, *Patrology* III, 481 and Altaner-Stuiber, 329.

41. Cf. Salaville, "L'épiclèse d'après saint Jean Chrysostome . . . ," 101–12: "La consecration eucharistique . . . ," 321–24; "Consécration et épiclèse . . . ," 10–16. Cf. also Renz, 406–407; Varaine, *L'épiclèse* . . . , 45–48 and Brunner, "Zur Lehre . . . ," 349.

42. Casel (Review of Atchley's *On the Epiclesis* . . .), 445–46.

43. Casel (Review of Brinktrine's "De epiclesi eucharistica"), 136 referring to p. 15 and de Jong, "Le rite de la commixtion . . .," 50–77, esp. 76–77. Cf. also, Bishop, "The Moment . . . ," 143; Dix, *The Shape* . . . , 281–82 and Trembelas, 176.

44. Kern, 174–75. Cf. Salaville, "Epiclèse eucharistique," 238.

45. Kern, 177–181.

teaching that the consecration power was in the words of the institution recited afresh at each celebration of the Eucharist. The theory that the consecration was effected by the priest's recital of our Lord's words is, according to these writers, a misunderstanding of the teaching of Chrysostom and the other Eastern Fathers. Such a misunderstanding ends up in ". . . changing the idea of the word *spoken once for all* yet ever effective, being brought into action (so to say) through the invocation, into that of the effect being produced at each mass by the celebrant's iteration of that word."[46] In reality Chrysostom was, according to the interpretation now under consideration, trying to show that in the last analysis it is Christ who is the "consecrator" and that the priest is merely the minister. The priest speaks the words but it is God who gives them their power. Thus the words, "This is my body," received divine power from God once and for all. The priest, nevertheless, has to apply them here and now to the offerings through the epiclesis.[47]

The journey through the maze of interpretations pertaining to Chrysostom and the epiclesis is complete. Not all of these interpretations are mutually exclusive. Their variety and nuances, however, underline once again the complexity of the epiclesis question in the patristic writings.

Theodore of Mopsuestia (d. 428)

The discovery and publication by Mingana in 1932–33 of a Syriac text of Theodore of Mopsuestia's sixteen *Catechetical Homilies* has pointed to the importance of this famous Antiochene who up till that point had received relatively little attention in regard to the epiclesis question.[48] The *Catechetical Homilies*, which probably date from 388–92,[49] enable

---

46. Atchley, *On the Epiclesis* . . . , 167.

47. This interpretation, which reflects that of Nicholas Cabasilas (cf. Cabasilas, 71–76 and Salaville, *Nicolas Cabasilas* . . . , 179–91, has found various shades of discipleship in SH 345, L'Huillier, 320 Chavasse, 202–204 and MacLean, 409 as well as in Atchley, *On the Epiclesis* . . . , 68.

48. Cf., for instance, Casel (Review of Atchley's *On the Epiclesis* . . . , 445) who notes that Atchley would have to add Theodore of Mopsuestia to the list of Fathers he has examined. Casel adds that Theodore is important because he bears witness to a petition for the coming of the Holy Spirit upon the people even before Narsai whom Atchley (54 n. 1, 124) claimed was the first witness to this.

49. Cf. Quasten *Patrology* III, 409 and Altaner-Stuiber, 321.

one to arrive at a fuller picture of Theodore's views on the Eucharist and especially on the epiclesis.

In the last two *Catechetical Homilies (Mystagogical Catecheses V and VI)* Theodore explains the liturgy to the newly baptized. His explanation is steeped with references to the resurrection of Christ. At one point, he draws the parallel between what took place in Christ's mortal body through the Holy Spirit in the Resurrection and what takes place in the bread and wine through the coming of the Spirit:

> Indeed, even the body of our Lord does not possess immortality and the power of bestowing immortality in its own nature, as this was given to it by the Holy Spirit; and at its resurrection from the dead it received close union with Divine nature and became immortal and instrumental for conferring immortality on others . . . If, therefore, the nature of the vivifying Spirit made the body of our Lord into what its nature did not possess before, we ought, . . . not to regard the elements merely as bread and cup, but as the body and blood of Christ, into which they were so transformed by the descent of the Holy Spirit . . .[50]

All of this will, in turn, Theodore goes on to say, one day lead to a similar resurrection for those who partake worthily in the Eucharist.[51] With this as a partial background, Theodore begins, in *Mystagogical Catechesis VI*, to explain the anaphora to his hearers. Having come to and having made mention of the institution of the Eucharist by our Lord and his instruction to the disciples to "commemorate by stages the death of Christ" Theodore turns to the epiclesis:

> . . . It is necessary, therefore, that our Lord should now rise from the dead by the power of the things which are taking place and that He should spread His grace over us. This cannot happen otherwise than by the coming of the grace of the Holy Spirit, through which the latter had also raised Him previously. . .

> . . . It is with great justice, therefore, that the priest offers, according to the rules of priesthood, prayer and supplication to God that the Holy Spirit may descend, and that grace may come therefrom upon the bread and wine that are laid (on the altar) so that they may be seen to be truly the body and the blood of our Lord . . .

---

50. *Mystagogical Catechesis* V, 10–11; according to the English text of Mingana, 75–76. Cf. also, Tonneau-DeVreesse, 475–77.

51. Cf., for instance, *Myst. Cat.* V, 8 and 18; Mingana 74-82 and Tonneau-DeVreesse, 473, 493.

In this same way, after the Holy Spirit has come here also, we believe that the elements of bread and wine have received a kind of an anointing from the grace that comes upon them, and we hold them to be henceforth immortal, incorruptible, impassible, and immutable by nature, as the body of our Lord was after the resurrection.

And the priest prays that the grace of the Holy Spirit may come also on all those present, in order that . . . they may be knit here as if into one body by the communion of the flesh of our Lord.[52]

Some authors see these texts as clearly witnessing to the epiclesis as the "moment of consecration" or "form" of the Eucharist.[53] There are others who see in the texts an indication that Theodore viewed the anaphora as having two phases: the first with its institution narrative and separation of the two species symbolizing the presence of the body and blood shed for us and the second with its epiclesis (and commixture rite) symbolizing the Resurrection of Christ and the presence of his risen body.[54] Within this framework some would tend to stress the institution narrative in their interpretation, thus making the epiclesis "post-consecratory,"[55] while others would seem to allow more for the possibility that Theodore saw the "consecration" as incomplete without the epiclesis.[56]

If one were forced to make an either-or judgment between the institution narrative and the epiclesis, and to make this judgment on the basis of the texts alone, the weight of evidence would seem to favor the epiclesis as the "moment of consecration." The following texts, cited by Quasten from Mingana, are cases in point:

We ought not to regard the elements merely as bread and cup, but as the body and the blood of Christ, into which they were so transformed by the descent of the Holy Spirit (*Cat. Hom.* 5, 76 Mingana).

---

52. *Myst. Cat.* VI, 11–13; Mingana 103–104 and Tonneau-DeVreesse, 551–55.

53. Cf. Quasten, *Patrology* III, 421-22 and Reine, 16–27, 35. Cf. also Mingana, 104 n. 3, who sees Thedore as making "allusions" in this direction.

54. Cf. de Jong, "Epiklese," 936; Jugie, *De forma* . . . , 43 and Lécuyer, "La théologie . . . ," 408–409.

55. Jugie, "Le 'Liber . . . ," 266–70, esp. 269. Lécuyer, "La théologie . . ." 408 n. 90 also cites, and tends to agree with, Jugie, *De forma* . . . , 42–43 as holding that the epiclesis in Theodore is "post-consecratory." There, however, Jugie admits that Theodore's view on the "moment of consecration" remains obscure (43).

56. Cf. de Jong, "Epiklese," 936.

Those who have been chosen as the priests of the New Testament are believed to perform sacramentally, by the descent of the Holy Spirit . . . these things which we believe that Christ our Lord performed and will perform in reality (ibid., 86 Mingana).

One is the bread and one is the body of Christ our Lord, into which the element of bread is changed; and it receives this great change from one descent of the Holy Spirit (*Cat. Hom.* 16, 110 Mingana).

It is indeed offered so that by the coming of the Holy Spirit it should become that which it is said to be: the body and blood of Christ (ibid., 111 Mingana).

Picture in your mind the nature of this oblation, which, by the coming of the Holy Spirit, is the body of Christ (ibid., 113 Mingana).

At first it is laid upon the altar as a mere bread and wine mixed with water; but by the coming of the Holy Spirit it is transformed into body and blood, and thus it is changed into the power of a spiritual and immortal nourishment (ibid., 118–119 Mingana).

One suspects, however, that precisions such as a "moment of consecration" were foreign to the mind of Theodore. When the texts are seen in their overall context it is far more probable that Theodore viewed the Eucharist and, in particular, the anaphora as a single whole and that he definitely considered the epiclesis necessary for the *full* "consecration" or realization of this mystery.[57]

Ambrose of Milan (d. 397)

At first glance Ambrose would seem to lack the ambivalence which many find in John Chrysostom. A number of his texts seem to indicate clearly that for Ambrose the words of institution are responsible for the transformation of the gifts in the Eucharist. In *De Mysteriis* IX, for instance, in the midst of trying to show his readers that if God could work wonders through the prophets, if he could create the world from nothing with a word, then it is reasonable to suppose he could change bread into Christ's body, Ambrose states:

For the sacrament, which you receive, is effected by the words of Christ . . . The Lord Jesus himself declares: "This is my body." Before the benediction

---

57. Cf. Havet, 61–93, esp. 89–91. Texts are cited in Quasten, Patrology III, 421.

of the heavenly words another species is mentioned; after the consecration the body is signified. He himself speaks of His blood. Before the consecration is it mentioned as something else; after the consecration it is called blood.[58]

Three other texts, however, at least raise the possibility that Ambrose considered some other prayer or prayers as having played a role in the transformation of the offerings. In *De fide* IV, 10, 124, discussing Christ's statement ". . . *et qui manducat me, et ipse vivit propter me*," Ambrose declares:

> And then he adds: *For my flesh is truly food and my blood truly drink.* You hear flesh, you hear blood, you know the sacraments of the Lord's death and do you misrepresent the divinity? Hear him saying it himself: *Because a spirit does not have flesh and bones.* We, however, as often as we receive these sacraments, which, through the mystery of the sacred prayer, are transformed into flesh and blood, proclaim "the death of the Lord."[59]

De Spiritu Sancto III, 16, 112, where Ambrose stresses the Spirit's equal sanctity with the Father and the Son, reads:

> How, then, does He not possess everything that is God's, who is named by priests together with the Father and the Son in baptism, and is invoked in oblations, is proclaimed by the Seraphim in heaven with the Father and the Son, dwells in the saints with the Father and the Son, is poured forth among the just, is infused within the Prophets.[60]

And in *De sacramentis* IV, 5, 21, in bringing out the fact that it is the "sermo Christi" that "consecrates" the bread and wine, he seems to include more than simply the words of institution in this "*sermo Christi*":

> Do you want to know by what divine words it is consecrated? Listen to what the words are. The priest speaks. "Make this offering approved, spiritual and acceptable for us. It is the figure ("figura") of the body and blood of our Lord Jesus Christ who, before he suffered, took bread into his holy hands, looked up to heaven to you, Holy Father almighty, everlasting God,

---

58. *De Mysteriis* IX, 50–54, especially 52-54 (CSEL 73:110–13). Cf. also *De Sacrementis* IV, 4, 14–17, 19; IV, 5, 21–23 (CSEL 73:53–56). English version from FC, XLIV, 25–26.

59. *De fide* IV, 10, 124 (CSEL 78:201). Blais, 582, lists the classical meaning of "oratio" as "language," "parole," and gives this passage as an example of this usage.

60. *De Spiritu Sancto* III, 16, 112 (CSEL 79:197–98). English version from FC, XLIV, 193.

and giving thanks, he blessed it, broke it and gave it broken to his disciples and apostles, saying: 'Take and eat of this, all of you; for this is my body which shall be broken for the many.'"[61]

Since many of the interpretations given to Ambrose parallel those just seen in conjunction with Chrysostom, there is no need to linger on them. One interpretation regards Ambrose as a clear witness to the institution words as what later will be termed the "form" of the Eucharist.[62] Another possibility is to see Ambrose as a parallel to Cyril of Jerusalem in attributing the consecration to the whole eucharistic prayer. Ambrose, however, stresses the institution narrative within this framework whereas Cyril emphasizes the Spirit epiclesis.[63] It is also possible to opt for the view that for Ambrose the declaration, "This is my body," uttered once and for all remains operative throughout the ages. "But the daily application of this divine word is through the "sacred prayer" and "blessing," in the course of which the Holy Ghost was invoked on the oblations."[64] The number and variety of these interpretations, although once again not always mutually exclusive, tend to confirm the suspicion that the patristic texts that pertain to the epiclesis question are not always as crystal clear as some authors would have us believe.

Augustine (d. 430)

Saint Augustine, Ambrose's disciple, provides a number of texts which seem to run the gamut of possibilities in regard to eucharistic consecration. He also affords an incentive for taking a second look even at those Fathers who at first glance seem to indicate clearly that this consecration takes place by the words of institution when repeated by the priest. In Sermon 227, a paschal sermon in which he explains the Eucharist to the newly baptized, the bishop of Hippo states:

---

61. *De Sacramentis* IV, 5, 21 (CSEL 73:75).

62. Jugie, *De forma* . . . , 95–96 and Varaine, *L'épiclèse* . . . , 60–66.

63. Casel, *Das christliche Opfermysterium*, 543. Bishop, "The Moment . . . ," 143, in his turn sees a parallel between Ambrose and Chrysostom. Both reflect the transition from the earlier lack of concern for a "moment of consecration" to the more precise conception of "form."

64. Atchley, *On the Epiclesis* . . . , 74. Cf. also, Chavasse, 205 and Rabau, 34 as well as T. Schermann, "Die pseudoambrosianische Schrift 'de sacramentis,'" *Romische Quartalschrift* 17 (1903), 248, 250–51.

. . . That Bread which you see on the altar, consecrated by the word of God, is the Body of Christ. That chalice, or rather, what the chalice holds, consecrated by the word of God, is the Blood of Christ.[65]

In Sermon 234, another Easter sermon, Augustine, speaking of Luke's resurrection account, says:

. . . The faithful understand what I am saying; they know Christ in the breaking of bread. For, not all bread, but only that which receives the blessing of Christ becomes the Body of Christ.[66]

In his treatise on the fourth Gospel Augustine relates the phrase, "*Iam vos mundi estis propter verbum quod locutus sum vobis*," to baptism and proclaims:

Take away the word and what is the water but water? The word comes to the element and it becomes a sacrament, a visible word as it were.[67]

This text is considered important because of its apparent clarity and because, in a work which may not be Augustine's but which is considered to reflect his thought,[68] one finds a similar statement in regard to the Eucharist:

. . . but this bread, and this wine, when the word comes to it, becomes the body and blood of the Word . . . For take away the word and it is bread and wine. Add the word and it is now something else. And this something else, what is it? The body of Christ and the blood of Christ. Take away the word, therefore, and it is bread and wine. Add the word and it becomes a sacrament. To this you say: "Amen. . . ."[69]

Warnings that the phrase "*verbum Dei*" is not always clear in Saint Augustine[70] call for caution when faced with statements similar to Salaville's:

Without being as explicit, Saint Augustine (d. 430) is certainly of the same opinion [as Ambrose]. Although he did not say it *ex professo*, he seems

---

65. SC, 116:234. English version from FC, XXXVIII, 196.

66. *Sermon 234* (PL., 38:1116). English version from FC, XXXVIII, 224.

67. *In Johannem* 80, 3 (CCL, 26:529).

68. Cf., for instance, Salaville, "Epiclèse eucharistique," 241–42 and Cabrol, "Epiclèse," 154 footnote 13, on the question of authenticity.

69. *Sermo 6*, 1 and 3 (PL 46:835–36).

70. Cf. Pourrat, 56–57; Varaine, L'épiclèse . . . , 66 and Rauschen, *Eucharistie und Bussakrament*, 124–25.

indeed to have had the idea of a precise moment of consecration and located this moment at the pronouncing of the words of Christ.[71]

Although he admits that certain passages, which we shall see in a moment, seem to refer to the whole eucharistic prayer as consecratory, Salaville maintains that they do not take away from the "*verbum Dei*" passages. These latter, he contends, reveal the words of institution as the "efficient cause" of the eucharistic "consecration."

> And this "word of God" certainly is not the entire canon, but indeed a very precise formula which veritably has the role of sacramental form, since as soon as it is united to the matter, the sacrament is realized . . .[72]

Despite categorical statements like this, such a position must face a barrage of questions: Do the "*verbum Dei*" texts of certain Fathers refer to "words" or to the personal Word of God, the Second Person of the Trinity? If these texts do refer to "words," is it reasonably certain that they refer only to the words of institution? And if they do refer to the words of institution, is it equally certain that they refer to these words as now repeated by the celebrant and not merely to these words *as spoken once and for all by our Lord at the Last Supper*?

Moreover, there are other texts which raise the question whether or not Augustine could have been thinking only of the words of institution when he spoke of the "*verbum Dei*" as transforming the bread and wine. In Sermon 227 he says:

> Then, after the consecration of the Holy Sacrifice of God, because He wished us also to be His sacrifice, a fact which was made clear when the Holy Sacrifice was first instituted, and because that Sacrifice is a sign of what we are, behold, when the Sacrifice is finished, we say the Lord's Prayer which you have received and recited.[73]

In a letter to Paulinus of Nola, when explaining terminology, he writes:

> I prefer to understand by these words what the entire, or almost the entire, Church observes: that we take as supplications [precationes] those prayers which are said in celebrating the Mysteries, before we begin to consecrate what lies on the table of the Lord; prayers [orationes] are said when it is

---

71. Salaville, "Epiclèse eucharistique," 241.

72. Ibid., Cf. also Jugie, *De forma* . . . , 100–101.

73. SC, 116–240. English version from FC, XXXVIII, 197.

blessed and sanctified and broken for distribution; and the whole Church, for the most part, closes this complete petition with the Lord's Prayer.[74]

Finally, in *De Trinitate* III, 4, 10, speaking of the invisible and spiritual at work in the material, he states:

> For when we speak of the body and blood of Christ, we certainly do not mean the tongue of the Apostle, or the parchment or the ink, or the vocalized sounds, or the alphabetical signs written on the skins. We are referring only to that which has been received from the fruits of the earth, has been consecrated by a mystical prayer, and has been duly taken for our spiritual health in memory of the Lord's passion. Although it is brought to that visible form by the hands of men, yet it is not sanctified so as to be so great a Sacrament, except by the Spirit of God working invisibly.[75]

These texts, while not excluding the interpretation that *"verbum Dei"* refers to the institution narrative as repeated by the priest, do seem to leave room for other interpretations. The first two quotations above would seem to combine to favor the view that the Fathers generally saw the whole anaphora as consecratory.[76] The quotation from *De Trinitate* may also refer to the whole eucharistic prayer.[77] In addition, the same quotation seems to allow room for the view that Augustine saw an epiclesis involved in the "consecration"[78] and that the *"verbum Dei"* meant for him the words spoken once and for all by Christ at the Last Supper.[79] Finally, the texts under consideration seem neither to prove nor to disprove the contention that Augustine, along with other Western writers, recognizes a sanctification of the oblations distinct from their consecration.[80]

---

74. *Epistola 149 ad Paulinum* 16 (CSEL 44:107). English version from FC, XX, 250–51.

75. CCL, 50:136. English version from FC, XLV, 104–105.

76. Casel, *Das christliche Opfermysterium*, 537–46, esp. 544. Cf. Cabrol, "Amen," DACL 1/1 (1924), 1556–60, esp. 1558.

77. Salaville, "Epiclèse eucharistique," 241; Blaise, 661 and Havet, 79.

78. Cf. Cabrol, "Epiclèse," 154; Atchley, *On the Epiclesis*, 83 and S. Salaville, "L'épiclèse africaine," EO 39 (1941/42), 268–82, esp. 272–74. B. Botte (Review of Salaville's "L'épiclèse africaine,") BTAM 5 (1947), 200 n. 578 raises the question whether Augustine may not have been eclipsing the epiclesis for theological reasons. Cf. also, W. C. Bishop, "The African Rite," JTS 13 (1911/12), 259–260.

79. MacLean, "Invocation," 409. Cf. Atchley, "The Epiclesis: A Criticism," 33 and L. Tarchier, *Le Sacrement de l'Eucharistie* (d'sapres saint Augustin) (Lyon, 1904), 104–05 as cited by Varaine, *L'épiclèse . . .* , 69.

80. Cf. A. Sage, "Saint Augustin et la prière du canon 'Supplices quaesumus,'" REB 11 (1953), 252–65. Cf. also, SH, 332 footnote 70 and Havet, 78–80.

Once again, then, a study of the texts which Augustine has left behind in regard to eucharistic "consecration" incline one to shy away from overly categorical statements on the meaning of these texts. The shortage of time and space again makes it impossible to give more than passing mention to such men as Pope Gelasius I, Fulgence of Ruspe, and Isidore of Seville.

Gelasius (d. 496) has left a letter to Bishop Elpidius of Volterra in which he poses the question "For how can the heavenly Spirit come who is invoked for the consecration of the divine mystery, if the priest, who calls upon him to be present, stands condemned because he is filled with wicked deeds?"[81] This quotation has raised some discussion among scholars. Suffice it to note here that Jungmann[82] follows Botte[83] in holding that Gelasius does not clearly witness to a Spirit epiclesis. The text of his letter does not postulate anything more explicit than the *Quam oblationem* of the Roman Canon.[84]

Although impossible to treat in detail, Fulgence of Ruspe is significant because, despite claims to the contrary,[85] the view that he witnesses to a Spirit epiclesis in the African liturgy has received strong backing.[86]

As for Isidore of Seville we shall have to content ourselves with a few remarks from Geiselmann's important study of Isidore and the Eucharist. The author notes that there are at least five different interpretations as to what constituted the "form" of consecration for Isidore.[87] Geiselmann himself holds that Isidore saw the "consecration" as more than simply making present the body and blood of Christ. This body and blood had to be linked to the Holy Spirit to become fully capable of sanctifying, i.e., to become fully a "sacrament."[88]

81. Fragmentum 7—Gelasius Elpidio episcopo Volaterrano, in A. Thiel, *Epistolae Romanorum Pontificium Genuinae* I: *A. S. Hilaro usque ad S. Hormisdam (461–523)* (Brunsbergae, 1868), 486.

82. Jungmann, *Missarum Sollemnia* II, 242.

83. B. Botte, *Le canon de la messe romaine* (Louvain, 1935), 60–61.

84. Ibid., 61. Cf. C. Callewaert, "Histoire positive du Canon Romain, Une épiclèse á Rome?" SE 2 (1949), 95–98.

85. Jugie, "Considérations générales sur la question de l'épiclèse," EO 35 (1936), 326–30.

86. Cabrol, "Epiclèse," 154–55; Salaville, "Epiclèse eucharistique," 244 and the same author's "L'épiclèse d'après saint Jean Chrysostome . . . ," 107–108 and "L'épiclèse africaine," 274–82 as well as Botte's (Review of Salaville's "L'épiclèse africaine") BTAM 5 (1947), 200; Burmester, 293; Renz, 285 ff.; cf. also Dix, *The Shape* . . . , 296–98 and Havet, 72–78.

87. J. R. Geiselmann, *Die Abendmahlslehre* (Munich, 1933), 5–8, 14–16.

88. Ibid., 244–45. Cf. Havet, 61 ff. and Cagin, *L'Eucharistia*, 50–51.

Finally, and perhaps most important for this study, Geiselmann
contends that while it is right to claim that the Fathers looked upon
the whole eucharistic prayer as consecratory, it is wrong to claim that
Isidore did not share this view. It was only much later—first in the
twelfth century—that the institution narrative was specified as the
essential and exclusive consecration form of the Eucharist.[89] In reality
Isidore has a foot in each of two epochs. In viewing the "consecration"
as an organic series of acts or prayers, he stood with the Fathers. In
splitting the Preface ("Illatio") from the rest of the eucharistic prayer,
he in a sense stood with the later developments of the Middle Ages.[90]

John Damascene (d. c. 749)

With John Damascene we come to the end of this survey of the
Fathers. John's importance lies in the lasting impact his writings will
have on the Orthodox position concerning the eucharistic epiclesis.
The texts which he has left behind seem to leave little doubt that he
viewed the epiclesis as consecratory.

In *De fide orthodoxa* IV, 13 he seeks to bring out the relationship
between the efficacy of God's word and the operation of the Holy
Spirit. In drawing a parallel between Creation, Incarnation, and
Eucharist, as Chrysostom had once done, he writes:

> . . . In the beginning He said: "Let the earth bring forth the green herb,"
> and even until now, when the rain falls, the earth brings forth its own
> shoots under the influence and power of the divine command. God said:
> "This is my body," and, "This is my blood," and, "This do in commemora-
> tion of me," and by His almighty command it is done, until He shall come,
> for what He said was "until he come." And through the invocation the
> overshadowing power of the Holy Ghost becomes rainfall for this new
> cultivation. For, just as all things whatsoever God made He made by the
> operation of the Holy Ghost, so also it is by the operation of the Spirit
> that these things are done which surpass nature and cannot be discerned
> except by faith alone. "How shall this be done to me," asked the blessed
> Virgin, "because I know not a man?" The archangel Gabriel answered,
> "The Holy Ghost shall come upon thee and the power of the Most High
> shall overshadow thee." And now you ask how the bread becomes the body
> of Christ and the wine and water the blood of Christ. And I tell you that

89. Geiselmann, 255 referring to Casel, "Die Eucharistielehre . . . ," 341.
90. Ibid., 245–47, 252 ff. Cf. Betz, *Die Eucharistie . . .* , 331.

the Holy Ghost comes down and works these things which are beyond description and understanding.[91]

And again:

. . . What is more, it is not amiss to say this, that just as bread by being eaten and wine and water by being drunk are naturally changed into the body of the person eating and drinking and yet do not become another body than that which the person had before, so in the same way are the bread of the offertory and the wine and water supernaturally changed into the body and blood of Christ by the invocation and coming down of the Holy Ghost, yet they are not two bodies, but one and the same.[92]

In *Homilia in sabbatum sanctum* he makes a similar statement:

Now the flesh of God from the grain, and the blood of God from the wine, truly and inexpressibly changed by the invocation, for the one promising is trustworthy.[93]

Finally, one passage of *De Fide orthodoxa* IV, 13 seems to have banished the doubts of even the most enthusiastic proponents of "consecration" through the institution narrative alone. Attempting to explain Basil's use of the word "antitype" Damascene states:

Moreover, although some may have called the bread and wine *antitypes* of the body and blood of the Lord, as did the inspired Basil, they did not say this as referring to after the consecration, but to before the consecration, and it was thus that they called the offertory bread itself.[94]

In view of this passage few authors would seem to go beyond Salaville who contends that *if* it were not for this quotation other passages from Damascene might be reconciled with the "Catholic doctrine" on the "form" of the eucharist.[95] Salaville admits, however, that Damascene's explanation of the word "antitype" bars the way to an interpretation favoring the exclusive consecratory value of the institution narrative. He maintains that it was the desire to defend the

---

91. PG, 94:1140–41. English version from FC, XXXVII, 357.

92. Ibid., 1145. English version from FC, XXXVII, 358.

93. PG, 96:637–40.

94. PG, 94:1142–53.

95. Salaville, "Epiclèse eucharistique," 250. Cf. Jugie, *De forma* . . . , 114–120. SH, 29 rightly lists T. Spacil, *Doctrina theologiae orientis separate de ss. Eucharistiae* II (= *Orientalia Christiana* 14 [1929], 5–173) (Rome, 1929), 54–57 as one of the exceptions who try to "latinize" Damascene.

"real presence" in the Eucharist against every purely symbolistic interpretation that led Damascene to overstress the role of the epiclesis. This
same desire hindered him from holding on to the "traditional doctrine,"
namely, "*la vertu exclusivement consécratoire des paroles du Christ . . .*"[96]

Faced with opponents who held that the word "antitype"
as used after the institution narrative in the Liturgy of Saint Basil
showed that the Eucharist was only a symbol or image of Christ,[97]
Damascene took a drastic step. He retorted by maintaining that
"antitype" in the sense of mere symbol or image was used after the
institution narrative because it was the epiclesis and not the words of
institution that consecrated. Thus Damascene played down the purely
symbolic interpretation and at the same time made the words of
institution appear to be a *conditio sine qua non* for "consecration."[98]

For a number of writers within the Catholic tradition John
Damascene's position in regard to eucharistic consecration in general
and to the word "antitype" in particular is not only fallible but in fact
false. They see Damascene as paving the way for an "absolute" view of
the epiclesis which will later hold sway in the East.[99] For Eastern
writers from his own day down to ours, however, John Damascene
has provided a strong influence and, especially centuries later with
the emergence of the dispute over the epiclesis and the "moment of
consecration," a constant basis of appeal.[100]

Conclusion to Patristic Survey

This patristic survey began with two questions: Did the Fathers
consider the epiclesis to be consecratory? If so, in what sense? Despite
the emphasis on the words of institution found among some of the
Fathers, the evidence indicates that at least in the East, the eucharistic
epiclesis was looked upon as consecratory and essential.

---

96. Salaville, ibid., cf. Cabrol, "Epiclèse," 152 and Brunner, "Zur Lehre . . . ," 350 footnote 361.

97. Cf. Dix, *The Shape* . . . , 292–93.

98. Cf. ibid. as well as Salaville, "Epiclèse eucharistique," 250–51 and Smit, 114.

99. Jugie, "L'épiclèse et le mot antitype . . . ," 196; Salaville, "Epiclèse eucharistique," 250 and
Salaville's article with the same title in *Catholicisme* 4 (1956), 307; Varaine, *L'épiclèse* . . . , 53–58;
and Smit, 114–15. Cf. Renz, I, 513 for a somewhat milder judgment.

100. Cf., for instance, Kern, 194. Cf. also, Salaville, "Epiclése eucharistique," 250–52; Smit,
114-15; Varaine, *L'épiclèse* . . . , 56–57; Trembelas, 176–177.

When one asks, in what sense and to what extent the epiclesis was consecratory and essential, however, any semblance of a clear-cut answer vanishes. Some Fathers seem to stress the institution narrative. Others tend to emphasize the epiclesis. Sometimes the same Father seems to look on now one, now the other as achieving the consecration. J. Laager sums up well the basic fuzziness of the patristic picture when he says:

> The consecration of the elements would often be attributed to the institution narrative—although in some patristic passages it is not always clear whether the institution narrative in the liturgy of the words of Christ at the Last Supper are meant—quite often, however, now to the epiclesis, now to the institution narrative.[101]

In short, this survey seems to confirm the contention that passages from the early Christian writers, while they have the advantage that one can date them more or less accurately, often allow of more than one interpretation. The meaning of the patristic texts when they are brought to bear on the epiclesis question often seems terribly elusive.

Despite all the obscurity of these texts, however, some clear lines do emerge. The Fathers generally saw the Holy Spirit as well as Christ playing an active role in the eucharistic "consecration." No amount of emphasis either on the words of institution or on the words of the "epiclesis," whatever that word meant to the different Fathers, can obscure the vital role attributed to the Holy Spirit in the eucharistic thought of the Fathers.[102] There is also widespread agreement that the Fathers generally tended to view the eucharistic prayer as a single consecratory whole.[103] A number of authors, as we have seen, would share the viewpoint that the Fathers saw two essential moments, namely, the institution narrative and the epiclesis, within this broader

---

101. J. Laager, "Epiklesis," RAC 5 (1962), 591. Cf. Rauschen, 123–24 and SH, 344.

102. Cf. Salaville, "Epiclèse eucharistique," 355 ff.; Vagaggini, *The Canon* . . . , 156–60, 176; Smit, 110–12, 118–20; Kern, 191–94; Dix, "The Origins . . . ," 127; Brightman, (Correspondence: Invocation . . .), 37–38.

103. Without in any way trying to give an exhaustive list, we might mention: Casel, "Die ostchristliche Opferfeier als Mysteriengeschehen," 68 and (Review of Elfers' *Die Kirchenordnung* . . .),120 as well as his "Neue Beiträge . . . ," 171–73 and elsewhere; de Jong, "Epiklese," 936; Laager, 587, 591; Betz, *Die Eucharistie* . . . , 332–33; Cabrol, "Amen," 1558 and "Epiclèse," 174; SH, 337–38, 341; Smit, 102–103; Rauschen, 121–24; Kern 180–81; Salaville, "Epiclèse eucharistique," 232; Geiselmann, 255; Stolz, 143–44; Schmaus, 308.

framework of the whole anaphora as consecratory.[104] In any event, one thing is clear, the Fathers did not brood over a "moment of consecration." Consequently, one should be most careful in even posing the question of a "moment of consecration" in regard to the early Christian writers and liturgies.

This apparent lack of concern for a particular "moment of consecration" seems to account for a final phenomenon which one can point to with a good degree of certainty. The question, whether it was at the moment of the institution narrative or at the moment of the epiclesis that the gifts were transformed, seems to have been foreign to the patristic way of thinking. At any rate, apparently contradictory statements as to the consecratory value of the words of institution and of the epiclesis—whether these statements occur in different authors or even at times in the writings of the same author—appear to have posed no problem for the Fathers.

It is one thing to claim that we can reconcile these apparent contradictions. It is another thing to say that the Fathers tried to do so. They did not. The problem of the epiclesis and the "moment of consecration" would have to wait centuries before surfacing.

THE EMERGENCE OF THE MOMENT OF CONSECRATION QUESTION

The fact is, that as long as no attempt was made to pinpoint a "moment of consecration," the catalyst for a real dispute over the consecratory value of the epiclesis was missing. John Damascene, for example, certainly took a firm stand in favor of a consecratory epiclesis. Yet he caused no stir by attributing a consecratory force to the epiclesis and proposing the words of institution as a sort of *conditio sine qua non* to the transformation of the gifts.

The deacon Epiphanius at the second Council of Nicea (737) seized upon Damascene's argumentation to affirm the reality of the Eucharist against the symbolism of the Iconoclasts. Epiphanius gave a clear exposition of Damascene's doctrine on the epiclesis. As was the case with Damascene he was seeking to demonstrate the fact that

---

104. Besides Casel, "Neue Beiträge . . . ," 173, cf. SH, 344, 353–54; de Jong, "Epiklese," 936 and Rauschen, 125.

Christ is really present in the Eucharist. He never sought to determine the moment of consecration and probably for this reason he, too, caused no stir in regard to the epiclesis.[105]

Even a frontal assault against the consecratory value of the institution narrative by Moses ben Kepha (813–903), an outstanding Jacobite scholar and author of numerous works in theology, exegesis, homiletics, and philosophy, found no echo among his contemporaries. According to a report of Dionysius ben Salîbî (d. 1171), Moses protested against the practice in the Syrian liturgy of Saint James of having the people say, "Amen," after the words of institution. He saw in this "Amen" an affirmation of a consecratory value in the institution words. The efforts of Moses ben Kepha to stir up opposition to this practice, however, met with little success as Dionysius ben Salîbî, a few centuries later, was to attest.[106]

Even in the midst of the heated disputes revolving around Photius (858–879) and Michael Cerularius (1043–58) neither side dreamed of making the epiclesis a point of dispute.[107] On the contrary, several texts among Greek, Syrian, and Armenian writers seem to indicate a continuing belief in the efficacy of the words of institution.[108]

In the West, the textual support P. Drews offers is rather slim for his sweeping statement, "That the Germans in the Middle Ages attributed the consecration only to the epiclesis and not to the institution narrative is evident from Gerbert, monum. veteris lit. Alem II, 285 u. 299."[109] A document dated February 11, 1079, and submitted to Berengar of Tours does indicate, however, that at least the mere recitation of the words of institution was not considered as exclusively responsible for the "consecration." The statement reads:

> I, Berengar, believe with my heart and confess with my lips that the bread and wine which are placed on the altar are substantially changed into the

---

105. Smit, 115; Salaville, "Epiclèse eucharistique," 252; SH, 329.

106. Jungmann, *Missarum Sollemnia* II, 254. Cf. SH, 330 and Smit, 97.

107. SH, 330; Smit, 97 and Salaville, "Epiclèse eucharistique," 252–53.

108. Salaville, ibid., 253–56.

109. P. Drews, *Zur Entstehungsgeschichte des Kanons* (= *Studien zur Geschichte des Gottesdienstes und des gottesdienstlichen Lebens* Heft I) (Tübingen, 1902), 28 footnote 3. Cf. A. Wilmart, "Expositio Missae," DACL 5/1 (1922), 1020–21 and the same author's "Un traité sur la messe copié en Angleterre vers l'an 800," EL 50 (1936), 133–39.

true and proper and life-giving flesh and blood of Jesus Christ, our Lord, *by the mystery of the sacred prayer and the words of our Redeemer.*[110]

Scholasticism and the Moment of Consecration

With the rise of Scholasticism came an almost overriding desire for precision,[111] which in turn was to set the stage for a clash over the epiclesis and the "moment of consecration." The Scholastics tended to stress rational speculation and the strict application of the hylomorphic theory to explain the make-up of the sacraments. They often did this, however, to the neglect of historical and liturgical data. As Pourrat puts it:

> . . . The scholars would be led to neglect the study of history; and, by *a priori* reasoning, they would determine the conditions of validity of the sacraments and the elements essential to each of them.[112]

Much attention was given to the question of the "matter" and "form" of the sacraments.[113] This concentration did provide some valuable insights. The danger of this approach, however, was that precisions of a purely physical order could take priority over the interest shown the redeeming activity of the Trinity and, especially, of the Holy Spirit. As this redeeming activity, now present in mystery, slipped into the background, a more static concept of the Eucharist tended to come to the fore.[114] Not only the theology but the spirituality and the liturgical practice, e.g., the elevation of the host, give evidence of the shifting mentality of the times.[115] In this context it was almost inevitable that the "moment of consecration" would receive a great deal of attention.

In this respect Thomas Aquinas (d. 1274) was a child of his times. He, too, tended to isolate and emphasize efficacious "moments" to what now seems to be an extreme degree:

---

110. DS, 700 (355). Italics mine. Cf. also Goldammer, 60–86.

111. Cf. D. van den Eynde, "The Theory of the Composition of the Sacraments in Early Scholasticism (1125–1240)," *Franciscan Studies* 12 (1952), 12, 19–20. Salaville, "Spiritus liturgiae . . . ," 132–33 seems to see only the positive side of this tendency to precision.

112. Pourrat, 68. Cf. Smit, 120.

113. Cf. van den Eynde, 1–26; SH 362–87.

114. Cf. Smit, 119–20.

115. Cf. Goldammer, 86 ff. and Jungmann, *Missarum Sollemnia* I, 156 ff.

Whence it must be said that if the priest utters only the aforementioned words ["Hoc est corpus meum"'] with the intention of confecting this sacrament, this sacrament will be effected; because the intention causes these words to be understood as though they were offered in Christ's person, *even if the words preceding this are not said.*[116]

   Statements such as these are, to say the least, disconcerting for the non-Scholastic mentality and have given rise to pointed remarks from those defending a consecratory value of the epiclesis.[117]

   On the other hand, Thomas clearly taught the principal role the Holy Spirit played in the "consecration,"[118] although he viewed this role apart from the liturgical context of an epiclesis.[119] Perhaps this very failure to place the role of the Holy Spirit in a liturgical setting accounts for the fact, bemoaned by Salaville, that Thomas never came to grips with the problem of the epiclesis and the "moment of consecration." Be that as it may, the fact remains that the epiclesis raised no problem for Thomas Aquinas. The same is true of the Council of Lyon (1274) when treating the question of reunion of the Church. Neither side raised the issue of the eucharistic epiclesis as a point of division.[120] Thus, up to the start of the fourteenth century no conflict over the consecratory value of the epiclesis had arisen between the East and the West. Yet a clash had now become inevitable. Why? Basically, it seems, because the Scholastics, concentrating attention on the question of the "matter" and "form" of the sacraments, were concentrating attention on a precise "moment of consecration." In trying to explain the "how" of the eucharistic transformation they appealed to "transubstantiation," the *instantaneous* replacing of one substance with another.[121] Once one limits oneself to an instantaneous transformation in the Eucharist and at the same time seeks to determine precisely what is the "form" responsible for this transformation one automatically tends to become exclusive.[122]

---

116. S.T. III, q. 78, a. 1 ad 4um. Italics are mine.
117. Kern 181–82 and L'Huillier, 317.
118. S.T. III, q. 75, a. 1 ad 1 and III, q. 78, a. 4. Cf. III, q. 82, a. 5 and 6.
119. Cf. Smit, 120 footnote 105.
120. Salaville, "Epiclèse eucharistique," 271–72; 256. Cf. Smit, 97.
121. Cf. Kern, 180.
122. Cf. Salaville, "Epiclèse eucharistique," 201–202.

As long as one remains in this type of Scholastic framework, a conflict with the East, with its emphasis on the eucharistic epiclesis, becomes inevitable. It is important to appreciate this framework to understand both the inevitability of the conflict and the efforts, especially of the Roman teaching authority, to protect the consecratory value of the words of institution in a context of instantaneous transubstantiation. It is hardly surprising to find a number of popes, immersed as they were in the Scholastic framework, speaking out on the consecratory value of the epiclesis.

Thus in the *Libellus "Cum dudum" ad Armenios* composed during the reign of Pope Benedict XII (1334–1342) and dated August 1341, the Armenians are accused of holding that through the words of the institution narrative, ". . . [the sacrament] is not confected and they do not intend to confect the body and blood of Christ, but they only say the words in a recitative manner, by reciting, to be sure, what the Lord did when he instituted the sacrament." There then follows the text of the epiclesis in use among the Armenians, with the reproach that the Armenians, ". . . believe that through these words, the body and blood of Christ are confected."[123] Although this document originally stemmed from an unofficial inquisition initiated by persons hostile to the Armenians,[124] it is interesting to note the twofold accusation. The words of institution are considered to be mere recitative; (*because*) the epiclesis is considered to be consecratory.

It is also interesting to note the response the Armenians made when they gathered together at the Council of Sis in 1344 or 1345.[125] Taking the *Libellum* article by article they set about refuting the accusations contained therein. In regard to the epiclesis those present at the Council cite the reproach contained in the *Libellum*. They admit that the *Libellum* is correct in regard to the wording of their epiclesis. They protest, however, that both Basil and John Chrysostom used such an epiclesis at this point in the Eucharist and directed that this practice be continued. The members of the Council then add:

> . . . therefore, and thus we ourselves have said that they taught and ordained these things. Nevertheless, we do not believe that the body and

---

123. DS, 1017 (543).
124. Ibid., p. 297 (note introducing 1006 [532] ff.).
125. Ibid.

blood are [thus] confected, as they say, since this takes place beforehand. And yet we do not know with what intention the aforementioned holy masters did these things and if something else seems better to you, which it is necessary to do, we are ready to do it . . .[126]

What is striking about the whole response of the Armenians is that neither the position nor the wording of their epiclesis seems to have been at all problematic for them. They appear unaware of any tension, more apparent to a precision-orientated, Scholastic mentality, between their epiclesis and their belief in the efficacy of the institution narrative.

Pope Clement VI (1342–1352), however, in a letter dated September 29, 1351, and addressed to the Catholicos of the Armenians, reflects a dogged determination to arrive at greater precision and clarity:

In chapter 42 you say that you believe and hold that the body of Christ, born of the Virgin and having died on the Cross, the body which now lives in heaven, that this body is in the Sacrament of the altar under the form and likeness of bread after the words consecrating the bread, viz., *Hoc est corpus meum*. On the basis of this we ask you: *First*, if you believe that the bread is transubstantiated into the body of Christ? *Second*: if after these words: *Hoc est corpus meum*, the priests in the Church of the Armenians use prayers in which they seem to pray that the bread be transformed and change into the body of Christ or that it be made into the body of Christ? and if you and the Armenians who obey you are prepared to drop prayers of this type completely and totally or at least to correct them to this extent that in beseeching [God] it be prayed that the body of Christ might be on the altar, after the body of Christ is really and truly in the Sacrament through the words of consecration?[127]

The real dispute between East and West over the epiclesis seems, however, to have been triggered by Western missionaries sojourning in the East around the beginning of the fourteenth century. These missionaries upon learning that the Greeks attributed a consecratory value to the epiclesis attacked this view as heretical. Nicholas Cabasilas and later Simon of Thessalonica eventually came to the defense of the Greek position and the battle was joined in earnest.[128]

---

126. Mansi, 25:1242–43.

127. A. Tautu, *Acta Clementis PP. VI* (= *Codicem Juris Canonici Orientalis*—Fontes III, Vol. 9) (Vatican, 1960), 311–12.

128. Cf. Salaville, "Epiclèse eucharistique," 256 and SH 330–31. Cf also Salaville, *Nicolas Cabasilas . . .* , 312.

Nicholas Cabasilas

Cabasilas, who lived from about 1320 to 1390,[129] defending the consecratory value of the epiclesis, left behind some very fine insights. It is important when reading his comments on the epiclesis to remember the context in which he was writing. Not only was he aware of the reproaches "certain Latins" had hurled at the Greek epiclesis; he was probably also aware of the exaggerated emphasis given to the eucharistic "form" by some Western theologians. Nothing could be so foreign to the Eastern mentality and so apt to aggravate the Eastern attitude toward the Latin position than isolating the words of institution from their liturgical context.[130] Yet this is exactly what some Western theologians, even one as great as Thomas Aquinas, were doing.[131]

First of all, Cabasilas notes the criticism made by "certain Latins" that:

> Those who rely more on their own prayer than on God's word are in the first place implying that his words lack effectiveness. They show that they put more trust in themselves, and in the third place they make the holy sacrament dependent on something uncertain, namely, human prayer, . . .[132]

Then the great Greek writer deftly counters this criticism, at the same time providing us with valuable insights into the attitude necessary in the Christian assembly:

> It is unreasonable to address reproaches like these to those who pray for the consecration of the offerings. Their confidence in their prayer is not confidence in self, but in God who has promised to grant what they are seeking. It is indeed the very contrary (to self-reliance) which is fundamental to the conception of prayer. For suppliants perform the act of prayer because they fail to trust themselves in the matters about which they pray and they believe that they can obtain their requests from God alone . . .[133]

The main objection of Cabasilas to the Latin viewpoint was that it placed the consecration *exclusively* in the words of institution as

---

129. Salaville, *Nicolas Cabasilas . . .* , 9.

130. Ibid., 35, 317.

131. S. T. III, q. 78, a. 1 ad 4um. Even a Thomist such as Roguet, *L'Eucharistie* I, 331–32 n. 101, to some extent recognizes this weakness in Thomas.

132. Nicholas Cabasilas, *A Commentary . . .* , 72. For the Greek text see Salaville's edition *Nicolas Cabasilas . . .* , 180.

133. Cabasilas, 73. Cf. Salaville, ibid., 182.

repeated by the priest. This exclusiveness he attacked with a vengeance. His words, however, do not indicate, as some at times imply, that the words of institution are merely a historical narrative with no consecratory value at all.[134] Rather, the point Cabasilas appears to be making is that these words *alone* are not enough to realize the Eucharist:

> . . . And in the same way, here in the liturgy we believe that the Lord's words do indeed accomplish the mystery, but through the medium of the priest, his invocation, and his prayer.[135]

And a little further on:

> . . . The words of the Lord about the holy mysteries were spoken in a narrative manner. None of the Apostles or teachers of the Church has ever appeared to say that they are sufficient to consecrate the offerings of sacraments. The blessed John (Chrysostom) himself said that, spoken once by Christ, and having actually been said by him, *they are always effective,* just as the word of the Creator is. *But it is nowhere taught that now, spoken by the priest, and by reason of being said by him, they have that efficacy . . .*[136]

For Cabasilas, then, the words of institution are of sacred and special significance for the "consecration." The words of institution were spoken once and for all at the Last Supper and they are always the basic instrument of "consecration." They need, however, to be applied or adapted here and now by the invocation and prayer. For Cabasilas, the "consecration" is completed when the priest pronounces the words of the epiclesis. Thus, Cabasilas, while acknowledging the value of the words of institution, seeks to underline the absolute necessity that the prayer of the priest accompany those words. He is primarily concerned with preserving the place of prayer in the realization of the sacraments. For Nicholas Cabasilas there can be no question of an either-or attitude toward the sacraments.

> . . . For God himself has said that he answers prayer and grants the Holy Spirit to those who ask, and nothing is impossible to those who pray in faith, and his assurance cannot be untrue. *It is nowhere stated that this will*

---

134. Cf. Salaville, *Nicolas Cabasilas . . .* , 35, 313. J. Kramp, *Die Opferanschauung der römischen Messliturgie* (Regensburg, 1924²), 146–47 footnote 1, remarks that he cannot share Salaville's interpretation (in "Epiclèse eucharistique," 256) of Cabasilas. Cf. also, Kern, "En marge . . . ," 194 and SH, 331.

135. Cabasilas, 72. For the Greek text see Salaville *Nicolas Cabasilas . . .* , 182.

136. Cabasilas, 76 (Italics mine) and Salaville, ibid., 190.

happen to those who simply speak this or that word. It is the tradition of
the Fathers who received this teaching from the Apostles and from their
successors, that the sacraments are rendered effective through prayer;
all the sacraments, as I have said, and particularly the Holy Eucharist.[137]

R. N. S. Craig sees Cabasilas as rejecting a similar Western
bent toward exclusiveness in regard to the roles which Christ and the
Holy Spirit play in the Eucharist. In bringing out the role of the Holy
Spirit in the Eucharist he in no way contradicts what he has said about
Christ being the consecrator. Rather, Craig maintains, he stands
opposed to the Western tendency to make an either-or choice between
the activity of Christ and that of the Holy Spirit.[138] Be that as it may,
it seems possible, and fair, to understand Nicholas Cabasilas only
against the backdrop of the, at times exaggerated, Scholastic mentality
which confronted him.

The Council of Florence

The events of the Council of Florence (1439) form another important
chapter in the history of the problem of eucharistic epiclesis and the
"moment of consecration." Powerful political pressures, among them
the continuing advance of the Turks, provided strong motivation to the
Greek Emperor to open negotiations on the reunion of the Churches.
The popes, for their part, sincerely wished union and were willing to
use political considerations for this purpose. To assure any success the
monks and the people had to be won over in the East. One way to do
this, it was hoped, was to arrange a General Council, and this Pope
Eugene IV did.[139] To maintain, as Smit at one point does, that after
a few hesitations on the part of the Greeks both sides felt that there was
such strong agreement on the question of the consecration formula
that it was not even taken up in the Council's decrees of union[140] is an
oversimplification. Simply to indicate the final statement of the Greeks
regarding the epiclesis, apart form the historical context, as though

---

137. Cabasilas, 75–76 (Italics mine) and Salaville, *Nicolas Cabasilas . . .* , 188, 190.
138. Craig, 22, 25–28.
139. Cf. Gill, esp. viii-xv, 1–15; Boularand, 241–73 and Biedermann, 23–43.
140. Smit, 98. Perhaps allowance has to be made here for the brevity of Smit's article.

this statement was proof that the Greeks really did see eye to eye with the Latins at that time, is equally an oversimplification.[141]

The "*quelques hesitations*" Smit speaks of were in fact the result of great reluctance on the part of the Greeks to go as far as the Latins wished them to go on the epiclesis question. The delay caused by this reluctance was both unexpected and aggravating for Pope Eugene IV (1431–1447) and his advisors. The fact that Torquemada, the papal theologian, did not seem to grasp the basic viewpoint of the Greeks and that they in turn definitely were not at home with his Scholastic categories appears to have complicated matters greatly.[142]

Salaville is correct in claiming that Isidore of Kiev sought to ward off a definition of the efficacy of the words of the institution narrative, maintaining that all the Greeks, even the simple faithful, held this.[143] Salaville also gives a good account of the nuances in Isidore's position. Isidore looked upon the institution narrative as a seed which the epiclesis made fruitful.[144] This understanding, however, was not enough to satisfy the Latins. They eventually prevailed upon the reluctant Greeks to go further. On July 5, 1439, Cardinal Bessarion, metropolitan at Nicea, in his own name and in the name of his compatriots, made an oral profession of faith. A notary recorded Bessarion's statement, the key passage of which reads as follows:

> And since we hear from all the holy doctors of the Church, especially from blessed John Chrysostom, who is very well known to us, that it is those words of the Lord which change and transubstantiate the bread and the wine into the true body and blood of Christ and that those divine words of the Saviour contain all the power of transubstantiation, we ourselves, by necessity, follow this most holy doctor and his opinion.[145]

Salaville contends that this statement can in no way be dismissed as the view of only five or six Greek bishops and that only

---

141. Cf. Salaville, "Epiclèse eucharistique," 198–99, 258–59; SH, 331–32 and Dix, "On the Origins of the Epiclesis," 201–202. Atchley, "The Epiclesis: A criticism," 34–35 rightly criticized Dix for neglecting the historical background and Dix later in *The Shape . . .* , 293 did in fact acknowledge the "dire political necessity" behind the statement.

142. Cf. Boularand, 253–79, esp. 225, 257, 268 and 270. Also Biedermann, 34, 36–37.

143. Salaville, "Epiclèse eucharistique," 198.

144. Ibid.

145. G. Hormann, *Concilium Florentinum: Documenta et Scriptores*, Series A, Vol. III, fascicle II: *Fragmenta Protocolli, Diaria Privata, Sermones* (Rome, 1951), 25.

an effort to avoid embarrassing the Easterners unnecessarily prevented it from taking the form of a definition.[146] What Salaville fails to bring out is the historical background. Serbia, Bulgaria, and Macedonia were in the hands of the Turks who only a few years before had made an unsuccessful attack on Constantinople itself. The emperor was in desperate straits. The union with Rome was for him a means to obtaining military aid. Yet despite pressure from the emperor to come to an agreement with the Latins the Eastern clergy did indeed show their reluctance. They hesitated to go beyond the statement that the institution narrative did consecrate the elements but that it was the epiclesis that here and now makes these words effective. Exactly how great the pressure was which led to their final statement, and exactly how such pressure may have affected their understanding of that statement, is hard to say.[147] Atchley seems close to the truth in writing:

> Of course, the whole trouble was that the union between East and West was sought for political reasons, and not spiritual and religious ones. The Eastern emperor wanted military help against the Turks, and the Pope wanted the prestige of a reunited Christendom to oppose the supporters of the Council of Basel. The Greeks and Russians never did accept the Latin scholastic position; some tried to make the Latins think they did, but neither side was really taken in . . .[148]

In any event, the circumstances are enough to raise doubts as to whether the Greeks and Latins understood the Bessarion statement in the same sense or whether that statement really represented the Greek position on the epiclesis. E. Boularand, for instance, sees the declarations by the Greeks as affirming implicitly, but not explicitly, that the words of institution alone "consecrate."[149] Dom B. Botte maintains that Florence only ratified (here we might add, at least in the mind of the Latins) the conviction of Western medieval theologians. It did not banish the problem posed by the Fathers and the liturgical texts.[150]

---

146. Salaville, "Epiclèse eucharistique," 197–99.

147. Cf. Gill, 1–15, esp. 11–13, 15 on the historical and political background of the Council and especially xi–xiii, 290–93 on the extenuating circumstances under which the Greeks signed the decree of union.

148. Atchley, "The Epiclesis: A Criticism," 25. Besides Atchley, ibid., a number of authors express similar reservations. Cf. T. Ware, *The Orthodox Church* (London, 1963), 80; Frere, *The Anaphora* . . . 186–90; Rauschen, 114 and Dix, *The Shape* . . . , 293.

149. Boularand, 273.

150. Botte, "L'épiclèse dans les liturgies syriennes orientales," 70 n. 1.

One thing, however, is certain. The Greeks lost little time in rejecting the declaration on transubstantiation which had been made at the Council. Soon after the Eastern representatives had returned home from Florence, Mark Eugenicus, the metropolitan of Ephesus, who had opposed the declaration on the eucharistic "form" to the very end,[151] went into action. He succeeded in spearheading a repudiation by the Greek populace of the Decree of Union and of the declaration on the Eucharist. Salaville and Smit accuse Eugenicus of pushing Cabasilas's doctrine on the epiclesis to its extreme. They imply that Eugenicus made the words of institution appear to be an empty narrative and that "transubstantiation" depends exclusively upon the epiclesis. Salaville even goes so far as to accuse the metropolitan of Ephesus of evident bad faith.[152] When one reads Eugenicus's short treatise on the question in the light of the exclusiveness of Western Scholastic teaching and also in the light of Western Communion practice then current, a milder judgment seems in order. Eugenicus seems to have concerned himself mainly with demonstrating that the gifts are sanctified *not only* by the words of institution but also, and especially, by the invocation of the priest and the power of the Holy Spirit.[153]

In the West, too, there seems to have been dissatisfaction with the vagueness of the Greek declaration at Florence. Eugene IV may have been trying to remedy this when he issued the *Decree for the Armenians* on November 22, 1439. The decree, the value of which is much disputed because of its statement that the *"traditio instrumentorum,"* was the "matter" of the sacrament of Orders,[154] definitely stems from a Scholastic framework. It had as its basis a small treatise of Thomas Aquinas entitled *De articulis fidei et Sacramentis Ecclesiae.*[155] The pertinent passage reads as follows:

The words of the Lord, by which he confects this sacrament, are the form of this sacrament; for the priest, speaking in the person of Christ, confects

---

151. Cf. Gill, 297.

152. Smit, 116–17; Salaville, "Epiclèse eucharistique," 259–60.

153. Cf. PG, 160:1080–89. Roguet, *L'Eucharistie* I, 387.

154. Cf. DS, 332 (note introducing 1310 [695] ff.) and 3857 (2301) ff. Cf. Salaville, "Epiclèse eucharistique," 197.

155. Roguet, *L'Eucharistie* I, 387.

this sacrament. For by virtue of these words, the substance of bread and the substance of wine are changed into the body and blood of Christ.[156]

Even such precision did not satisfy some. It was deemed necessary to make explicit the fact that the "*verba Salvatoris*" referred to the words, *"Hoc est enim corpus meum," "Hic est enim calix sanguinis mei . . ."* This was done on February 4, 1442, in the *Decree for the Jacobites.*[157]

Before leaving the events which surround the Council of Florence we might point out one more factor in the Western teaching on the sacraments and especially on the Eucharist. In the *Decree for the Armenians* we read:

All these sacraments are realized by three things, namely, by things as matter, by words as form and by the person of the minister conferring the sacrament with the intention of doing what the Church does; if any of these are lacking, the sacrament is not realized.[158]

With all its concentration on the "form" of the sacrament, with all its exclusiveness in regard to the "form" of the Eucharist, the Scholastic mentality still recognized that something else was necessary on the part of humans. The words of institution without the "*intentio ecclesiae*" could have provided a starting point in the search for deep-seated agreement. Bessarion did in fact suggest it,[159] but in vain. For both East and West, immersed as they were in the political tensions of the time, found it difficult to approach their basic differences of mentality objectively. It was hard for both sides to understand one another much less to unite with one another.

One might grant that the Easterners in general did not seem to preoccupy themselves with the precise *moment* of consecration until goaded in this direction by the Latins. One would, however, hesitate to agree with Boularand that the Easterners did not try to distinguish essential from secondary.[160] In general they seem to have recognized the words of institution as essential *but* not exclusively so. They acknowledged that the "intention" of the Church to realize the sacra-

---

156. DS, 1321 (689).
157. Ibid., 1352 (715). Cf. Roguet, *L'Eucharistie* I, 387–88.
158. DS, 1312 (695).
159. Cf. SH, 332.
160. Boularand, 270.

ment here and now and the intervention of the Holy Spirit were also essential for this purpose. In addition, for them the epiclesis proper, which gives expression to the intervention of the Holy Spirit and the praying, believing Church, was also essential.

On the other hand, we have less hesitation in accepting Boularand's conclusion that much of the difficulty lay in the differing mentalities of East and West.[161] It is this difference of mentality in regard to the sacraments which seems to account for much of the growing divergence between East and West in the centuries to come. The Roman tradition whose position was already hardened to some extent by the rigid application of the hylomorphic theory to the sacraments would continue to move in the same direction. The Orthodox tradition would experience an increasing hardening and at times an untraditional[162] precision in its position *vis-à-vis* Rome. The treatment of the epiclesis by both sides will consequently suffer. All too often it will be dragged into and limited to the polemic over the "moment of consecration."

Trent

In the West the teaching concerning the consecration continued to follow basically the course it had taken around the time of the Council of Florence. It is true that with the rise of a more positive theology, liturgical data in general and the liturgical fact of the epiclesis received more attention. With this growing attention paid to the epiclesis, periodic proponents of a consecratory role for the epiclesis arose in the West, especially from the sixteenth century on.[163] In the shadow of controversy between the followers of Martin Luther and Roman Catholic authorities, Pope Paul III convoked the nineteenth Ecumenical Council in Trent, Italy. The aim of the Council, which was to last from 1545 to 1563, was to order and clarify Catholic doctrine and to

---

161. Ibid.

162. L'Huillier, 319.

163. Cf. Smit, 100, footnote 15 for a list of some of the better known among these. Considerations of time and space imposed certain limitations in the following sections. The failure to trace Anglican and Reformed thought during this period, for instance, implies no value judgment on the contribution of these traditions to the history of the epiclesis question. The main reason for choosing the Roman Catholic and Orthodox traditions is that the clash over the epiclesis, and therefore the underlying issues, comes into particularly sharp focus in the relationship of these two.

legislate reforms in the Church. Around this time, a Dominican named Ambrosius Catharinus (born Lancelot Politi) was teaching that in the East the epiclesis, conditioned by the words of institution, was the "consecration rite." In the West, he maintained, it was the words of the institution determined by the *"Quam oblationem"* which formed the rite of transubstantiation.[164] It seems that Catharinus even submitted his writings, which eventually ended up on the Index of Forbidden Books, to the Council's judgment.[165]

Nevertheless, the Council of Trent did not directly treat the eucharistic epiclesis. The closest Trent came to the question was in its statement:

> . . . and this belief was always in the Church of God, that immediately *after the consecration* the real body of our Lord and his real blood existed, together with his soul and divinity, under the form of bread and wine; but the body is indeed under the form of bread and the blood under the form of wine *by virtue of the words* . . .[166]

This statement, however, and statements similar to it were directly concerned with Protestant denials of the "real presence" of Christ in the Eucharist. Thus Trent took a direct stand neither for nor against the consecratory value of the epiclesis, although the Council Fathers were generally thinking of the "consecration" in Scholastic categories. In other words, although they generally considered the "consecration" as taking place through the institution narrative or words of institution, they were not trying to define this. Here as at Florence the documents simply reflect the appreciation of the sacramental formula then current in the Latin Church.[167]

Position of Post-Tridentine Teaching Authority: Roman and Orthodox

Much the same may be said for papal documents on the consecration question which appeared in the following centuries. Pohle's comment on

---

164. Cf. SH, 332 citing *Quaestio quibusnam verbis Christus divinum Eucharistiae sacramentum confecerit* (Rome, 1552).

165. Cf. Salaville, "Epiclèse eucharistique," 231; SH, 332, 334 and Smit, 100, 122.

166. DS, 1640 (876) (Italics mine).

167. SH, 333-34. Cf. Schillebeeckx, *Christ the Sacrament*, 158–59 n. 2.

Pius VII's letter to the Melchite Patriarch in 1822[168] would seem to apply equally well to similar statements issued by Clement XI in 1716,[169] Benedict XIII in 1729,[170] and Benedict XIV in 1741.[171] Pohle writes:

> . . . to say, then, that the epiclesis produces the change is nothing short of deferring the (instantaneous) change until the epiclesis and thereby robbing the institution narrative of the consecratory force attributed to it. This inescapable logic explains the strict prohibition which Pope Pius VII directed against the Antiochene Patriarch of the Melchites in May 1822, insisting, "under obedience," that no one support, publicly or privately, the teaching spread among the schismatics, viz., that the form, by which the life-giving sacrament is realized, does not consist in only the words of Jesus Christ . . .[172]

In the East, once the attempt of the Council of Florence to effect a lasting union had failed, the doctrine of Cabasilas on the epiclesis gained a widespread acceptance. In the sixteenth century this doctrine began to make its appearance in official documents such as the letters of Patriarch Jeremias II to the German Lutherans (1576–1581).[173]

The milestone in the formation of the Orthodox position was, however, *The Orthodox Confession of the Catholic and Apostolic Eastern Church* drawn up by Peter Moghila, Metropolitan of Kiev, in 1640. There are some who claim that Moghila's original version stated that the words of institution consecrate. Miletius Syrigos, they maintain, produced a modified translation into Greek. The Russians, desiring the speedy approbation of the work, yielded to pressure and accepted the Greek view that the epiclesis is consecratory.[174] Be that as it may, the Greek translation was approved by the Council of Jassy in 1642, by the Patriarchs of Constantinople, Alexandria, Antioch and Jerusalem in 1643 and by the Council of Jerusalem in 1672. The English of the text reads as follows:

---

168. CL, 2:550–51. Cf. DS, 2718.

169. Cf. CL, 2:439.

170. CL, 2:439–40.

171. CL, 2:196–97. Cf. also DS footnote to 3556 (2147a) and Bornert, 237 n. 1.

172. Pohle, III (1922⁷) 252. Cf. also for other examples of this viewpoint, A. D'Ales, *De sanctissima Eucharistia* (Paris, 1929), 128 and E. Hugon, *La sainte Eucharistie* (Paris, 1916¹), 222.

173. Cf. Salaville, "Epiclèse eucharistique," 260; SH, 332.

174. Salaville, ibid.; J. Parboire, "Meletios Syrigos, sa vie et ses oeuvres," EO 12 (1909), 25; Dix, *The Shape* . . . , 294.

The priest must know that at the moment when he consecrates the gifts, the substance (ουσια) itself of the bread and the substance of the wine are changed (μεταβαλλεται) into the substance of the real body and blood of Christ through the operation of the Holy Ghost, whom the priest invokes at that time, consecrating this mystery by praying and saying, "Send down Thy Holy Ghost on us and on these gifts set before Thee and make this bread the precious body of Thy Christ and that which is in this cup the precious blood of Thy Christ, changing (μεταβαλον) them by the Holy Ghost." For immediately after these words the transubstantiation (μετουσιοσισ) takes place, and the bread is changed into the real body of Christ, and the wine into His real blood.[175]

What is striking here is the accent on a particular "moment of consecration." It is this accent which leads Pohle to claim, perhaps unjustly, that Moghila's position like that of Catharinus is not merely contrary to the common teaching of the Church but contrary to the Church's faith. According to Pohle, Moghila's *Confession* no longer allows room even for a co-consecratory role for the words of institution.[176] It is true that this portion of the *Confession* does not mention the words of institution and that it definitely attributes the "moment of consecration" to the epiclesis. Nevertheless, it does not necessarily follow that the institution narrative loses all consecratory value. The epiclesis could, it seems, at least in the view of the Eastern writers, play an essential role. It could even be the "moment of consecration," without making the words of institution non-essential. For instance, Isidore of Kiev's view that the institution narrative was like a seed which the epiclesis makes fruitful, seems to allow for such a possibility.

Despite the fact that the Russians yielded to pressure and accepted the Greek translation of Moghila's statement, Kiev formed, according to Salaville, a pocket of resistance to the Greek doctrine up to the beginning of the eighteenth century. Moghila and the Russians of Kiev, Salaville contends, continued to believe and teach that the consecration takes place through the words of institution.[177]

---

175. P. Palmer (ed.), *Sources of Christian Theology I: Sacraments and Worship* (London, paperback edition, 1957), 261. For the Greek text see J. Michaelcescu, *Die Bekenntnisse und die wichtigsten Glaubenzeugnisse der griechisch-orientalischen Kirche* (Leipzig, 1904), 72.

176. Pohle III (1960[10]), 282.

177. Salaville, "Epiclèse eucharistique," 261–63.

With the passage of time the viewpoint of Nicholas Cabasilas gradually formed the basis for the Orthodox postion.[178] Both in Moghila's *Confession* and in the profession of faith demanded of those about to be consecrated bishop, among the Russians the epiclesis and the "moment of consecration" were considered identical.[179] Nevertheless, it does not seem that Cabasilas, as we have already noted, or those following him, understood this in such a way as to make the words of institution non-essential or to deprive them of all consecratory worth. L'Huillier states that to the best of his knowledge no Orthodox theologian has ever upheld a theory of consecration by the epiclesis independent of its context in the eucharistic prayer. He flatly rejects Jugie's claim[180] that some Orthodox theologians hold for consecration by the epiclesis alone.[181]

The Russian *Longer Catechism* based on the *Confession* approved at the Council of Jerusalem (1672) and in its turn approved in both a Russian and a Greek version by Orthodox authorities tends, to some extent, to confirm L'Huillier's contention. It reads:

What is the most essential act in the Liturgy of the Faithful:

The utterance of the Words which Jesus Christ spake in instituting the Sacrament, *Take, eat, this is My Body. Drink ye all of it, for this is My Blood of the new Covenant* (Matthew 24: 27–28); and after this the Invocation of the Holy Ghost, and the blessing of the gifts, that is the bread and wine which have been offered. Why is this so essential? Because at the moment of this act the bread and wine are changed, or transubstantiated, into the very Body of Christ and into the very Blood of Christ.[182]

Since then, the response of the Patriarch and Synod of Constantinople to the encyclical on union of Leo XIII in 1894 may have provided a highpoint in tension between the two teaching authorities on the epiclesis question. The response affirmed that the gifts are consecrated by the prayer invoking the Holy Spirit and that the Roman Church had innovated in proclaiming the moment in

---

178. SH, 332.

179. Jugie, *De forma . . .* , 56.

180. Cf. ibid., 58 and Jugie's *Theologia Dogmatica . . .* III, 290 to which L'Huillier is referring in particular.

181. L'Huillier, 317 n. 33. Cf. also Kern, "En marge . . . ," 181–82.

182. Frere, *The Anaphora*, 193 citing the English translation from Blackmore in *The Doctrine of the Russian Church* (1845), 91–92.

which the words of institution are pronounced to be the "moment of consecration."[183]

Before closing this survey of the emergence of the problem of the epiclesis and the "moment of consecration," it would be well to examine briefly a statement made by Pius X on the question. The statement, it is true, appeared in 1910 and therefore belongs to the very period that is to form the main object of our study. It sums up, however, much of the papal thought on the epiclesis question up to 1900 and seems to underscore some of the basic issues at stake. This statement would certainly have had great impact on many Roman Catholic writers treating the epiclesis question after 1910.

The occasion for Pius X's declaration was an article by Maximilian of Saxony. In the article, which appeared in *Roma e l'Oriente* in 1910, the author bemoans the division between the Eastern and Western Churches. He appeals for truth and charity. In this context he raises some of the issues which underlie the division. One of the issues which he touches upon is that of the epiclesis. He maintains that the Western treatments of transubstantiation have taken for their basis the liturgy of the Roman rite. The universality of the epiclesis and the antiquity of the doctrine (e.g., in the writings of Cyril of Jerusalem which sees it as the principal component of the consecration) have been, he claims, disregarded. This leads him to the statement which was to earn for him a sharp rebuke from Pius X. Maximilian contends:

> . . . Nevertheless, it would be so easy to reconcile the two points of view. One would only have to say that it is the words of our Lord which cause the sacrament, because they ought to correspond to the truth, but that these words produce their effect in consequence of the consecration of the Church and because of her intention. Since, then, *in the Roman liturgy the consecration consists solely of our Lord's words, these produce their effect immediately, as soon as they are pronounced.* Since, on the other hand, in the oriental Church, and according to her intentions, the epiclesis, which follows our Lord's words, is the principal part of the consecration and its completion, it follows that *in the East the words produce their effect through the epiclesis* and that our Lord is only present when the epiclesis is concluded.[184]

---

183. Salaville, "Epiclèse eucharistique," 260–61 and Smit, 117. For the Greek text of this document cf. Ἐκκλησιαστικὴ Ἀλήθεια 15 (1895/96), 244.

184. Maximilian of Saxony, "Pensées sur la question de l'union des Eglises," *Roma e l'Orient* 1 (1910), 25. (Italics mine).

More important than Maximilian of Saxony's statement, however, is Pius X's response to it:

> But the Catholic doctrine on the most holy sacrament of the Eucharist is not left intact when one resolutely teaches that it is possible to hold the opinion which maintains that, among the Greeks, the consecratory words do not produce their effect unless that prayer, which they call the epiclesis, has already been offered. *For it is certain that the rights of the Church in no way make her competent to alter the substance of the sacrament in any respect;. . .*[185]

A number of points in Pius X's statement are noteworthy. First of all, he does not expressly deny that the epiclesis *could* have a value of its own. He simply rejects the putting off of the "moment of consecration" until the epiclesis proper.[186] Secondly, the Pope does not say that the epiclesis never formed a "co-consecratory moment" in the past but simply that it does not *now* form a necessary "moment of consecration." He does, however, seem to presuppose that at no time in the past was the epiclesis considered to have had a consecratory value. This leads us to the third important point, the Pope's reason for refusing the epiclesis a share in the "moment of consecration." He contends that to acknowledge such a role for the epiclesis would be to change the "substance of the sacrament," something which Trent defined the Church has no right to do. Pius X's argumentation seems to presuppose then that Christ himself intended the words of institution as a liturgical consecration formula and that, as a result, this specific "form" or formula belongs to the unchangeable substance of the sacrament. In other words, he seems to be arguing that this specific "form" is, and *always has been*, the *exclusive* consecratory moment in the Eucharist.[187]

An examination of the place of the eucharistic epiclesis in patristic writings and in later debates over the "moment of consecration" inclines one to treat such presuppositions with great reserve.[188] In examining the emergence and intensification of the "moment of consecration" problem and its effect on the epiclesis question we have tried to remain aware of the background of the statements made in

---

185. DS, 3556 (2147a) (Italics mine). Cf. EO, 14 (1911), 7.
186. Cf. SH, 334 and Smit, 123.
187. SH, 334–35.
188. Cf. ibid., and Smit, 123.

regard to this problem. An attempt has been made to be objective in pointing out, for instance, the extenuating circumstances surrounding the Greek declaration at Florence and the weakness, at least in some parts, of the *Decree for the Armenians*. E. Schillebeeckx and others seem correct in the judgement that, "None of these documents supports a de-fide argument that the essentially sacramental significance belongs exclusively to the words of institution."[189]

Nevertheless, despite reservations in regard to various declarations of the Roman teaching authority pertinent to the epiclesis question, one thing is clear. There is no question that this teaching authority, while not *defining* that the institution narrative alone has "consecratory" value, did in fact officially teach this. It is important to bear this in mind during the study of the eucharistic epiclesis between 1900 and 1966. For during the greater part of this period the authority and influence of papal statements, encyclicals, etc., seems to have reached a high point in the thinking of many Roman Catholic theologians. This is especially true of those writing theological manuals. It seems scarcely to have been conceivable in the first few decades of the twentieth century that within the Roman tradition one would call into question the basis or presuppositions of papal statements or even attempt a "hermeneutical" study of the same. Thus for many Roman Catholic theologians the epiclesis question seems to have become practically an open and shut case in view of numerous papal statements regarding the "moment of consecration."

Was it impossible to ask *why* the official teaching authority took the stand that it did within the Roman Tradition? Was it, perhaps, because in a Scholastic, "transubstantiation" framework it could take no other stand without, in its eyes, denying *any* consecratory value to the institution narrative? B. Schultze's claim that the Scholastic mentality did not provide the starting point for the Catholic teaching on the epiclesis, seems unacceptable. The Scholastic mentality did, indeed, affect the outlook on the Eucharist as a whole. Schultze's own view of the Eucharist appears at times to betray this fact.[190] One can

189. Schillebeeckx, *Christ the Sacrament*, 159 n. 2, 114 n. 2 and SH, 388–91. Cf. also, for instance, Salaville, "Epiclèse eucharistique," 197; Smit, 123; J. Höller, "Die Stellung der Päpste zur Epiklese der griechischorientalischen Liturgien," TPQS 66 (1913), 315; Jugie, *De forma . . .*, 38–39.

190. Schultze, "Zum Problem der Epiclese . . . ," 391 n. 1. and 392. Cf. Kern, 185 n. 1.

hope to grasp the official teaching on the epiclesis only when one situates this teaching within its Scholastic setting.

The Roman teaching authority for centuries lay embedded in Scholastic thought patterns. This is especially true of the centuries in which the problem of the epiclesis and the "moment of consecration" became most acute. If one accepts the contention that it is necessary to situate the official statements that touch on the epiclesis question in a Scholastic context of instantaneous transubstantiation, one raises the question already alluded to. Given the either-or nature of this context as regards the "moment of consecration," did the teaching authority really have much choice in the matter? In this context must it not have seemed necessary in order to protect the consecratory value of the words of institution (and this seems throughout to have been the main purpose) to deprive the epiclesis proper of any consecratory value? We shall return to this question later on in this study. At this point, however, it might be helpful to summarize what has been seen so far.

SUMMARY

First of all, we have examined a number of patristic texts pertaining to the question whether or not the Fathers saw the eucharistic epiclesis as "consecrating." At first glance a number of these texts seem to be clear. When subjected to closer scrutiny, however, they allow various interpretations and have, in fact, received widely varying interpretations. Some of the early Christian writers, Ambrose and Augustine for instance, seem to stress the consecratory value of the institution words. Others, Cyril of Jerusalem and John Damascene, for example, seem to stress the consecratory value of the epiclesis. The frequent uncertainty as to the exact meaning of the patristic texts, therefore, tends to make one wary of overly categorical and overly consistent interpretations of the pertinent patristic passages.

Some clear lines do, however, emerge from an examination of the patristic texts. In the eyes of the Fathers, the action of the Holy Spirit is an absolute necessity for the realization of the Eucharist. There is also general agreement that the Fathers regarded the whole eucharistic prayer as consecratory. It is possible that the Fathers viewed the words of institution and the epiclesis as two consecratory "moments" or highpoints within this larger framework of the entire canon.

Despite all the ambiguities, one thing is certain. The "moment of consecration" was not an issue for the early Christian writers. As a consequence, there was for them no problem of the epiclesis and the "moment of consecration."

In fact, up to the beginning of the fourteenth century we find little or no evidence of a conflict over the epiclesis. Neither Photius nor Michael Cerularius, neither Thomas Aquinas nor the Council of Lyon made an issue of the eucharistic epiclesis.

The rise of Scholasticism had, however, brought with it a growing interest in the "moment of consecration." Thomas Aquinas is a case in point. A number of papal statements and the reaction of Western missionaries to the Eastern use of the epiclesis also reflect this interest.

A response from the East was inevitable. Nicholas Cabasilas, who was to set the tone for later Orthodox thought on the epiclesis, ought to be understood against a backdrop of Scholasticism. He inveighed against making the words of institution *alone* sufficient for consecration. In stressing the need for prayer (the epiclesis), however, he does not appear to have denied all consecratory value to the words of institution.

Both East and West, immersed as they were in the political tensions of the time, found it difficult to approach their basic differences of mentality objectively. The events subsequent to the Councils of Florence and Trent reflect a hardening of position on both sides.

The Orthodox tradition, perhaps in over-reaction to the Roman position, increasingly stressed the epiclesis and revealed, at times, an untraditional precision in regard to the "moment of consecration." The Roman tradition, on the other hand, continued to mirror the Scholastic mentality and to insist on the *exclusive* consecratory value of the words of institution. The conciliar and papal statements to this effect thus reflect the Scholastic appreciation of the sacramental formula and ought to be interpreted in the light of this appreciation.

Part II

Modern Liturgists and Theologians: "Moment of Consecration"

With the data of the early anaphoras and a historical survey of the eucharistic epiclesis—especially of its entanglement with the "moment of consecration" problem—as a basis, it is now possible to turn to the twentieth-century writers. Chapter 3 will examine the terminology which these writers use. Chapter 4 will focus on some of the attempts to reconstruct the early development of the epiclesis. These attempts often carry with them implications which are important for the theology of the epiclesis. Chapter 5 will examine and try to evaluate some of the theological explanations the writers of this century have proposed in regard to the epiclesis.

Finally, chapter 6 will study briefly the structure of the sacraments in the light of the epiclesis and thus prepare the way for a better understanding of two more theological explanations of the epiclesis proposed in the twentieth century. All too often one will detect the "moment of consecration" problem overshadowing and influencing the theology of the epiclesis in this period. Hence the title of Part Two.

Chapter 3

Understanding the Terminology of Modern Writers

The terminology that the writers of the twentieth century use has a twofold importance. First, it forms a necessary condition for, and at times even an obstacle to, understanding the discussion over the epiclesis. For instance, what do twentieth-century writers have in mind when they use the term "epiclesis" in conjunction with the primitive Christian community, and what do they have in mind when they use this same term to refer to the fully developed epiclesis as found in the early anaphoras? In addition, this terminology often carries with it important theological implications and insights.

EPICLESIS IN MODERN WRITINGS

Before examining the various definitions and descriptions which the twentieth-century writers have applied to the developed form of the eucharistic epiclesis as seen in Chapter 1, it would be well to survey the valuable discussion revolving around the *primitive* meaning of the word "epiclesis."

In 1917 J. W. Tyrer, the great Anglican scholar, published a book entitled, *The Eucharistic Epiclesis.* At the outset of this work he makes a statement that was to pave the way for an extremely fruitful exchange of views over the meaning of "epiclesis." Tyrer declares that, "Εὐχαριστια definitely signifies a *thanksgiving;* ἐπίκλησις equally definitely a solemn *petition.*"[1]

It was this point that R.H. Connolly, the British Benedictine and noted liturgical scholar, was to single out for special criticism a

---

1. Tyrer, *The Eucharistic Epiclesis,* 5–6 (Italics mine).

number of years later in an article published in *Downside Review* in 1923.[2] In so doing Connolly touched off a running battle between himself and Tyrer over this question. He began by challenging Tyrer's description of "epiclesis" as a "solemn appeal . . . a solemn *petition*":

> I do not know of any passage in an ante-Nicene writer which can be held to justify the statement that *epiclesis* signifies a *petition* . . . It is certain at least that, both in ante-Nicene times and after, words denoting invocation were freely used with reference to formulae into which petition need not and often did not, enter at all.[3]

So began the fruitful debate.

One could sum up Connolly's position as follows: In speaking of the epiclesis we often seem to presume that it is, and was originally, a *petition* for God to intervene and make the sacrament what he intended it to be. On the basis of this presumption we often interpret some of the pre-Nicene Fathers as witnessing to an epiclesis proper in their day. What we need, maintains Connolly, is a philological study of the word "epiclesis" as it was understood in the early days of Christianity. Such a study, the broad lines of which he himself attempts to sketch,[4] would seem to indicate that "epiclesis" in those days was not an appeal or petition for someone to come upon or onto the oblations (or water or oil). "Epiclesis" was rather used to designate a certain religious formula involving the use of names. This is the way the word is to be understood in Irenaeus, Origen, the Gnostic *Acts of John,* Ambrose, and probably even in Cyril of Jerusalem's use of the expression, "the epiclesis of the Holy Spirit."

Connolly appeals to early Christian as well as to classical Greek usage to support his argument. If the baptismal formula and the eucharistic prayers can both be described by the term "invocation," the common factor, he contends, cannot be the notion of petition. Such descriptions could be explained, however, if the terms *epiclesis* and *invocatio*, ". . . came into the Christian vocabulary with a strong sense of the power inherent in a divine Name, and the virtue attaching to the mere pronouncing the name in connection with religious acts."[5]

---

2. Connolly, "On the Meaning . . . ," 28–43.
3. Ibid., 29.
4. Ibid., 28–43.
5. Ibid., 30.

In classical Greek, it is true, both the verb and noun (ἐπικαλεῖν, ἐπίκλησις) occasionally referred to an appeal for help. The most common meaning, however, was related to a surname, a title, etc., or the giving of such. "It will now be only a short step forward if we find epiclesis uniting both the meanings just noticed, and signifying the invocation *of a name*, or an appeal by name."[6] All these facts tend to confirm Connolly in his viewpoint, namely:

> My thesis is that here the characteristic use of the words "invocation" "invoke," is not to express the idea of petition, but to designate this or that religious formula as one involving the use of names—whether it be names or titles given to God, . . . or any other supernatural powers: and whether the formula be pious and orthodox, or profane and superstitious.[7]

In his response, however, Tyrer maintains his original position. Writing in 1924, he contends that the characteristic and primary use of the words ἐπικαλεῖσθαι and ἐπίκλησις is to express the idea of petition. A secondary meaning was acquired and the term "epiclesis" came to be used of religious formulas other than petitions, e.g., formulas for Christian baptism, as well as heretical and magical incantations.[8] To substantiate this claim Tyrer musters an impressive collection of biblical and patristic texts and comes to a twofold conclusion. First, we have to be aware of the fact that the same writer may use the word "epiclesis" in different places with different meanings. It does not follow, for instance, that when he uses this word in regard to the Eucharist that it has the same meaning as when he uses it in regard to baptism. Second, since the verb επικαλεισθαι definitely expresses the idea of petition, the noun "epiclesis" is also most likely to have this primary and normal meaning. This is especially true when these two words are used in close proximity and in connection with the same subject.[9]

Connolly's reply is no less firm but it contains a clarification which is important for the question at hand. He points out that he did not deny that the term "epiclesis" could be applied to a "formula" that

---

6. Ibid., 31–32.

7. Ibid., 33.

8. Tyrer, "The Meaning . . . ," 140–41. Cf. also, Brightman (Correspondence: Invocation . . .), 34–35.

9. Tyrer, ibid., 146–47.

is a prayer, even a prayer of petition. What he did deny was that it is the petition rather than the address (the naming) that is essential to "epiclesis."[10]

The importance of the answer to the question is that it influences our judgment on the presence or absence of the "epiclesis" in the strict sense at the time of and in the writings of the first three centuries, e.g., in the writings of Irenaeus.

> If then a writer like St. Irenaeus can say that the bread, on 'receiving the *epiclesis* of God, is no longer bread but Eucharist' . . . , does he not mean that it becomes 'Eucharist' in answer to an express petition to God that it may be made so? The inference which we are expected to draw is that that is his meaning; but the justice of the inference depends, *inter alia*, on the correctness of the definition of ἐπίκλησις as "a petition."[11]

In the meantime O. Casel of Maria Laach was making his contribution to the whole question. Writing in 1923, he outlined his basic position which can be summed up as follows: In classical antiquity, and therefore in early Christianity which has its roots in this antiquity, the essence of the epiclesis consisted in the naming of a divine name (upon a person or a thing). This has as its basis the belief, which continued on in Christianity, that such a naming called upon or (in magical rites) forced the person named to be actively present to or in the person or thing he was "called down upon." Thus implied in, or tightly bound up with, the naming of the name was an "epiphany of the divinity." Examples of the epiclesis in this sense are the baptismal formula, the consecration of the baptismal water and fundamentally the Prefaces in the Eucharist. All involve the naming of the divine person or persons (the Trinity, for instance) so that these persons might come to be *actively, effectively* present. The prime example of this was the Canon of the Mass, at once Eucharist and *epiclesis* in the ancient and broad sense of this word. It is a naming, in praise, of the Trinity.[12]

Returning to the question in 1924 after reading the exchange between Connolly and Tyrer, Casel takes the role of a distant but involved referee of sorts. Tyrer goes too far when he maintains that the term epiclesis could only refer to a petitionary form:

---

10. Connolly, "The Meaning . . . ," 341–42. Cf. Robinson, "Invocation . . . ," 89–93.
11. Connolly, ibid., 340.
12. Casel, "Zur Epiklese . . . ," 100–101.

Rather, the ἐπίκλησις is a naming of the divine name *and* a calling
down. . . . Sometimes one comes to the forefront, sometimes the other. The
baptismal formula is, therefore, a real ἐπίκλησις because the divine name
is pronounced over the one being baptized, even though no 'invocation,' in
the sense of a petition, takes place.[13]

As for Connolly, Casel notes that in his reply to Tyrer,
Connolly admits that the naming of the name could be in conjunction
with an appeal. As long as Connolly concedes this point, Casel feels
that he and Connolly are saying the same thing but that he himself
said it more clearly in his earlier article.

The calling down (not: petitioning) belongs to the essence of the epiclesis
and can, but does not have to be, made explicit.[14]

Basically then Casel objects to Connolly trying to play down
too much the petitionary character of the epiclesis, just as he objected
to Tyrer for stressing too much the same petitionary aspect to the
detriment of the naming of the name. Casel's attempt to give proper
weight to each of these aspects was an important contribution to the
whole discussion.

In 1949, F. Nötscher was to enter the picture. In an article
published in *Biblica*, Nötscher complains that Connolly, Tyrer, and Casel
and Pascher[15] look to the history of religions, early Christian and
profane Greek and Roman literature, and Hellenism in general, for the
origin of the epiclesis. They should have been looking more to the Bible
and especially the Old Testament for the source of this element of
early Christian worship. There they would find that the idea of calling
someone's name upon a person or a thing is very much at home in the
Old Testament. Hand in hand with this calling or naming goes
a certain possession by the one named of the person or thing upon
which the name is invoked. This in turn implies a dependence on the
person named but also a confidence that when that person is called
upon, e.g., in prayer, he will respond with help and protection.[16]

---

13. Casel, "Neue Beiträge . . . ," 170.

14. Ibid., 172. Cf. also Casel's (Review of Elfers' *Die Kirchenordnung* . . .), 129 and (Review
of Frere's *Primitive Consecration Prayer*), 174 and SH, 308.

15. Pascher, *Eucharistia*, 116.

16. Nötscher, 401–403. Cf. Schmidt-Lauber, 156, n. 165 for a similar critique of Casel.
Cf. also, Bartsch, 160–61.

In his study of the real presence prior to Nicea, which first appeared in 1955, J. Betz attempts a synthesis of the aforementioned positions. Betz sees Nötscher's position, derived from the Bible and stressing the taking of possession by God of the person or thing over which God's name is spoken, as complementary to the three-cornered contribution of Connolly, Tyrer, and Casel. The epiclesis presents the transfer to, or the taking over of the elements by, God. This takes place through the naming of God's name over the gifts. This naming of the name implies a calling upon God to be present here and now and to take these gifts into his possession, fill them with his power and thus transform them into the body and blood of Christ. Thus Tyrer's stressing of the appeal character of the epiclesis brings out its existential aspect. Connolly's emphasis on the naming of the name underlines its objective character and Nötscher calls attention to the purpose of the epiclesis.[17]

We would agree with Betz that Tyrer and Connolly have respectively brought out the existential and objective character of the epiclesis. We would simply add here that Casel deserves credit for his efforts to balance both these aspects. In giving his analysis of the purpose of the epiclesis as the transformation of the gifts into the body and blood of Christ, however, Betz has carried us into the realm of the more developed epiclesis. He has also touched upon a problem in regard to terminology by describing the purpose of this more developed form solely in terms of a transformation of the gifts. It is to the terminology relating to the more developed epiclesis, and the problems associated with this terminology, that attention now turns.

Modern Descriptions of
the Developed Epiclesis

When we speak in this study of the more developed epiclesis, we are referring to the epicleses or possible epicleses found in the early Christian anaphoras. As soon as one attempts to go further, however, one realizes that the problem of terminology already looms large.

When H. Lietzmann, for instance, in his famous *Messe und Herrenmahl* published in 1926, speaks of the *Te igitur* and certain

---

17. Betz, *Die Eucharistie* . . . , 320–28.

Gallican prayers as epicleses, it is on the basis of terminology that Casel challenges him.[18] It is on the same basis that Jungmann at times takes Bouyer's *Eucharistie* to task.[19]

E. Bishop's treatment of the moment of consecration reflects the problem well. According to Bishop, writing in 1909 the *Supplices* is clearly a prayer for the communicants and therefore not equivalent to the Eastern epicleses which are prayers calling for the consecration. As for the *Quam oblationem* one must distinguish: If one asks, "Does it contain an 'invocation' on the bread and wine?" the answer is definitely, "Yes." If one asks, "Does it contain an 'invocation' of the Holy Spirit' on the bread and wine?" the answer is just as definitely, "No."[20]

Bishop's statements illustrate well how one's concept or definition of an epiclesis proper affects one's choice of what in fact is an epiclesis in the text. Here, for instance, if one considers the epiclesis proper as only looking to the consecration and not to the reception of Communion the case for *Quam oblationem* as an epiclesis becomes stronger and that for the *Supplices* weaker. If the stress were on the epiclesis being an appeal for worthy Communion, then the strength of the case for the *Supplices* becomes stronger and that for the *Quam oblationem* weaker. If, moreover, one considers the mention of the Holy Spirit as necessary for an epiclesis then the case for either of these being an epiclesis proper vanishes.

M. Jugie in an article which appeared in *Echos d'Orient* in 1936 is thus correct in seeing terminology as one of the greatest difficulties in tracing the historical evolution of the epiclesis.[21] This same difficulty arises when one seeks a theological explanation for the epiclesis.

Recalling the results of our examination of the earlier Christian anaphoras, let us now look at the terminology that some of the twentieth-century writers employ in regard to the eucharistic epiclesis.

A number of authors limit themselves to a very general description of the epiclesis. J. J. Von Allmen is a recent case in point. In his *Essai sur le Repas du Seigneur*, he describes the epiclesis as

---

18. Casel (Review of Lietzmann's *Messe und Herrenmahl*), 210–12. Cf. also, Casel's *Das christliche Opfermysterium*, 547.

19. Jungmann (Review of Bouyer's *Eucharistie*), 465.

20. Bishop, "The Moment . . . ," 131–36. Cf. Renz, 532, 539.

21. Jugie, "Considérations générales . . . ," 324. Cf. also, Cabrol, "Epiclèse," 144; Vagaggini, *The Canon . . .* , 91 n. 6 and Ware, *Eustratios Argenti*, 132.

". . . the prayer which asks the Holy Spirit to intervene so that the Lord's Supper might really become what Jesus Christ intended it to be when he instituted it."[22] J. Laager follows a similar course in an article which appeared in the *Reallexikon für Antike und Christentum* in 1962. After criticizing those who restrict the definition of the epiclesis to that of a full-blown epiclesis asking for the Holy Spirit to change the gifts and, as a rule, to work in the communicants, he suggests that the most general form of epiclesis simply be described as an invocation ("Anrufung") over the eucharistic gifts.[23] Such general descriptions have the advantage that they are broad enough to embrace a number of the variants found in liturgical texts. They also preclude an overemphasis of one or other aspect in the fully developed epiclesis. They only vaguely reflect, however, the actual data which the early anaphoras offer.

A number of authors give an epiclesis definition or description whose one-sidedness seems to reflect traces of the "moment of consecration" problem. A. Fortesque provides us with an example of this when he states: "The Epiklesis (ἐπίκλησις, *invocatio*) is, as now understood, an invocation of the Holy Ghost that he may change the bread and wine into the body and blood of Christ."[24] P. Brunner, writing in 1954, and F. Cabrol, in an article which first appeared in 1922, underline what seems to be the cause of the one-sidedness. Brunner rightly points out the twofold content of the developed eucharistic epiclesis, namely, the appeal for the transformation of the gifts and for the fruitful reception of Communion. He hastens to add, however, that since the appeal for the fruitful reception of Communion poses no dogmatic problem he will limit himself to the appeal for "consecration" and this is what the word "epiclesis" will connote throughout his article.[25] In a similar vein, Cabrol distinguishes between the definition that today seems to fit the data and the more restricted meaning which is usually understood in discussions or debates on the epiclesis and its relationship to the "moment of consecration."[26]

---

22. Von Allmen, *Essai* . . . , 31.

23. Laager, 585. The description Stählin, 45 proposes fits into a similar category.

24. Fortescue, 402. For similar descriptions, cf. Srawley, 196; MacLean, 407; Varaine, "L'épiclèse eucharistique," 121; Merk, *Der Konsekrations text* . . . , 103.

25. Brunner, "Zur Lehre . . . ," 348–49.

26. Cf. Cabrol, "Epiclèse," 143–44.

A number of authors have rightly leveled criticism at such restricted definitions as not doing justice to the liturgical data of the early anphoras.[27] In the anaphoras examined earlier, the epiclesis or possible epiclesis that does not contain a clear reference to the communicants is a rare exception. There have, however, been a good number of twentieth-century writers who have succeeded in better balancing the various elements of the fully developed epiclesis in their definitions or descriptions. Although it is practically impossible to include in a single description of the epiclesis all the variations, seen in Chapter 1, a number of good attempts have been made. Cabrol, for instance, offers the following definition:

> [The eucharistic epiclesis is] one of the prayers of the canon in which the priest asks God to send his Word or his Holy Spirit upon the elements to transform them into the body and blood of Christ and to produce the effects of communion in the faithful.[28]

For Cabrol, then, there are three principal elements to an epiclesis: an invocation to God; a request to transform the bread and wine into Christ's body and blood; a request to apply the effects of the eucharistic sacrament to the faithful. He hastens to add, however, that often one or the other of these elements is missing.

G. C. Smit, in an article which appeared in Dutch in 1950 and in French translation in 1958, provides an even more detailed description:

> . . . that invocation from the eucharistic anaphora or canon, which—through the intervention of the Word and of the Holy Spirit or not—expressly appeals for: 1) the transformation of the gifts presented on the altar into the Body and Blood of Christ; 2) a salutary action of the gifts (considered as already consecrated) upon those who partake of them—i.e., a worthy and fruitful Communion; 3) the sanctification of the gifts (always regarded as consecrated) as salutary instruments—consequently, an objective sanctification of the gifts in order to constitute the "sacramentum."[29]

---

27. Cf. Dinesen, 72 n. 24, 79–80, 84; Laager, 585; Cabrol, ibid. Cf. also, Jugie, *De forma* . . . , 14.

28. Cabrol, "Epiclèse," 143–44. Cf. also, Salaville, "Epiclèse eucharistique," 194.

29. Smit, 95. "Sacramentum" is here understood in the sense of an *objective* instrument suited for, adapted to, subjective reception. It does not include, as does the usual use of the word "sacrament," the subjective element, i.e., the attitude of those partaking. Cf. 95 n. 3.

The epiclesis is, then, a prayer which forms part of the great eucharistic prayer or anaphora and which looks to either a transformation (1) or a sanctification (2, 3).[30]

While similar to Cabrol's definition in many ways, Smit's description insists on neither an explicit mention of the Holy Spirit (or the Word) nor an explicit appeal for the transformation of the gifts into Christ's body and blood. It can thus cover more of the variations which we have seen in the epicleses of the early Christian anaphoras.

Still another attempt to describe the full-blown epiclesis is that which H. C. Schmidt-Lauber proposed in 1957:

> (The epiclesis is) the prayer for the coming of the Holy Spirit upon those celebrating (1) and upon the gifts of bread and wine (2) so that they fulfill the function which Christ instituted for them by becoming, in the course of the Eucharist, Christ's body and blood (3) and so that through them the faithful may be given a fuller participation in the "whole Christ" and in his work (4) so that the faithful in turn, might reveal themselves as the one Body of Christ (5) and might not partake of this food unworthily.[31]

This description reflects, among other things, those epicleses that underscore the key role that the Holy Spirit plays as life-principle ("Lebensprinzip") of the New Covenant, enlivening and increasing the bond between the glorified body of the risen Lord and his mystical Body, the community.

A final example is the definition which P. Dinesen, professor at the University of Aarhus, Denmark, puts forth in his 1962 article in the periodical *Studia Theologica*:

> The epiclesis is an appeal to God (1) for his intervention through the Holy Spirit (2) in regard to the elements of the Thanksgiving, the bread and wine (3) that they manifest (5) the body and blood of Christ (4) and in regard to those partaking in the Lord's Supper (6) that they might be one (7) and attain (among other things) (10) forgiveness of sins (8) and eternal life (9).[32]

Dinesen uses the term "manifest" ("offenbaren") instead of more definite terms such as "make" which the fully developed epicleses

---

30. Ibid., 95–96.
31. Schmidt-Lauber, 155–56.
32. Dinesen, 72. Cf. 73–75.

often employ in regard to the transition of bread and wine into the body and blood of Christ. This reflects his desire to underline what he considers to be the vague, non-philosophical character of the expressions used to describe this transition. In addition, he does not bring out as clearly as Schmidt-Lauber, for instance, the relationship between the transformation of the gifts and the benefits desired for the communicants. The transformation generally is asked for, as we have seen, *so that* those partaking may receive these benefits. Otherwise, Dinesen's definition represents one of the finest composite pictures of the epiclesis in the early anaphoras.

From the examples just seen, it should be fairly clear that the better descriptions or definitions of the eucharistic epiclesis have in common three basic facets which *generally* turn up in the full-blown epiclesis, namely, an appeal for the Holy Spirit (1) to transform or sanctify the bread and wine (2) so that they may benefit those who partake of them worthily (3).[33] In addition, a number of authors have succeeded in capturing, as Dinesen has, the frequently recurrent elements which the liturgical data reveals and in presenting these elements in the form of more detailed descriptions of the eucharistic epiclesis.

Before closing this section on the terminology, it is necessary to glance at some further precisions used in conjunction with the more developed epiclesis. The Glossary provided some preliminary terminology which included an explanation of the terms *Spirit epiclesis, Logos epiclesis, consecratory epiclesis,* and *epiclesis of sanctification.* There is no need to return to these now. In addition to this terminology some authors refer to a *pre-consecration* and a *post-consecration* epiclesis. The pre-consecration epiclesis would refer to an epiclesis which precedes the institution narrative. The post-consecration epiclesis would in turn refer to an epiclesis that follows this institution narrative.[34] Whenever possible we have avoided using this terminology. Its use often carries with it a twofold connotation. First, it seems to presume that the eucharistic consecration involves only the transformation of bread and wine into the body and blood of Christ. Secondly, such terminology

---

33. For examples of such descriptions, in addition to those we have already mentioned, cf. SH, 307; Rauschen, 111–12; Spacil, *Doctrina theologiae Orientis* . . . , 5–6; Vagaggini, *The Canon* . . . , 15, 91.

34. Cf., for instance, Smit, 107 n. 47 and Baumstark, "Zu den Problemen . . . ," 341 referring to Höller, *Die Epiklese* . . .

seems to presume that the words of institution alone are responsible for this eucharistic consecration or, in other words, that they alone represent the moment of consecration. Whatever one may think of such presuppositions, they could be prejudicial to an open examination of the epiclesis question since they threaten once again to keep the epiclesis under the shadow of the moment of consecration issue.

If at times it is necessary to avail oneself of such concise terms to denote the epicleses which come before or after the institution words, it would be well to follow M. Jugie's lead. Jugie distinguishes between "antecedent (before the institution words) epicleses" and "subsequent (after the institution words) epicleses."[35] Such terminology, or something similar to it, might help avoid certain prejudices, at least in one's terminology.

Summary

The *primitive* meaning of the word epiclesis seems to have involved basically the naming of a name upon a person or a thing. Implied in this naming, however, was an appeal that the person invoked be actively, effectively present to, and in a sense take possession of, the person or thing upon which s/he was invoked.

Those definitions of the *more developed epiclesis* which limit themselves to the appeal for the transformation of the gifts hardly do justice to the liturgical data. Definitions such as that of Dinesen, on the other hand, give us a good composite picture of the epiclesis in the early anaphoras. In any case, three basic facets *generally* turn up in the fully developed epiclesis, namely; an appeal for the Holy Spirit (1) to transform or sanctify the bread and wine (2) so that they may benefit those who partake of them worthily (3), and these three deserve mention in a description of the developed epiclesis.

---

35. Jugie, "Considérations générales . . . ," 324–25. Jugie also uses the term "merely impetratory epiclesis" for what we have termed "epiclesis of sanctification."

Chapter 4

Reconstructions of the History of the Eucharistic Epiclesis

We have repeatedly stated that the main interest of this study is the theology of the eucharistic epiclesis as expressed by the writers of the modern period. At this point someone might raise the question, "Is it necessary then to examine numerous attempts to reconstruct historically the origin and development of the epiclesis?" We think that the answer to that question is a definite "Yes."

To begin with, the historical data found in these reconstructions can serve at least as a negative criterion by ruling out any theological explanations that contradict this data. Moreover, a theological explanation to the degree that it rests on a historical reconstruction remains only as strong as that reconstruction. It would be helpful, then, to be aware of the gist and strength of the historical reconstructions upon which certain theological explanations of the epiclesis seem to rest. Finally, examining such historical reconstructions often carries with it theological insights that enable us better to grasp the theology of the epiclesis in modern writings.

To admit the need of a study of these historical reconstructions is, however, not to deny the difficulty of such a study. The hypotheses are myriad. Even no less an authority than Edmund Bishop, while acknowledging the value of examining such reconstructions, had to admit ". . . the difficulty there is in keeping a clear head among them all."[1] Once again we have tried to limit ourselves to those hypotheses which seem most important for an understanding of the modern theology of the epiclesis.

---

1. Bishop, "Notes and Studies: Liturgical Comments and Memoranda II," 593.

FROM LOGOS TO SPIRIT EPICLESIS

As has been seen in Chapter 2, in conjunction with the treatment of Justin and Irenaeus, a number of authors, among them F. J. Dölger and E. Bishop, hold that the primitive Logos epiclesis gave way to a Spirit epiclesis only in the fourth century. They argue from the nature of second-century theology, which tended to attribute to the Logos what post-Nicene theology attributed to the Holy Spirit, and from fourth-century echoes of a Logos epiclesis, e.g., in Sarapion, Athanasius, etc.[2] Bishop also appeals to the silence of the Cappadocians in regard to a Spirit epiclesis during the Pneumatomachian controversy.[3] Even when we find references to "the Holy Spirit" in Christian writers and liturgies, e.g., in Justin and in the *Apostolic Tradition*, this term could have been understood as referring to the Logos.[4]

W. H. Frere, Anglican bishop of Truro and eminent liturgical scholar, offers a reconstruction which although similar in its starting point, namely, the relationship between the Logos and Spirit epicleses, and in a number of details, displays some striking differences from the viewpoint just mentioned.

Frere, in two fine works, *The Primitive Consecration Prayer* and *The Anaphora or Great Eucharistic Prayer* published in 1922 and 1933 respectively, sees the development as follows: The original epicleses contained a certain ambiguity as to whether it was the Holy Spirit or the Logos who was invoked. Both a Logos and a Spirit form were used and both were acceptable. As yet there was not a clear differentiation between the Logos and the Spirit.[5] This differentiation came in the fourth century[6] and with it came two tendencies. The one was to stress the invocation of the Holy Spirit and make it an explicit appeal for the consecration of the gifts. The other tendency was to stress the role of the Word and thus to center the idea of consecration around the Second Person of the Trinity. In the course of time the consecration was associated not simply with the Word but with his spoken words,

---

2. Cf. Dölger, I, 73–79, 81: II, 497–502. Cf. also MELV 62–63 n. 5; Bishop, "The Moment . . . ," 160 and Rauschen, 112–13.

3. Bishop, ibid., 140–43. Cf. Dix. "The Origins . . . ," 197–98 and N. Abercrombie, *The Life and Work of Edmund Bishop* (London, 1959), 391–392.

4. Cf. Bishop, ibid., 158–63, esp. 160.

5. Frere, *The Primitive* . . . , 19. Cf. also his *The Anaphora* . . . , 42–44.

6. Cf. Frere, *The Anaphora* . . . , 68–75 and *The Primitive* . . . , 20.

i.e., in this case, the institution narrative. The ambiguity of the term *verbum* lent itself to this. For instance, Augustine's "Accedit verbum ad elementum et fit sacramentum" can refer to either the personal Word or to his words of institution or to both. "It is susceptible of either interpretation or of both; but in practice the second came to supercede the first."[7] Thus the "consecration" could be explained as the result of the invocation of the Holy Spirit or as the result of the recital of the words of institution and for a long time these two possibilities were not regarded as mutually exlusive.[8]

Now if one chose to explain the "consecration" by the invocation of the Holy Spirit, then the liturgical face of the epiclesis caused no embarrassment. If, however, one explained it by the institution narrative then the epiclesis could prove embarrassing. Two solutions seem to have been tried to avoid this embarrassment. One was to banish the invocation of the Holy Spirit *after* the institution narrative in favor of a prayer asking that the offerings be borne up to the heavenly altar, e.g., as in the *Supplices*. The other was to move the invocation up to *before* the institution narrative. Both Alexandria and Rome seemed to have tried this one and neither was satisfied. Alexandria went back to the usual Eastern arrangement and Rome watered down the invocation for the Spirit to a *Quam oblationem* form.[9]

> Thus doctrinal consistency was secured; but at the cost of making a break with Christian tradition, and of having a Canon which, apart from doxologies, is devoid of any specific mention of the Holy Spirit.[10]

The basis, then, for the development as Frere sees it is the doctrinal stress either on the role of the Holy Spirit or on the role of the Word in the consecration.

G. Dix, another eminent Anglican scholar, in "The Origins of the Epiclesis," written for *Theology* in 1934, also sees the difference in doctrinal emphasis as accounting for different viewpoints in regard to the epiclesis. He contends, however, that the theology of eucharistic consecration by the Word through the institution narrative is not merely a "Western Tradition," as some claim. Originally Africa, Asia

---

7. Frere, *The Primitive* . . . , 20. Cf. *The Anaphora* . . . , 161–62.

8. Frere, *The Primitive* . . . , 20–21. Cf. *The Anaphora* . . . , 172.

9. Frere, *The Primitive* . . . , 21–22. Cf. *The Anaphora* . . . , 169–70.

10. Frere, *The Primitive* . . . , 22.

Minor, Egypt, and Antiochene Syria shared this view.[11] Furthermore the so-called Western Tradition, that the Eucharist is consecrated by the Logos and some form of the institution narrative, is indeed the primitive tradition.[12]

None of these reconstructions, whether they take as their starting point a primitive Logos epiclesis or Logos and Spirit epicleses flourishing side by side, commands unreserved acceptance. Claims that Fathers such as Justin and Irenaeus and the Euchologium of Sarapion witness to a primitive, widespread Logos epiclesis have come under fire. So has the argument from the silence of the Cappadocians in regard to a Spirit epiclesis. Moreover, a great part of the development as Frere outlines it presumes that an invocation of the Holy Spirit originally was widespread in the Latin West—in Spain, Gaul, Africa, and very probably in Rome itself. Gelasius is singled out as a witness to the latter probability.[13] Here again the argumentation for an explicit spirit epiclesis is not absolutely conclusive.

It is not in the details of these historical reconstructions, however, that their significance for the present study lies. It is rather in the fact that, despite their differences, these reconstructions and others which we are about to see agree that the doctrinal development of the role of the Holy Spirit in the Eucharist led to the Spirit epiclesis and/or the tension between the East and West over the Spirit epiclesis. This is an important insight because it underlines the fact that any important attempt to work out a theology of the epiclesis will have to face the apparent tension between the role of the Holy Spirit and the role of Christ in the Eucharist.

FROM SANCTIFICATION TO CONSECRATORY EPICLESIS

A number of authors contend that the primitive form of epiclesis was consecratory. F. Varaine, for instance, in a dissertation published in 1910 in Lyon, claims that originally there was a petition for transformation of the gifts. This developed into a Logos epiclesis and this in

---

11. Dix, "The Origins . . . ," 187–99.

12. Ibid., 199–202.

13. Frere, *The Primitive* . . . , 18–19.

turn developed into a Spirit epiclesis.[14] W. C. Bishop, in an article which appeared two years earlier in the *Church Quarterly Review*, also maintains that originally the epiclesis was consecratory. He contends, moreover, that this epiclesis was essential and appeals to parallels between the Eucharist and other sacraments to support his case.[15]

A far greater number of authors, however, view the development as a transition from an epiclesis of sanctification to a consecratory epiclesis. One of the proponents of this view is J. Brinktrine. In an article written for the *Zeitschrift für Katholische Theologie* in 1918, he reconstructs the development as follows: The first stage took the form of prayers of blessing for objects in daily use. From ancient times the Church had the custom of sanctifying materials from daily life, e.g., oil, cheese, olives, etc. This was especially true of those materials used for sacraments, e.g., water, oil. Therefore, it was quite natural to sanctify the elements used in the Eucharist in the same way before partaking of them.[16]

This led to the second stage which consisted of prayers asking for the blessing, sanctifying, and descent of the Holy Spirit upon the materials used in the sacraments, prayers asking for the "transformatio corporis et sanguinis Christi," and prayers asking for the acceptance, assumption, etc. of the materials (gifts) brought to the altar. Despite their great variety of forms these prayers are basically identical in content.[17] The appeal for the sanctifying, blessing of, and the descent of the Holy Spirit upon the offerings is, however, primary. Out of this grew the appeal for acceptance, assumption, etc. In all these cases we are still dealing with an epiclesis of sanctification.[18]

The next stage is that in which these epicleses of sanctification came to be regarded as necessary to the Eucharist. How did that take place? The primary factor was, according to Brinktrine, the comparison which the Fathers often made between the Eucharist and the other sacraments, and especially between the consecration of the water for

---

14. Varaine, *L'épiclèse eucharistique*, 139 ff. Cf. Brinktrine, "Zur Entstehung . . . ," 513–14 for a critique of this position.

15. Cf. W. C. Bishop, "The Primitive Form . . . ," 385–404, esp. 399–400, 403–404. Cf. Batiffol, "La question . . .," 647, who opposes Bishop.

16. Brinktrine, "Zur Entstehung . . . ," 483–87.

17. Ibid., 307–17.

18. Ibid., 302–17, esp. 307 n. 1; 487, 491–92.

baptism and the consecration of bread and wine for the Eucharist. This led to the belief that the blessing formula was necessary for the realization of the sacrament.[19]

In addition to the parallel drawn between the sacraments, two other factors also played a subordinate role in the transition from an epiclesis of sanctification to a consecratory epiclesis. The appeal for the Holy Spirit in some blessing formulas ("Segensgebete") could lend itself to the belief that he was coming to make Christ present in the Eucharist, i.e., to effect the eucharistic presence. Moreover, the notion that all consecrations, blessings, etc., involved a certain transformation or change was also a contributing factor.[20] Once the view that the epiclesis of sanctification was necessary had been accepted, it was a short step to the final stage of development. This final stage takes the form of a prayer appealing to God to effect the eucharistic presence, i.e., a consecratory epiclesis.[21]

Some authors go along with the view that the epiclesis developed from an epiclesis of sanctification to a consecratory one. They emphasize, however, the communion orientation of the original plea for sanctification. Originally, they contend, the epiclesis was a plea not to change the elements into the body and blood of Christ but "to fill them with hallowing power (or 'Spirit') for the communicants."[22] In maintaining that only later was it directed toward "consecration," some would even go so far as to say that this later development was something "fundamentally different" from the epiclesis's original purpose.[23]

Of a more philological bent is the reconstruction which sees the consecratory epiclesis evolving out of a misunderstanding of key words in the epiclesis of sanctification. J. Höller provides one of the most complete presentations of this position.[24] Höller begins his

19. Ibid., 511. Cf. 502–11 and also the same author's "De epiclesi eucharistica," 111–14. Cf. also Batiffol, "La question . . . ," 658.

20. Brinktrine, "Zur Entstehung . . . ," 515.

21. Ibid., 512. Cf. 516–18 for a fine summary of the development as Brinktrine sees it. Cf. also Gutberlet, 56–67; Merk, "Die Epiklese . . . ," 367 ff. Batiffol, "La question . . . ," 661–62 and Laager, 588–89.

22. Cf. Richardson, "The Origin . . . ," 148–53. Cf. also Baumstark, "Zu den Problemen . . . ," 341.

23. Cf., for instance, Woolley, 93–120, esp. 111, 117–18.

24. This he has done both in a book entitled *Die Epiklese der griechisch-orientalischen Liturgien,* published in 1912 and in an article with a similar title which he published in 1914 and in which he summarized his earlier position.

article by noting the apparent dilemma of liturgical data revealing
a consecratory epiclesis after the institution narrative and a strong
tradition teaching that the consecration takes place through the institution narrative alone. He maintains that it is not simply a dogmatic
question. Dogmatic studies can only lead to a negative solution, i.e.,
they can show us that the epiclesis does *not* possess any consecratory
value. For the positive significance or meaning of the epiclesis a
historical study is needed.[25]

Such a historical study reveals that the most ancient liturgies,
namely, the "Clementine" liturgy of *The Apostolic Constitutions* and the
Syriac liturgy of Saint James, call for the Holy Spirit to "manifest" the
already consecrated gifts and not to "transform" or "make" them into
the body and blood of Christ. These ancient epicleses look more to the
Communion than to the consecration. Only later was this acceptable
meaning obscured by additions, emendations, misunderstanding, etc.,
of such key words as ἀποφήνῃ and ἀναδεῖξαι. When a double
epiclesis is present then the first was originally the appeal for the
transformation of the gifts, and the second (after the institution
narrative) merely for the "manifestation" of the gifts as the body and
blood of Christ and for fruitful communion. Moreover, it is not true
that the later development, which used terms indicating the post-
institution narrative epiclesis as consecratory, was tacitly accepted by
Rome for many centuries. Rome never accepted these terms as imply-
ing a dogmatic necessity of the epiclesis for the "consecration." The
appeal to *lex precandi, lex credendi* does not hold here.[26]

The basis of Höller's position rests, then, in his claim that
words like ἀποφήνῃ and ἀναδεῖξαι contain no consecratory significance, no appeal for a change in the gifts. J. Brinktrine, while not
going along with Höller on a number of details, does see the epicleses
which contain these words as a transition from the earlier appeals for
sanctification *toward* the consecratory epiclesis.[27] Jugie, too, at one
time seemed to argue that such words merely expressed the "manifestation" of a consecration which had already taken place.[28]

---

25. Höller, "Die Epiklese . . . ," 110–16.

26. Höller, *Die Epiklese* . . . , 110–34 and the same author's "Die Epiklese . . . ," 118–22, 126.

27. Brinktrine, "Zur Entstehung . . . ," 494, 514–15.

28. Jugie, "Le 'Liber . . . ,'" 266–67.

As noted in Chapter 1, however, the number of authors who opt for a consecratory meaning in the words ἀποφήνη and ἀναδεῖξαι is impressive. A. Baumstark, for instance, in a 1916 review of Höller's two works on the epiclesis, rejects outright the claim that these words meant something else than ποιήσῃ. Consequently, he rejects the claim that it was through a misunderstanding of the meaning of words that the epiclesis properly so called found its way into all the later Eastern liturgies.[29] E.G.C. Atchley, too, sees little difference between the ποιήσῃ in Cyril's epiclesis and ἀποφήνη and ἀναδεῖξαι in the epicleses of the Basil liturgy and *The Apostolic Constitutions*.[30] Even M. Jugie, while continuing to underscore the notion of manifesting and showing contained in these words and to maintain that they do not *per se* indicate a physical conversion, acknowledges their consecratory content.[31]

One final example of the sanctification to consecratory reconstructions is that which G. C. Smit offers. Smit stresses the doctrinal background of this transition in a manner similar to some of the reconstructions which we have seen in the preceding section. Moreover, contrary to the view of authors such as Wooley and Brinktrine, he sees the transition itself as a continuation of, rather than a break with, earlier tradition. The attention, the emphasis given to the epiclesis, he contends, seems to vary in direct proportion to the development in pneumatology. To begin with, the East and West had contrasting yet complementary orientations. In the East, Sabellianism led theologians to underline the distinction between the divine Persons (in this case Father and Son). In the West, Monarchianism led to a stress on the unity of the divine essence.

The original orientation continued to influence the later development of dogma. In the East, where the disputes over the Person of the Holy Spirit raged most fiercely, pneumatology became far more precise. The "appropriation" of certain functions to the Holy Spirit found in the indisputable liturgical fact of the epiclesis a means of concrete expression. As the understanding of the role of the Holy

---

29. Baumstark, "Zu den Problemen . . . ," 341–42.

30. Atchley, "The Epiclesis," 95–96, and the same author's *On the Epiclesis* . . . , 114–15, 134, 137 n. 4. Cf. Casel's (Review of Atchley's *On the Epiclesis* . . .), 445.

31. Jugie, *De forma* . . . , 17–18, 30 n. 26 and "De epiclesi . . . Basilium Magnum," 205–207 in response to Botte's (Review of Jugie's *De forma* . . .), 246.

Spirit evolved, the role of the epiclesis and its relation to the Holy
Spirit also became more precise.[32] Thus we should not regard the
transition in the East from an epiclesis of sanctification to a consecratory epiclesis as a novelty. Rather such a transition was a logical
consequence of the growing precision in pneumatology. Only those
who contend, *a priori*, that the institution narrative alone can be the
form of the sacrament, are unable to admit such a development.[33]

In tracing the theories regarding a development from a
sanctification to consecratory epiclesis one often senses the influence
of the "moment of consecration" problem on these theories. Apart
from certain details contained in these reconstructions, however, it is
hard to discount them entirely. The fact that what appear to be some
of the most ancient forms of the epiclesis that have come down to us,
e.g., those of Hippolytus and Addai and Mari, do not contain an
appeal for the transformation of the gifts seems to favor these theories.

On the other hand, as A. Raes pointed out in 1960, the
evidence does not exclude the possibility that the need to *express* the
transforming action of the Holy Spirit was felt only later.[34] It may well
be that such transforming action was implicit even in the simpler
forms of Hippolytus and Addai and Mari. The absence of any outcry
against the explicit mention of a transformation in later epicleses
would even seem to favor Smit and Atchley[35] who, contrary to Wooley
and Brinktrine, see here a continuation and making explicit of an
earlier tradition.

From Epiclesis to "Epiclesis"

The position which we have entitled Epiclesis to "Epiclesis" has long
been associated with the name of Odo Casel. The starting point for
the development as Casel sees it is the primitive meaning of the term
"epiclesis," i.e., the naming of a divine name (upon a person or a
thing). Implied in this naming, as we have seen, was the belief that

---

32. Smit, 110–11, 124–25.

33. Ibid., 111.

34. Cf. Raes, "Un nouveau document . . . ," 407. Cf. also, SH, 327 and Casel (Review of
Brinktrine's "De epiclesis eucharistica"), 136.

35. Cf. Atchley, *On the Epiclesis* . . . , 199–200 citing de la Taille, *Mysterium Fidei* (Paris,
1924), 444 as holding the same opinion.

the person named would be actively present to or in the person or thing he was "called down upon." Thus the naming involved a calling upon the divine person to be present ("ein Herbeirufen") and an expectation of a divine "epiphany" of some sort. Casel offers a number of examples of epicleses in this sense, including the baptismal formula, the formula for consecrating baptismal water, and the eucharistic Prefaces. The prime example of such a naming was the Canon of the Mass which was at once Eucharist and Epiclesis in the ancient and broad sense of the word. It is a naming in praise of the Trinity.[36]

Since, then, such namings could take on different forms and different purposes, there had to be some specification to make it clear what the intended purpose of this particular naming was. In the eucharistic prayer of Hippolytus, for instance, the prayer "petimus ut mittas spiritum tuum sanctum in oblationem sanctae ecclesiae" made it clear that the *object* of God's active, effective presence was to be the elements of bread and wine. The institution narrative, on the other hand, made it clear what the *purpose* of the naming and the active presence was, namely, that the bread and wine become the body and blood of Christ.[37] In the fourth century the tendency arose, especially in the East, to express both the object and the purpose of the naming in one prayer. The assembly prayed that God send his Logos or Holy Spirit upon the gifts so that the bread and wine might become the body and blood of Christ. In this way the "epiclesis" ("die 'Epiklese'") in the strict sense was born.[38]

---

36. Cf. Casel, "Zur Epiklese," 100–101. Cf. Crehan, "Epiklesis," 223–24.

37. Ibid., 101 and Casel's "Die ostchristliche Opferfeier . . . ," 68. Cf. also Frere, *The Anaphora* . . . , 28; SH, 337–38, 343–44; and Spacil, "Lis de epiclesi . . . ," 100–101 who records G. Kosteljnik's view that the "form" of the Eucharist is the whole canon in which the institution narrative and the epiclesis play necessary and complementary roles (53, 121–24).

38. Casel, ibid., 101. Cf. SH, 344. A note on Casel's terminology seems called for here:
1. Epiclesis in general ("die Epiklese")—refers to the naming of a name (upon a person or a thing) with its implied calling upon the person named to be actively, effectively present. Casel usually refers to this as the epiclesis in the ancient sense of the word.
2. Epiclesis (also "die Epiklese")—in regard to the Eucharist refers to the whole canon as a naming of the Trinity and thus a calling upon the Trinity to be actively, effectively present in the Eucharist. This EPICLESIS is a prime example of the epiclesis in the ancient sense (cf. 1) above).
3. "Epiclesis" (in quotes) ("die 'Epiklese'")—refers to what is often called the epiclesis in the strict sense, namely, the calling for the Logos or Holy Spirit so that he might change the bread and wine into the body and blood of Christ.
4. The old epiclesis ("die alte Epiklese")—at least once ("Zur Epiklese," 102) he uses this term to refer to a particular prayer similar to one in Hippolytus's canon which asks God

Thus we have the epiclesis in the ancient sense of that word, i.e., a naming of a name (upon a person or a thing) with its implied calling upon the person named to be actively, effectively present. A prime instance of the epiclesis in this sense is the whole eucharistic prayer, the Epiclesis, which in its entirety was consecratory and which seems from the very beginning to have included an appeal for the Logos or Spirit. This appeal in turn formed the basis for the "epiclesis" in the strict sense which arose in the fourth century. Cyril of Jerusalem thus witnesses to a stage where old and new, Epiclesis in the sense of the whole Canon as consecratory and "epiclesis" in the strict sense (with an appeal for the Logos or Holy Spirit to change the bread and wine into Christ's body and blood) stood side by side.[39] With the birth of the "epiclesis" in the strict sense came the danger of playing down the importance and function of the institution narrative. Perhaps it was with this danger in mind that Rome never adopted this "epiclesis." In fact, apparently in protest against the overemphasis given the "epiclesis" in the East, Rome almost completely effaced the old epiclesis prayer as it has stood in Hippolytus.[40]

Nevertheless, the whole Canon with its naming of the Trinity still remained the Epiclesis in the ancient sense. The institution narrative remained, too, and took on an increasingly important character in the West.[41] As long as the "epiclesis" in the strict sense remained in the context of the ancient concept of the whole eucharistic prayer as consecratory, its position mattered little and it raised no great problem. When the West, however, began to stress the institution narrative as *alone* consecratory and some in the East began to regard the same institution narrative as *merely* narrative, the "epiclesis" became the object of heated dispute and painful division.[42] Casel adds that the Western view is closer to the original understanding which saw the whole eucharistic prayer as consecratory and the institution narrative as making precise the immediate purpose of this "consecration," namely, the presence of body and blood of Christ. On the other hand, he

---

to send the Holy Spirit upon the oblation of the Church, but which does not explicitly ask for a transformation of the gifts.

39. Casel, "Neue Beiträge . . . ," 171 referring to Cyril's *Mystagogical Catecheses* I, 7; III, 3; V, 7.

40. Casel, "Zur Epiklese," 101–102. Cf. von Allmen, *Essai . . .* , 32.

41. Casel, ibid.

42. Cf. Casel, "Die ostchristliche Opferfeier . . . ," 69.

admits that the East has preserved the primitive attribution of this transformation to the divine Spirit.[43]

As was the case for other historical reconstructions examined, the details of Casel's theory are hard to prove or disprove entirely. The fact that it has met with opposition from some authors is not surprising.[44] Nevertheless, the basic outlines of Casel's theory are attractive, if for no other reason than that they could explain the ambiguity found in certain Fathers who seem to attribute the "consecration" at times to the institution narrative and at times to the epiclesis proper.

From Appeal for Unity to Epiclesis Proper

L. Bouyer has recently put forth in his *Eucharistie*, which first appeared in 1966, still another theory on the origin and development of the eucharistic epiclesis. To understand Bouyer's theory on the epiclesis, however, it is necessary to situate it within his theory on the formation of the primitive eucharistic prayer. Bouyer maintains that originally the Christians had their "liturgy of the word" in the synagogue. Their "liturgy of the Eucharist" or eucharistic prayer was held separately and modeled on the three final Jewish meal *berakoth*. The early Addai and Mari text reflects this. The anaphora of Hippolytus is an anachronistic attempt to return to this ancient ("archaique") form.[45]

Later the service of readings was joined to the eucharistic meal to form a single whole. With this union the Christian form of the *Qeduschah* with the blessings framing it and of the *Tefillah*, both of which had accompanied the Christian reading service, were joined to the meal *berakoth*. Hence, ". . . the universal presence of the *Sanctus* and the thanksgiving preceding it, and of the detailed intercessions and commemorations of the saints in the set texts of the eucharist that appear from the fourth century on comes from the now customary conjunction of the service of readings and prayers with the eucharistic

---

43. Ibid, Cf. also Casel's "Zur Epiklese," 102 and, for a good summary of the basic elements in his reconstruction, his "neue Beiträge . . . ," 178. Smit, 101–105, 110–111, 124–25 traces the development along the same basic lines as Casel, although he stresses the role of pneumatology in this development.

44. Cf., for instance, Brinktrine, "Neue Beiträge . . . ," 440–41.

45. Bouyer, *Eucharistie,* 146–81, esp. 181 (146–82, esp. 182).

meal." The Alexandrian and Roman anaphoras reflect this development which took place at an early date, even before Hippolytus.[46]

It is against this background that Bouyer constructs his theory
on the origin and development of the epiclesis, the broad lines of which
run as follows: The primitive form of the eucharistic prayer, based on
the three meal *berakoth*, alone, already contained the transition from
praise to prayer. Recalling the wonderful works of God (the "mirabilia
Dei") it asks that these wonderful works have their eschatological
fulfilment in us so that we all achieve perfect unity in the whole Christ,
Head and members perfectly united for the glory of God. This prayer
had its basis in the third *berakah* of the Jewish meals. The notion and
the prayer for the unity of those gathered together for the Eucharist
and for the unity of all people for the glorification of the Father
through the Son, quite naturally lead to the *mention* of the Holy Spirit,
the seal of unity and the "Spirit of glory." This *mention* of the Spirit
appears for the first time, ". . . beneath the original text of Hippolytus,
as the author of the *Testamentum Domini* must have read it."[47]

Later, in the second half of the fourth century, when it was
thought necessary to specify the role of the Holy Spirit and stress his
equal divinity, the *mention* became an *invocation* of the Holy Spirit to
produce the fruit of the eucharistic celebration in the communicants.
This fruit was "the completion of the Church in unity in order to
glorify for ever the Father, through the Son, in (or with) the Spirit."[48]
Meanwhile, the prayer for the acceptance of the sacrifice which had
come from the *Abodah* prayer concluding the Jewish *Tefillah* had given
rise to a formal petition for the "consecration" of the elements. With
the breaking up and systematic reassembling in West Syria of the
ancient eucharistic prayers, this prayer was repositioned and fused
with the epiclesis of the Holy Spirit at the end of the anamnesis.[49]

---

46. Ibid., 198, 211–212, and esp. 299–300 (199, 213–14, esp. 309–10). Cf. Casel (Review
of Atchley's *On the Epiclesis . . .*), 446 and Abercrombie, 435 for other claims that the Roman
canon was primitive or at least of very great antiquity. Cf. Jungmann (Review of Bouyer's
Eucharistie), 462–63 for a critique of this position.

47. Bouyer, ibid., 176 (177). Cf. 182–84 (183–84), 300–303 (310–13). On the other hand,
Botte, "L'Epiclèse de l'Anaphore d'Hippolyte," 247 maintains that the appeal for the Holy Spirit
on the faithful is, rather, a consequence of the appeal for his descent upon the gifts.

48. Bouyer, ibid., 183–84 (184). Cf. 176, 301 (177, 311).

49. Ibid., 211–12, 303 (213–214, 312–13).

From this moment on, the epiclesis became a threefold petition for: the acceptance of the sacrifice-memorial, the consecration of the bread and wine into the body and blood of Christ, "and finally (which alone is original), that this descent of the Spirit, uniting us all in the body of Christ which is the Church, permit us all in this unity to glorify the Father eternally."[50] In the course of time, the central (and most recent) element, the appeal for the "consecration" of the offerings, gained increasing prominence.

Two of the most characteristic features of Bouyer's theory, namely, the Jewish *berakoth* as starting point for, and the appeal for unity as the original basis of, the later epiclesis development, have found numerous adherents in this century. For instance, both G. Dix in his *The Shape of the Liturgy* published in 1945, and L. Ligier, writing in 1966, look to the Jewish *berakoth* for the origins of the epiclesis.[51] In addition to Ligier, F. Cabrol, P. Cagin, and J. Souben, among others, see the epiclesis stemming from an appeal for unity.[52] As we have seen in Chapter 1, the anaphora of Hippolytus and a number of the anaphoras of the Antiochene type offer a certain amount of support for the claim that an appeal for unity played an important role in the formation of the eucharistic epiclesis. They at least allow us to verify the presence of such an appeal in a good number of the more developed epicleses which have come down to us.

There are still large gaps in the data, however, and as Bouyer himself admits the further back one attempts to go the larger these gaps become.[53] This is especially true of the attempts to trace the epiclesis back to the Jewish *berakoth*. There are extremely interesting parallels between the Christian and Jewish prayer forms. Parallels, however, are not necessarily dependences. A number of the details of Bouyer's reconstruction of the origin of the eucharistic prayer in general

---

50. Ibid., 303 (313).

51. Cf. Dix, *The Shape* . . . , 182–84 and Chadwick in Dix's *The Treatise* . . . , l–m as well as Ligier's "De la cène . . .," 36, 42–46. Cf. also Buchwald, 21–56.

52. Cf. Ligier, ibid., 46; Cabrol, "Epilcèse," 174; Cagin, *L'Anaphore* . . . , 234–47, esp. 234–36; J. Souben, "Le canon primitive de la messe," *Les Questions écclesaiastiques* 1 (1909), 326. Cf. also Chadwick in Dix's *The Treatise* . . , 1; Connolly, "The Eucharistic Prayer of Hippolytus," 367 and L. Labauche, *Leçons de théologie dogmatique* IV: *Les sacrements* (Paris, 1918), 341 n. 1.

53. Bouyer, "The Different Forms . . . ," 158.

are difficult to accept in the light of current historical research.[54] Still others, and this holds true for some of his claims in regard to the epiclesis and the *berakoth,* are hard to control on the basis of the available data.[55] This latter is perhaps the greatest difficulty with Bouyer's admirable attempt to trace a relationship between epiclesis and *berakah,* and it leads to the first of our final remarks before closing this section.

It is important once again to recall that throughout this section one has been dealing with hypotheses—hypotheses which, although they appeal for support to certain historical facts, remain nonetheless hypotheses. It is necessary to be continually on one's guard against confusing these theories with the facts upon which they rest. Botte's reminder is in place here, that one must remember that even now insufficient light has been shed on many of these—at times ingenious—hypotheses to satisfy the critical historian. Such hypotheses are necessary for scientific progress. The challenge is to avoid being carried away by them to the point of confusing reality with theory.[56]

In addition, it would be well to keep in mind the fact that these hypotheses are not all mutually exclusive. It is no coincidence, for instance, that we have cited G. C. Smit under three different categories of historical reconstruction. For it is possible to conceive of a development which began with the whole eucharistic prayer, Epiclesis in Casel's sense, as consecratory, led to a Logos and/or Spirit epiclesis of sanctification and eventually issued in a consecratory Spirit epiclesis. Other such combinations of these reconstructions are also within the realm of possibility.

Finally, no matter how one reconstructs the origin and development of the eucharistic epicleses one has to face up to the fact that we have in recognized, official liturgies, epicleses which follow the institution narrative and which nevertheless appeal for the Holy Spirit to transform the elements. Moreover, there is good evidence that a number

---

54. For instance, Bouyer's claim in *Eucharistie,* 309–318 (320–29) that the primary layer of the Gallican and Mozarabic prayer formularies reveals an early—mid-fourth century—Syrian influence before the improvisation which later characterized these Western liturgies. Jungmann (Review of Bouyer's *Eucharistie*), 464 remarks that to exclude the possibility of Eastern influence in Gaul and Spain between the fifth and ninth century, as Bouyer seems to do, is to ignore the historical data. Cf. also in this regard, Casel, "Neue Beiträge . . . ," 177–78 n. 9 and the same author's (Review of Lietzmann's *Messe . . .*), 211; Porter, 186–94; Gamber, 381–82 and Abercrombie, 395–96.

55. Cf. Botte (Review of Bouyer's *Eucharistie*), 173.

56. Botte, *Le Canon . . . ,* 27.

of the Fathers consider the epiclesis an essential part of the anaphora and affirm its consecratory value.[57] Thus the "moment of consecration" issue has not only cast its shadow over many of the historical hypotheses just examined, but it also seems to demand that one go further and seek a theological explanation which will do justice to the historical data.[58] It is to the attempts of modern authors to come up with a satisfying theological explanation for the epiclesis that we now turn. First, however, it might be helpful to summarize the findings of this chapter.

SUMMARY

A number of attempted reconstructions of the history of the epiclesis agree that it was the doctrinal development concerning the role of the Holy Spirit in the Eucharist that eventually led to the Spirit epiclesis and/or the tension between East and West over the Spirit epiclesis. This agreement highlights the need, in seeking to solve the epiclesis question, to resolve the apparent tension between the role of the Holy Spirit and that of Christ in the Eucharist.

The evidence, while far form being conclusive, seems to favor the theory that the consecratory epiclesis developed from an earlier epiclesis of sanctification but that the latter already *implicitly* contained the notion of the Holy Spirit's transforming, consecratory action.

The theory that the primitive notion of Epiclesis, i.e., the whole canon as consecratory, paved the way for the fully developed epiclesis proper, has the advantage that it could help explain the ambiguity of certain Fathers who seem to attribute the "consecration" at times to the words of institution and at times to the epiclesis proper.

The link with the Jewish *berakah* and with the basic theme of unity makes the theory that the epiclesis was originally an appeal for unity modeled after the third Jewish meal *berakah* alluring. The major drawback of this theory seems to be that it is hard to control with the data now available.

Once again, these reconstructions, while not all mutually exclusive, remain hypotheses and are only as strong as the historical facts upon which they rest. In addition, they need to be supplemented by theological explanations, a number of which we shall now examine.

57. Cf. Botte, "L'épiclèse . . . syriennes orientales," 69; Cabrol, "Epiclèse," 173–74; Betz, *Die Eucharistie . . .* , 328 and J. Gouillard in Salaville, *Nicolas Cabasilas*, 32.

58. Cf. Cabrol, ibid., 177; Brinktrine, "Neue Beiträge . . . ," 450; SH, 328–29.

Chapter 5

Theological Explanations of the Eucharistic Epiclesis

Just as Höller once maintained that historical studies offer the only avenue for discovering the positive meaning of the epiclesis,[1] there are others who claim that only dogmatic theology can end the search for this meaning.[2] Once again one cannot hope to treat all the variant attempts to give a theological explanation for the eucharistic epiclesis. We have therefore chosen those explanations which seem to hold the most promise for a theological understanding of the epiclesis.[3]

EPICLESIS AS A CONSECRATION FORMULA

Any attempt to classify the different explanations of the epiclesis runs the risk of oversimplifying and, consequently, of being unfair to their proponents. This is immediately evident when one tries to classify the explanation of a number of Orthodox theologians. A. Maltzew, for instance, writing in 1902 cites *Confessio orthodoxa* Th. I as expressing the Orthodox position that the transformation first takes place in the Eucharist after the priest has said the epiclesis: ". . . After these words the consecration immediately takes place."[4] P. N. Trembelas, in a volume which first appeared in 1961, also seems to indicate the epiclesis proper as the moment of consecration when he speaks of the mention

---

1. Höller, "Die Epiklese . . . ," 116.

2. Cf., for instance, Brinktrine, "Neue Beiträge . . . ," 450 and Crehan, "Theological Trends," in *Theology in Transition,* ed. by E. O'Brien (New York, 1964), 24.

3. For a more complete list of the main attempts prior to and during the twentieth century to explain the epiclesis cf. Salaville, "Epiclèse eucharistique," 277–91; Dinesen, 75–107 and Brinktrine, "De epiclesi . . . ," 159–64. Cf. also Spacil, *Doctrina theologiae . . . ,* 58–76.

4. Maltzew, 421.

of the "antitypes" in the prayer of the Basil Liturgy "before the consecration."[5]

For many, especially those schooled in Western thought patterns alone, an either-or situation has thus been set up by the Orthodox. The epiclesis has become the essential form or formula of consecration and this in a sense robs the institution narrative of its consecratory value. Thus P. Brunner maintains that it is impossible to place a consecratory epiclesis *after* the institution narrative without at the same time fixing the moment of consecration in this epiclesis.[6] For similar reasons, G. Rauschen in 1910 could see dropping the traditional form of the epiclesis from the liturgy altogether as the only solution to the epiclesis question.[7]

Few, if any, modern Orthodox theologians, however, would seem to hold that the epiclesis alone consecrates. Maltzew, for instance, despite his emphasis on the epiclesis, notes that the institution narrative does play an essential role in the consecration. He cites Gregory of Nyssa, John Chrysostom, and Ambrose to support the view that the institution narrative is filled with divine power and that the epiclesis without the institution narrative would not be efficacious.

> In the words, with which the Lord instituted the holy mystery of his body and blood, an almighty power (δύναμις) lies hidden. Through the descent of the Holy Spirit, in consequence of the epiclesis, this power is brought to activity (ἐνέργια).[8]

Trembelas takes even more pains to bring out the mutual role of the institution words and the epiclesis in the consecration. [9]

If, then, one were to try to sum up the general Orthodox position in this regard, one might express it as follows: *If* one must speak of a moment of consecration in the Eucharist then the epiclesis would have to be it. *If* one must refer to a single formula of consecration, once again the epiclesis would be that formula. In neither case, however,

---

5. Trembelas, 23.

6. Brunner, "Zur Lehre . . . ," 357.

7. Rauschen, 126. Cf. P. Hüls, *Liturgik des Heiligen Messopfers* (Münster, 1915), 199 as well as our discussion in Chapter 2 of papal teachings on the question.

8. Maltzew, 427.

9. Trembelas, 177–78 who cites J. Karmiris, *Synopsis . . .* , (Athens, 1957), 101 n. 1 and M. Siotis, θεία Εὐχαριστία (Salonika, 1957), 14–15 as following similar lines. Cf. also, Evdokimov, *L'Orthodoxie,* 250; Schmaus, 311–12 and Rauschen, 115.

is the epiclesis to be thought of as independent of the institution narrative.[10] Moreover, the very term formula has connotations which many Orthodox find unacceptable.[11]

In regard to the epiclesis as a formula, P. Dinesen has brought out some important considerations. Faced with the question, "Is the epiclesis the *formula* which brings about the transition of the bread and wine into the body and blood of Christ?" he turns to the data of the early anaphoras for an answer. There he finds that neither the place of the elements in the epiclesis nor the description itself of the transition from bread and wine to body and blood nor the presence of formula-like expressions enable one to consider the epiclesis as a consecratory formula.

The place of the elements in the epiclesis varies in the different liturgies. Sometimes it is in the foreground; sometimes in the background. The elements play an important role but not the most important role. Moreover, if the epiclesis were a consecration formula one would expect a certain unity in the verbs used to describe the transition. This is certainly not the case in the anaphoras examined. There we find eight different verbs used in various combinations. Also, if the basic function of the epiclesis were to consecrate one would expect at least one *formula* in the epiclesis which has for its purpose the marking off, or bringing about, of this wonder. In fact, the epiclesis is basically a *prayer* or a series of *prayers*. Even if there were a *formula* present one would expect related liturgies to agree more or less on it, and that is not the case in the texts examined. And if it were a consecration formula, the epiclesis would ordinarily form an absolute highpoint which would not be repeated elsewhere in the eucharistic prayer. This condition is also absent in the texts examined.[12]

Dinesen sums up his argument thus far by saying:

> Above all, the epiclesis does not correspond to the picture that one would have of a consecration formula: We do not find any absolute concentration on the elements which are to "become" the body and blood of Christ. The epiclesis contains more than this. Moreover, the miracle itself of the Lord's Supper is described with such imprecise and changeable terminology that

---

10. This would also seem to be true of Atchley whom Casel (Review of Atchley's *On the Epiclesis* . . .), 445 sees as defending the thesis that the epiclesis proper is the "forma consecrationis."

11. Cf. for instance, Kern, 182–83. Cf. also Meyendorf, "Notes . . . ," 28.

12. Dinesen, 89–92.

it is difficult to imagine that a moment of consecration is supposed to be marked off as taking place here and now. Finally, the epicleses in no way bear the stamp of a ritual formula, which is supposed to bring about a specific occurrence during the Lord's Supper.[13]

Furthermore, to classify the epiclesis as a consecration formula would be to overlook two essential facets of the epiclesis. First, it is essentially a prayer expressing the helplessness, the dependence of the assembly in regard to the wonder of the Eucharist. Secondly, the Communion facet of the epiclesis would certainly seem to play as integral a part in the overall makeup of the epiclesis as the appeal for God's intervention in regard to the elements.[14] Dinesen concludes his treatment of the epiclesis as a possible consecration formula by stating that it is only possible to come to a correct understanding of this prayer by taking all of its characteristic features into consideration. Taking the notion of a consecration formula as a starting point, however, would be to doom one's efforts to failure at the very outset.

J. Betz's attempt to use the Incarnation as a basis for understanding the epiclesis[15] draws similar reservations from Dinesen. Betz claims that the Fathers saw the Eucharist as the making present of the Incarnation of Christ. This conception he terms the "eucharistic Incarnation principle." As we have already seen, Betz regards the epiclesis as the representation of the transfer of the gifts to God and his adoption of them. This takes place through the naming of God's name over the gifts. This naming of the name implies an appeal for God to be present here and now and to take these gifts into his possession, fill them with his power and thus transform them into the Body and Blood of Christ.[16]

The epiclesis is the transfer of the elements to Christ, through a Spirit-borne, invocatory naming of his name, so that he will realize his sacramental Incarnation in them. Viewed according to its result, the epiclesis brings about the consecration . . . . The epiclesis is, according to the patristic theology, a consecration form.[17]

---

13. Ibid., 93.
14. Ibid.
15. Cf. also Ritter, 169; Goldammer, 39; Wetter, I, 79.
16. Betz, 261 and 320–27. Cf. Schmaus, 305.
17. Betz, 328.

Dinesen acknowledges the fact that Betz has tried to underscore the basic invocatory or prayer character of the epiclesis and to bring out its link with the "thanks offering" which has led up to it. The attempt to explain the epiclesis as a new Incarnation, however, he rejects on the basis of the threefold context and the content of the epiclesis. He finds neither in the context with its narration of the wonderful deeds of God, its institution narrative and its Communion section, nor in the wording of the epiclesis itself anything that allows us to see the Incarnation as a key to understanding the epiclesis.[18]

In particular he finds fault with Betz's use of the term "consecration form" in regard to the epiclesis proper.[19] Perhaps here Dinesen has not given Betz enough credit for his effort to point out that for the pre-Nicene Fathers the whole eucharistic prayer was an Epiclesis and that the whole eucharistic prayer was the "Konsekrationsform."[20] Perhaps, too, one could accuse Dinesen of quibbling over terminology and even of being himself too one-sided in regard to a consecratory role of the epiclesis, a point to which we shall return shortly. Nevertheless, on one point he seems perfectly justified. That is when he criticizes Betz for limiting himself almost completely to the transformation of the elements in his discussion of the epiclesis.[21] This seems to stem more from the fact that this approach best ties in with Betz's parallel between Incarnation and epiclesis than from any preoccupation with the moment of consecration issue. Nevertheless the end product is equally misleading. The liturgical data indicates rather clearly that to the extent that any explanation of the eucharistic epiclesis neglects the Communion aspect it is unsatisfactory.

Epiclesis: Expression of the Church's Consecratory Intention

Somewhat akin to the position that sees the epiclesis as a sort of consecration formula is the view that the epiclesis expresses the intention of the Church to apply the perennial efficacy of the institution narrative to the eucharistic celebration at hand.

---

18. Dinesen, 93–94 n. 58, 82–87.
19. Ibid., 94 n. 58.
20. Betz, 332-33.
21. Cf. Dinesen, 86, 87 n. 45, 93.

It has already been noted in Chapter 2 that E.G.C. Atchley, writing in 1938, E. Schillebeeckx, in his *De Sacramentele Heilseconomie* published in 1952 and P. L'Huillier, in an article published in *Verbum Caro* in 1960, among others, interpret part of Chrysostom's two homilies *De Protitione Judae* along a similar vein. These authors contend that Chrysostom was not teaching that the "consecration" took place by reason of the mere repetition of the institution words by the priest. Rather, they contend that he was trying to show that it is Christ who is the consecrator and the priest is merely the minister. The priest speaks the words but it is Christ who gives them power. Thus Christ has given divine power once and for all to the institution narrative. Nevertheless, through the epiclesis the priest has to apply these words here and now to the offerings.[22]

Certain modern authors have taken a similar tack in their efforts to give a general theological explanation to the epiclesis. A. Chavasse, for instance, in an article written in 1946, begins his explanation by noting that Catholic dogma teaches that the intention to apply the words of institution here and now to the bread and wine on the altar is necessary to realize the Eucharist. This intention could be applied either through a purely internal act—the simple intention to apply the words to *this* bread and *this* wine—or through some addition to the text of the institution narrative. The Roman tradition seems to have solved the question of applying the words of institution, acknowledged by most to have a narrative character, by appealing to the internal intention of the minister.[23]

The ancient oriental liturgies also perceived the problem of realizing here and now what is contained in the institution narrative. They solved the problem with a prayer, the epiclesis, which appeals to God for this here and now realization. Thus the only difference between East and West in this area is that the Westerners content themselves with an internal intention whereas the Orientals have chosen to express this intention without equivocation in a special prayer—the epiclesis. In other words, the Roman tradition recognizes the fact that

22. This interpretation, which reflects that of Nicholas Cabasilas (cf. Cabasilas, 71–76 and Salaville, *Nicolas Cabasilas* . . . , 179–91), has found various shades of discipleship in SH, 345, L'Huillier, 320, Chavasse, 202–204 and MacLean, 409 as well as in Atchley, *On the Epiclesis* . . . , 68.

23. Chavasse, 198–200.

the intention to apply the words of the institution narrative here and now is necessary for the realization of the Eucharist, for "validity." The same tradition maintains, however, that the *explicit* expression of this intention, i.e., in an epiclesis proper, is not necessary.[24]

In fact, if one considers the *Quam oblationem* in the Roman canon as an expression of the "intention applicatrice," the only difference is that the Roman tradition expresses this intention before the words of institution while the Eastern tradition does it after.[25]

The approach which P. Dinesen takes to explain the epiclesis is somewhat similar to that of Chavasse. Dinesen maintains that the best way to grasp the meaning of the epiclesis is to regard it as a prayer *sui generis*. He begins his treatment by situating the epiclesis in its liturgical setting.

First of all, we have the "thanks-offering" ("Dankopfer"), i.e., the offering of the gifts and the first part of the eucharistic prayer. Here the assembly acknowledges the redemption, one of the high-points of which is the institution of the Lord's Supper. The assembly proclaims the fact that now, grateful and obedient to Christ's command, it is celebrating this same wonder, the Lord's Supper. Next comes the *anamnesis* which, when present, rounds out the thanks-offering and leads into the epiclesis proper.[26]

In the epiclesis one finds a concentration upon the present situation, upon the elements and upon those about to partake of the eucharistic meal. Here, too, however, the community gazes beyond the confines of the present situation. Having recalled the events of saving history and having made grateful acknowledgment for these events, it now draws the consequences. In view of Christ and in view of his promise at the Last Supper it expects God to act here and now in regard to the bread and wine and those about to partake of them. This expectation takes the form of a prayer in which the assembly submits its appeal to the power of God. No prayer that indicates that the epiclesis-prayer has been heard, and that it therefore makes sense to

---

24. Ibid., 200, 204–204 n. 1.

25. Ibid., 205. Salaville, "Epiclèse eucharistique," 280, cites Bossuet, *Explication de quelques difficultés sur les priers de la messe à un nouveau catholique* (Paris, 1710), as having proposed a similar explanation of the necessity of the epiclesis.

26. Dinesen, 47, 103.

partake of these gifts, comes between the epiclesis and the actual reception of Communion.[27]

The fact that, in this sense, the Communion follows directly upon the epiclesis shows that the epiclesis is a real prayer ("echtes Bitt-Gebet"). The assembly appeals to God to intervene in regard to the elements and those partaking and then leaves the rest in his hands. How and when this intervention is to take place is God's concern. In a spirit of trust and faith the community turns to what is its concern, namely, partaking in the eucharistic meal through Communion.[28]

Once one has fully grasped the prayer character of the epiclesis, one is in a position to understand the function of this prayer. In the epiclesis the community takes the logical step from the grateful acknowledgment of the miracle of the Last Supper as such to the appeal that this wonder might take place here and now with these elements and this community.[29]

The function of the epiclesis is, then, not to *realize* the wonder of the Lord's Supper but to give expression to the community's absolute confidence in, and its faith and dependence upon, God's intervention during the Eucharist.[30]

Dinesen has succeeded very well in bringing out the fact that the epiclesis is a prayer, a prayer which expresses the faith of the assembly and its appeal that God actualize the Lord's Supper here and now. In this he differs only somewhat from Chavasse. Where he differs greatly, however, is in his tendency to shy away from attributing any share in the realization of the Eucharist to the assembly itself. We shall take up this point again in the next section.

EPICLESIS WITHIN THE FRAMEWORK OF A CONSECRATORY EPICLESIS

Closely allied to the two explanations just treated is the view that the epiclesis and the institution narrative form an inseparable unit within the framework of the whole eucharistic prayer, the Epiclesis, as consecratory. Besides underlining the tight bond between the institution

27. Ibid., 103–106.

28. Dinesen, 105–106.

29. Ibid., 106.

30. Ibid., 106–107.

narrative and the epiclesis proper, explanations of this type generally tend to acknowledge a certain consecratory value in the epiclesis.

Odo Casel, as seen in the section on the reconstructions of the history of the epiclesis, has greatly influenced such explanations. Casel, in a series of articles and conferences which began to appear around 1923, maintains that the whole eucharistic prayer was originally an Epiclesis (capital E) in the sense of a naming of a name (upon a person or a thing) with its implied calling upon the person named to be actively, effectively present. Within the framework of this consecratory prayer the institution narrative and the Hippolytus-type epiclesis played integral, complementary roles by indicating the object and the purpose of the naming and of the consequent active presence.[31] The more developed epiclesis proper was basically only the expression of what the entire eucharistic prayer contained.[32]

It seems to be partly due to the influence of Casel that A. Stolz, in a fascicle of his *Manuale Theologiae Dogmaticae* which appeared in 1943, displays a stance in regard to the form of the Eucharist which is surprisingly open for a Catholic manual.[33] Stolz begins by noting that the Fathers of the Church saw the whole eucharistic prayer as a consecratory unit. Only the Scholastics really raised the question of a moment of consecration. The Roman Catholic magisterium, it is true, has sanctioned the decision in favor of the institution narrative as the essential form of the Eucharist. Not only, however, did the Fathers regard the eucharistic prayer as a single consecratory whole, but we even have ancient liturgical texts proclaiming the presence of Christ by dint of an invocation of the Holy Spirit or of the Logos.[34]

Faced with this apparent dilemma Stolz turns to the basic meaning of the term "epiclesis" (small e) for an answer. As we have seen, in its technical sense "epiclesis" refers to the naming of the divine name so that God might be present. In this sense, then, every prayer, every cultic act which constitutes communion with God, through which God becomes present to us, is an epiclesis of sorts. In this sense, too, the whole eucharistic prayer through which Christ becomes present to the assembly in a special way is an epiclesis. Thus the institution

---

31. Cf. Casel, "Zur Epiklese," 100–101. Cf. also, SH, 337–379, 343–44.

32. Cf. Casel, *Das christliche Opfermysterium*, 546–47.

33. Cf. B. Neunheuser's review in ALW 1 (1050), 151.

34. Stolz, 143–44. Cf. Schmaus, 308.

narrative and/or the epiclesis proper are simply expressing what takes place through the whole anaphora.[35]

To pose the question whether it is the institution narrative *or* the epiclesis which realizes the mystery of the Eucharist is, therefore to pose a false question. The sacrificial action is formally present through the words of institution but continues throughout the canon and reaches its completion in the Communion. The Orthodox tradition which regards the institution narrative and the epiclesis as an inseparable unit both components of which play a part in the realization of the eucharistic mystery is, concludes Stolz, in perfect agreement with the solution which he proposes for the epiclesis question.[36]

A. Fortescue, writing in 1913, takes a position virtually identical with the one just outlined. One can best summarize Fortescue's view by quoting two passages of his in regard to the epiclesis and eucharistic consecration:

> In all such cases we say that at whatever moment of our time God gives the Sacramental grace, he gives it in answer to the whole prayer or group of prayers, which, of course, take time to say.[37]

> So we can suggest a simple and (as far as it goes) sufficient explanation of the Epiklesis. It is merely a rather prominent case of the common idea. We remember again that the liturgy, especially the Consecration-prayer is one thing, one united prayer, in answer to which God consecrates . . . Naturally in that prayer we ask him, maybe repeatedly, to do so; the exact position of such petitions in the course of the prayers matters little. The form of asking him to send his Holy Spirit is a natural result of the development of the idea of the Holy Ghost as a source of grace, of the attribution to the third Person of divine operations *ad extra* which spread in the IVth century, and the place of the Epiklesis is perhaps fixed by the idea of Pentecost at the end of the Anamnesis.[38]

As a final example of the approach is P. Trembelas who gives voice to the opinion of most modern Orthodox writers when he stresses the essential role of the institution narrative as well as the consecratory value of the epiclesis. The whole anaphora is consecratory

---

35. Ibid., 144–45.
36. Ibid., 145.
37. Fortescue, 353 n. 3.
38. Ibid., 404.

but it has two highpoints or principal elements. Without the institution narrative the assembly would run the risk of not having what Christ bequeathed to it. Without the epiclesis, it would run the risk of not having the "consecration" and transformation of the gifts.[39]

P. Dinesen has also taken up the question of the relationship between the institution narrative and the epiclesis. The basic role or function of the institution narrative, he maintains, is to recall a specific event in saving history, namely, the event of the Last Supper. This provides the basis or reason for what is now taking place, i.e., the Eucharist with its epiclesis. The institution narrative thus does two things: it witnesses to a specific event in saving history for which the community wishes to express its thanks and it acts indirectly as the basis for the Eucharist which is taking place here and now. At the same time it serves as an assurance that the epiclesis has a historical basis and that it makes sense to pray the epiclesis. The assembly prays that God will intervene here and now in its celebration of the Eucharist and realize the promise which Christ once made. It prays with assurance because, thanks to the institution narrative, its gaze focuses on the basis of its hope, the Last Supper and the promise Christ made there.[40]

Dinesen shows himself extremely reluctant, however, when it comes to allowing the institution narrative or the epiclesis, or both together, a role in the "consecration." He notes that a number of modern authors have taken the stand that it is not a single moment in the eucharistic prayer that consecrates but the eucharistic prayer as a whole. It is only a short step, he contends, from this view to the position that the tight bond between the institution narrative and the epiclesis is the result of their common function, namely, that of inducing the wonder of the Eucharist.[41]

Dinesen then proceeds to show with reference to his earlier section on "Consecration and Epiclesis" (the main lines of which we have seen in our treatment of the "Epiclesis as a Consecratory Formula")

---

39. Cf. Trembelas, 177–78 who also cites J. Karmiris, *Synopsis* . . . (Athens, 1957), 101 n. 1 and M. Siotis, Θεία Ἐυχαριστία (Salonika, 1957), 14–15 as holding the same view; cf. also 173. Cf. also, Evdokimov, *L'Orthodoxie,* 250; Rauschen, 115; Schmidt-Lauber, 157, 132; Ritter, 163 ff.; Goldammer, 27, 38-39; SH, 345 and Smit, 125.

40. Dinesen, 99–101.

41. Ibid., 95.

and the reasoning contained there, that the prayer of thanksgiving (Dankgebet) with its institution narrative and the epiclesis do not form a consecration *formula*. The soundness of his reasoning, however, gives way to a conclusion which seems too sweeping when he states:

> *Negative* . . . if one views the prayer of thanksgiving and the epiclesis as a formula of consecration. The prayer of thanksgiving is just that, a prayer of thanksgiving and should fulfill no other liturgical function . . . we have already seen that, in regard to the epiclesis, it is impossible to conceive of the prayer of thanksgiving as a factor in the consecration. . .[42]

To deny that the eucharistic prayer as a whole or the "prayer of thanksgiving" and epiclesis (taken either together or individually) are a consecration *formula* is one thing. This seems to be justified on the basis of the texts Dinesen has examined. To deny that the eucharistic prayer as a whole or the "prayer of thanksgiving" with its institution narrative and/or the epiclesis can indeed play some role in the realization of the "Abendmahlswunder" [wonder of the Lord's Supper] is another thing. This does not seem justified on the basis of the texts Dinesen has examined.

Dinesen has brought out well the community aspect of the epiclesis as well as the attitude of faith and total dependence which it expresses. His stress on the absolute sovereignty of God in causing the transition from bread and wine to the body and blood of Christ is equally commendable. At times, however, he seems to be in danger of going to the other extreme. Perhaps in reaction to exaggerations in this area, he seems to deny that the community's prayer and gestures while expressing its thanks, praise, helplessness and faith could also play a role, however subordinate, in the realization of the Eucharist. To deny this possibility would be to go beyond, and at times perhaps even against, the historical data. Yet with such expressions as "should fulfill *no other* liturgical function" and "in regard to the epiclesis," it is *impossible* to conceive of the prayer of thanksgiving as a *factor* in the consecration,[43] Dinesen seems to be in danger of denying just that. Perhaps we have here an unfortunate by-product of the controversy over the moment of consecration. Perhaps we also have an instance of

---

42. Ibid., 98.

43. Ibid., (Italics mine). These expressions appear despite the fact that Dinesen himself (93 n. 57) has criticized Wetter, 69 ff. for going too far in the same direction.

the danger of limiting oneself to the early liturgical texts alone.[44] Numerous extra-liturgical texts from the patristic period, for instance, would seem to indicate a belief in a consecratory function of either the institution narrative or the epiclesis or, at times, both together within the framework of the whole eucharistic prayer.

Epiclesis as Realizing the "Sacramentum"

The theological explanations examined up to this point have all tended to accord the epiclesis a certain role in the consecration, i.e., in the transformation of the bread and wine into Christ's body and blood. A number of authors propose an explanation which stresses the function of the epiclesis in the adaptation of the already present body and blood in view of its reception by the faithful.

E. Schillebeeckx, for instance, in his *De Sacramentele Heilseconomie* sees Chavasse's theory, that the epiclesis expresses the necessary intention of the Church, as insufficient. The liturgical data which reveals a consecratory epiclesis after the institution narrative and the patristic testimony to the epiclesis as an essential moment in the consecration rite still pose a problem. In the framework of transubstantiation the transformation of the bread and wine necessarily takes place in an instant, not gradually. According to the present Roman teaching one cannot solve the problem by putting off Christ's eucharistic presence until the epiclesis *after* the institution narrative has been consummated.[45]

Schillebeeckx suggests that we look for a possible solution in the direction of a sanctifying epiclesis that makes the already present body and blood of Christ into a *sacramentum*, i.e., an objective source of sanctification for those receiving them. One would then have a twofold ritual moment that realizes the Eucharist both as sacrifice and as sacrament. Both aspects belong to a complete Eucharist and both are therefore necessary although not always simultaneously in the foreground. The institution narrative is the consecration realizing the presence of the body and blood of Christ, the *corpus eucharisticum*. The epiclesis, in turn, realizes the objective sanctification of this body and

---

44. Cf. ibid., 43 where Dinesen excludes extraliturgical texts from the main field of his investigation.

45. SH, 348–52.

blood in view of those about to partake of it. Both the institution narrative and the epiclesis, in some form, make up the *forma Eucharistiae* and therefore are necessary for a complete Eucharist.[46]

Schillebeeckx illustrates his point by drawing a parallel between the Eucharist and the sacraments of baptism and confirmation. In baptism and confirmation the water and the oil by reason of the epiclesis become *sacramentum* so that whoever comes into contact with these "sacramentalized" objects will be sanctified. So too, through the epiclesis the symbolic form of sacrificial food becomes a *sacramentum*. In other words, just as the historical Christ received the Holy Spirit for our sakes, so too, the *Christus eucharisticus* receives the Holy Spirit for our sakes. Thus it is that the epiclesis of sanctification, in this sense, is most often completed by an epiclesis asking that we partake worthily in the "sanctified *oblata*."[47]

Schillebeeckx admits that this explanation does not, perhaps, solve the problem completely if one insists that the Fathers were speaking of the epiclesis as essential to the *forma transsubstantiationis* which makes Christ's body and blood first present. At the very least, however, it gives us a good explanation of the consecratory epiclesis *before*, and the epiclesis of sanctification (in the sense just outlined) *after* the institution narrative. It also gives a good insight into some characteristic features of the patristic understanding of the Eucharist.[48]

J. P. de Jong, in a number of articles published in 1956–57, offers an explanation similar to that of Schillebeeckx while at the same time stressing the relationship between the epiclesis and the rite of consignation.[49] De Jong begins by remarking that one will always fail to find a solution to the epiclesis problem as long as one continues to regard it in relation to the metaphysical concept of transubstantiation.

---

46. SH, 352; cf. 353–54.

47. SH, 352.

48. SH, 353. Cf. also Havet, 61–93, esp. 61, 65, 68–69, 72–73, 82 who gives a more detailed presentation of this possibility in conjunction with the eucharistic thought of Isidore of Seville. Cf. also Salaville, "Epiclèse eucharistique," 278–79, 285–90 and Cagin, *Eucharistia*, 50–51.

49. Cf. de Jong, "La Connexion . . . ," 29–34 and "Le rite . . . ," 245–78, 33–79. By "consignation" de Jong understands the rite of tracing the sign of the cross with one species over the other and more especially when this is done in view of uniting the two, e.g., in the Roman commixtion or commixture.

One should rather consider the epiclesis on the plane of sacramental "figuration."[50]

He claims that the canon of Hippolytus presents the most ancient form of an epiclesis, a "Communion epiclesis." Hippolytus, therefore, becomes the point of departure for de Jong's study. There are two phases in the canon of Hippolytus. First, there is the representation of the sacrifice of Christ, symbolized by the separation of the elements and the words of institution. Secondly, there is the transfiguration of the offering as a preparation for Communion. This transfiguration is evoked by the epiclesis and signified by the consignation or commixture. De Jong has coined the word "transfiguration" to distinguish the aforementioned process from "transubstantiation" which takes place on the metaphysical level. Transfiguration, on the other hand, takes place on the *sacramental* level. One sacramental figure replaces another; the figure of the sacrificial death of Christ, or his body and blood given for man, gives way to the figure of Christ's glorified body and blood given to man as divine nourishment, as the nourishment of immortality. This does not, however, exclude the sacramental presence of Christ before the epiclesis which evokes the transfiguration.[51]

Thus through the epiclesis the eucharistic elements become a symbol of a new sacramental reality. This reality is in turn externally manifested by the symbolic gesture ("figuration sacrementelle") of the commixture. In other words, the commixture does with actions what the epiclesis does in words. The relationship, then, between the epiclesis and the consignation or commixture is a relationship between word pronounced and word signified ("figurée"). Both serve as a preparation for Communion.[52]

Closely aligned to the explanations offered by Schillebeeckx and de Jong is that which the Benedictine P. Rupprecht put forth in an article which appeared in *Divus Thomas* in 1937. An examination of texts from the ancient liturgies, the Fathers and the Councils, he contends, shows that the ancient understanding of the eucharistic "consecration" involved more than simply the changing of the gifts into the body and blood of Christ. Rather, the more ancient and

---

50. de Jong, "La Connexion . . . ," 29.

51. de Jong, "Le rite . . . ," 253, 257–58, 268.

52. Ibid., 268–69 and "La Connexion . . . ," 30–33.

deeper meaning of "consecration" encompassed the distributing and devout partaking of the Eucharist by the faithful.[53]

This is the reason why the assembly takes up the appeal for the acceptance and *full* "consecration" of the gifts even after their transformation. It thereby hopes to awaken in those present the faith and devotion necessary for a fruitful reception of the Eucharist. It recognizes that the transformation of the gifts is of itself not enough. It is only a means to a greater end, namely, the building up of the Mystical Body and the filling of this body with the life of Christ.[54] Thus there is in reality a double consecration, at least when it is a question of the building up of the Mystical Body of Christ.[55] It is not a question here of a new essential change (Wesensverwandlung). But it is rather a new intervention of the Holy Spirit in the consecratory process, an intervention in view of those about to partake.[56] Rupprecht sees in this return to the original ideas of "consecration" a means to resolving the conflict of the West with the East over the epiclesis.[57]

The three explanations outlined in this section, as well as those similar to them, have the common advantage of highlighting the purpose of the eucharistic transformation, namely, the worthy Communion of the faithful. In so doing they underline the basic unity which exists between the consecration, as it is usually understood, and the Communion. It is to this unity and its relation to the epiclesis that we now turn.

EPICLESIS: BOND BETWEEN CONSECRATION AND COMMUNION

The fact that one can include J. P. de Jong in the present section as well as in the previous one is a good reminder that one is dealing here

---

53. Rupprecht, "Zum Vollbegriff der eucharistischen Konsekration," 371, 377–78, 380, 385–86, 396, 401–402, 412–13.

54. Ibid., 401–402; cf. 396, 408–409 and 413.

55. Ibid., 412.

56. Ibid., 393–94.

57. Ibid., 412–13 and Salaville, "Epiclèse eucharistique," 284–85, 288–90. Cf. also, L'écuyer, "La théologie . . . . ," 408–10 who in the light of Theodore of Mopsuestia and John Chrysostom gives a similar explanation. The epiclesis works a "sacramental resurrection" aimed at communicating the life of the risen Christ to the faithful and thus uniting them more deeply with Christ and with one another.

with complementary, not opposing, viewpoints. De Jong, for instance, in conjunction with a treatment of the eucharistic teaching of Saint Irenaeus written in 1965, brings out an aspect which is complementary to the position that the epiclesis shares in the realization of the *sacramentum*. According to Irenaeus, maintains de Jong, Christ has taken on our flesh, our humanity, and through his sacrificial death and glorification has perfectly united it to ("mixed it with") his divinity.[58]

In the Eucharist God takes our offerings (bread and wine) and unites them to the offering of Christ, now made present (body and blood) and accepted because it is Christ's. God then returns our now "divinized" gifts to us and we, by partaking in them, partake also in the "mixing" (later called *commercium*) of human and divine in Christ. It is this twofold process of uniting our offering to that of Christ and then, in Communion, of uniting our humanity to Christ's divinized humanity that the epiclesis and the rite of commixture express symbolically.[59]

For Irenaeus, then, the epiclesis (and the rite of commixture) manifests symbolically the union between the human and divine, in the sacrifice, *and* our share in this union in Communion. One must therefore regard the epiclesis primarily as a connecting link between the eucharistic sacrifice and the eucharistic food.[60]

> From the writings of St. Irenaeus it is already clear why the Logos is called down upon the eucharistic sacrifice . . . This Logos epiclesis is apparently related to the Eucharist as a sacrament, *in sensu stricto*, and must be viewed above all else as the connecting link between the eucharistic offering and the eucharistic food.[61]

It is precisely because the epiclesis (and the commixture rite) form the connecting link which binds the consecration and Communion together that the symbolic meaning of the epiclesis can be grasped only in the light of the eucharistic celebration as a whole.[62]

B. Bobrinskoy, writing in 1962, also underlines the function of the epiclesis as highlighting the organic bond between consecration and Communion. The failure to see these two moments in the

---

58. de Jong, "Der ursprüngliche Sinn . . . ," 40–44.

59. Ibid., 32–39, 44–45. For de Jong this symbolism, however, *is* somehow what it signifies (45).

60. Ibid., 28, 37–39, 44–45.

61. Ibid., 37 (Italics mine).

62. Ibid., 28.

Eucharist as a unity has led to the view that Communion is a fruit of the eucharistic mystery rather than an integral, culminating point of a communal eucharistic celebration. The epiclesis proper, as the ancient Church has presented it, cries out against the practice, common to just about all the Christian traditions, of celebrating the Eucharist without all the faithful who are present normally receiving Communion. The rediscovery of the epicletic and pneumatological element in the Eucharist should do much to underline the abnormality of this arrangement. The Holy Spirit is invoked upon the gifts *and* upon the faithful. The consecration of the gifts is in view of their reception by those assembled. The Holy Spirit is to work on both.[63]

> The gifts are sanctified and transformed into the Body of Christ by the power of the Holy Spirit, in order to become divine nourishment and to transform the eucharistic assembly into the Body of Christ.[64]

E. G. C. Atchley, too, brings out the close ties between consecration and Communion—ties which the epiclesis expresses well. There is no basic difference, he maintains, between the fully developed Eastern epiclesis, with its explicit appeal for the transformation of the gifts, and the Hippolytus type in which it is simply asked that the Holy Spirit come on or into the oblation. The Eastern epiclesis is merely more explicit. Western writers, however, are quite definite in teaching that a transformation of the gifts takes place through the Holy Spirit. Moreover, both East and West are in agreement that this transformation has a profitable Communion as its goal.

> . . . Both East and West believe that the Holy Spirit makes the bread the body and the mingled cup the blood of Christ, and both believe that the purpose of His so doing is that the faithful may profitably communicate thereof.[65]

It might simply be noted in passing that this conclusion of Atchley might have been more forceful had he cited the full epiclesis

---

63. Bobrinskoy, "Le Saint-Esprit dans la liturgie," 58–59.

64. Ibid., 59. Cf. also the same author's "Présence réele . . . .," 409–13 which, although it falls outside the sphere of the time limits we have imposed, expresses the point at issue very well. Cf. also, Renz, 348; L'Huillier, 311–13; J. Danielou, *The Bible and the Liturgy* (Notre Dame, Ind., 1956), 138–41; Smit, 125–26; Kavanagh, "Thoughts on the New Eucharistic Prayers," 6, 9–11; Bulgakov, "Das eucharistische Dogma," 83, 43 and Afanassieff, 211–212.

65. Atchley, *On the Epiclesis* . . . , 199–200.

text throughout his study. Most often he cites the epiclesis texts only
up to and not including the point where reference is made to the fruits
desired for those partaking.[66]

Finally, it is interesting to note that with all their weaknesses
in treating the epiclesis question many of the theological manuals
within the Roman Catholic tradition do stress the two-directional
character of the epiclesis. While allowing the epiclesis no consecratory
value they do link it to the consecration in a fashion which we shall see
shortly. In addition, they often manage to bring out the Communion-
oriented facet of the epiclesis. J. Pohle is particularly articulate in this
regard.[67] Although other manuals may not express it so clearly, the
view that the epiclesis links "consecration" and Communion often
manages to surface in them.[68]

EPICLESIS: AN APPEAL FOR UNITY

Somewhat related to the preceding position, in that it looks to the
effect of eucharistic Communion in the faithful, is the view that the
epiclesis is basically an appeal for unity. L. Bouyer is of the opinion
that such an appeal already had a basis in the transition from praise to
prayer in the Jewish meal *berakoth*. The primitive Christian eucharistic
prayer, he maintains, after recalling the wonderful works of God asked
that these wonderful works have their eschatological fulfillment in
the present celebration of the Eucharist. This fulfillment will take the
form of unity in the whole Christ, with Head and members being
perfectly united for the glory of God. The notion of unity which lay at
the root of the epiclesis quite naturally led to the mention of the Holy
Spirit, the bond of unity. Although in the course of time an appeal for
the acceptance of the sacrifice-memorial and the consecration of the
bread and wine into the body and blood of Christ joined the appeal

---

66. He does this in the case of Sarapion n. 2 (89), Mark (99), *The Apostolic Constitutions* (115),
Greek James and to some extent Syriac James (119–120), Basil (134) and Chrysostom (135).

67. Pohle (19104), 290. In the 196010 Pohle-Gummersbach edition the exact quote is not
there but the basic content has remained (283–85).

68. Cf., for instance, Gutberlet, 56–57; Pesch, *De Sacramentis* Pars I: *De sacramentis in
genere* . . . (Greiburg i. Br., 19144), 370–71 and the same author's *Compendium Theologiae
Dogmaticae* IV (Freiburg i. Br., 19222), 114; B. J. Otten, *Institutiones Dogmaticae* V: *De sacramentis
in genere* . . . (Chicago, 1923), 482–83; J. B. Heinrich and K. Gutberlet, *Dogmatische Theologie*
IX: *Von den Heiligen Sakramenten* (Mainz, 1901), 729–37; E. Hugon, *Tractatus Dogmatici* IV: *De
Sacramentis in Communi* . . . (Paris, 19275), 406–407. Cf. also, Brinktrine, "De epiclesi . . . ," 162.

for unity, it is in this latter appeal that we find the original and basic meaning of the epiclesis.[69]

L. Ligier also sees the origin of the epiclesis in the Jewish *berakoth* and seems to be in agreement with Bouyer on the basic meaning of the epiclesis. He maintains that despite later additions and modifications the Church never lost sight of the basic signification of the epiclesis, namely, the restoration and gathering together of the people of God around the *Shekinah* or divine presence.[70]

H. de Lubac is another modern author who stresses the unity aspect of the epiclesis. In his *Catholicisme*, when treating the sacraments he generally emphasizes their social, ecclesial aspect. This holds true especially for his references to the Eucharist, "the sacrament of unity."

> All the sacraments are basically 'sacraments in the Church'; in her alone they produce their full effect, for in her alone, 'in the Community of the Spirit', one normally participates in the Gift of the Spirit.[71]

For if it is from the Church that the sacraments draw their efficacy, it is also in view of the Church that this efficacy is bestowed on the sacraments by God.[72]

This social, ecclesial aspect of the sacraments is particularly striking in the case of the Eucharist which has for its primary function the formation of the Mystical Body of Christ by producing unity among its members. There are a number of elements in the Eucharist which bring out this unifying function. The epiclesis, however, does so in a special way:

> . . . But besides that, one can note that in the ancient liturgies, and even today in the Eastern rites, petitions looking to unity form the crowning point of the epiclesis. Now the whole sacrifice, but in a manner that is usually more explicit, the epiclesis, stands under the sign of the Holy Spirit. It is the Spirit, whose divine action prepared for Christ his corporeal body, who also intervenes in the realization of the Eucharist for the formation of his mystical body.[73]

---

69. Cf. Bouyer, *Eucharistie*, 176 (177), 182–84 (183–84), 300–303 (310–13).

70. Ligier, "De la cène . . . ," 46 cf. 44–45. Cf. also, Oesterly, 217–19. 223–29.

71. Cf. de Lubac, *Catholicisme*, 55–56.

72. Ibid., 57.

73. Ibid., 79.

Finally, there is A. Kavanagh who holds a similar view in regard to the eucharistic epiclesis. For him the epiclesis is basically a prayer for unity with the Father and with each other through Jesus Christ:

> . . . a prayer for the community's assimilation or integration with God above all things and the members one with another through this action of thanksgiving in Christ.[74]

> . . . what is ultimately being prayed for is oneness with the Father—that oneness he has made available in Jesus and extends to all men through Jesus' body, the Church.[75]

Thus once it has narrated the *mirabilia Dei* and has responded to this "good news," the assembly prays that all those who share in this Eucharist—*ex hac altaris participatione*—will receive reconciliation with the Father through Christ. We find in *Didache* 9 an expression of this same notion: "As this broken bread was scattered upon the mountains, but was brought together from the ends of the earth into thy kingdom, etc." The assembly appeals for this unity here and now in the present celebration and even more fully in the future, and it prays with the awareness that it is this union of all with the Father through Jesus Christ that builds up the Church.[76]

This view would, according to Kavanagh, show the epiclesis *after* the institution narrative to flow naturally and smoothly from the proclaiming of the wonderful deeds of God (*mirabilia Dei*) and the Church's response to those wonders in the anamnesis. It would also explain how the *Supra quae* and the *Supplices* of the Roman canon could be regarded as an "epicletic unit," forming as they do a petition that the divine acceptance of the assembly's action bring about a deeper union between the assembly and God and among the assembled themselves. Finally, this view would help explain how the Holy Spirit, as the body of unity and "source of κοινονια," came to be invoked in this prayer and how the epiclesis in turn naturally leads to prayers of intercession.[77]

We have already noted, in conjunction with Bouyer's reconstruction of the history of the epiclesis in the preceding section, the

---

74. Kavanagh, "Thoughts on the Roman Anaphora," 7.
75. Ibid., 8.
76. Cf. ibid., 5–8; also 528–29.
77. Ibid., 5, 7, 528–29.

degree of support that the liturgical data provides for the view that the epiclesis is basically an appeal for unity. This basic approach, especially as de Lubac and Kavanagh present it, has the advantage of linking the epiclesis to the goal of the Eucharist in general. If one sees the Eucharist as geared to the sanctification of the faithful or, more specifically, to the unity of the faithful with God and with each other, then the epiclesis becomes an appeal for God to realize here and now the end for which Christ instituted the Eucharist.[78]

S. Salaville's attitude toward a similar position is of interest here. Referring, in an article which appeared in the 1941–42 volume of *Echos d'Orient*, to Fulgence of Ruspe's statement that the Church in invoking the Holy Spirit to sanctify the sacrifice is in reality appealing for unity in charity,[79] Salaville comments:

> Unity of Christ's mystical body by means of charity, through the grace of the Holy Spirit; this is certainly one of the intentions envisaged by the eucharistic invocation of the Holy Spirit; this, however, is only secondary and attendant upon the primary divine action which is the transubstantiation itself.[80]

On the one hand, the liturgical data examined in Chapter 1 does reveal that, as Salaville maintains, the unity and other benefits requested for the faithful are usually consequent to and dependent upon the transformation of the gifts. On the other hand, one has to be on guard against a danger which lurks beneath his criticism, a danger which can stem from an over-concentration on the moment of consecration. The danger would lie in seeing transubstantiation no longer as a means of deepening Christ's presence in, and unity among, the faithful but rather almost as an end in itself. Such a viewpoint would be a far cry from that of an Aquinas and a Cabasilas who saw the sanctification of the faithful and the unity of the Mystical Body, and not transubstantiation, as the ultimate purpose of the Eucharist.[81] The approach one adopts here has important consequences for one's

---

78. Cf. Von Allmen, *Essai* . . . , 31.

79. *Ad Monimum* liber II, 9 (PL 65:187).

80. Salaville, "L'épiclèse africaine," 277.

81. S. T. III, q. 73, a. 3 and Cabasilas, 25. Cf. also, Schillebeeckx, *The Eucharist*, 137–51; Smit, 125–26 and Rahner, "The Presence . . . ," 309–11.

understanding of the eucharistic epiclesis as well as for one's understanding of the Eucharist as a whole.

Suffice it to note here that the position of Aquinas and
Cabasilas conforms to the liturgical data. In the more developed
epiclesis when the transformation of the bread and wine into Christ's
body and blood is requested it is almost invariably requested *so that*
those partaking might benefit. To give short shrift to this relationship
within the Eucharist and within the epiclesis is to run the risk of being
lopsided in one's interpretation of both.

Epiclesis: Phenomenon of Liturgical Language

In treating a number of the attempts at a historical reconstruction
or a theological explanation of the eucharistic epiclesis, we have had
occasion to note the possible influence of the moment of consecration
question upon these theories. In the theories about to be discussed
such an influence seems even more obvious. These theories start out
with the presumption that the institution narrative and that alone is
the moment of consecration. Roman Catholic teaching authority in
recent centuries has been rather outspoken in this regard. The statements of a number of the patristic writers and especially the liturgical
fact of an epiclesis appealing for the transformation of the gifts *after*
the institution narrative seems to be a cause of evident embarrassment
for many modern writers within the Roman tradition. Very often their
attempts to explain, or explain away, this liturgical fact takes the form
of an appeal to liturgical style or liturgical language.

Writing in 1943, M. Jugie maintains, for instance, that the
true explanation of the eucharistic epiclesis, and the only one really
necessary, is that the Church cannot implore all the various effects of
the Eucharist simultaneously. Therefore she often appeals for an effect
even after this effect has been realized through the essential rite.

Other explanations, e.g., that the Church is appealing basically
for the communicants in the epiclesis, or that the epiclesis expresses
the intention of the Church, are merely complementary to this one.[82]

J. Brinktrine, in an article written in 1923, offers virtually the
same explanation although with a slightly different nuance. He claims

---

82. Jugies, *De forma . . .* , 128–33.

that the epiclesis is the accidental or secondary form of the Eucharist. Its function is to express more clearly what has taken place by means of the institution narrative. Brinktrine hastens to add, however, that the epiclesis is more than a mere explanation of the essential form. For *if* Christ had not himself instituted a form for the Eucharist, the epiclesis would be entirely sufficient and appropriate as the sacramental form.[83]

Brinktrine illustrates this explanation by drawing an analogy between the eucharistic epiclesis and the now secondary rites in the sacraments of Orders and baptism. In the ordination rite, for instance, the handing over of the instruments interprets and illustrates what is now essential, namely, the imposition of hands. Baptism, too, offers a certain analogy that is helpful for understanding the signification of the eucharistic epiclesis. Although the blessing of the baptismal waters is in no way necessary for the validity of the sacrament, since Christ himself determined water as the element for this sacrament, the Church at times acts as though the blessing were necessary. Similarly in the Eucharist, although the consecration has taken place through the institution narrative, the wording of the epiclesis makes it sound as though it has not taken place.[84]

In concluding, Brinktrine reveals a tendency to bog down on only one aspect of the epiclesis, a tendency which may once again reflect the presence of the moment of consecration problem.

> . . . This theory [Bessarion's], therefore, needs to be supplemented by another, according to which the epiclesis is understood not as an explicitation of one truth or another contained only implicitly in the essential form but simply as a secondary form—in the sense, of course, that the sacramental sign would be entirely adequate, *if* Christ himself had not determined the form of this august sacrament but had left its institution to his Church.[85]

That is a big "if," however, and one wonders whether Brinktrine, despite such terminology as "secondary or accidental form," has said much more than that the epiclesis makes explicit what is already implicit in the "essential form."[86]

---

83. Brinktrine, "De epiclesi . . . ," 157.
84. Ibid.,157–158.
85. Ibid., 164 (Italics mine).
86. Cf. Casel (Review of Brinktrine's "De epiclesi . . ."), 137 on Brinktrine's explanation.

One of the most important attempts to explain the epiclesis in terms of liturgical style or language is that of S. Salaville in his classical study of the eucharistic epiclesis that appeared in *Dictionnaire de théologie catholique* in 1913. At the very outset of his article Salaville states his purpose, namely, to demonstrate that it is the formulas, "Hoc est enim corpus meum, etc." which constitute the form of the Eucharist and that in no way is it the epiclesis.[87] This aim sets the tone for the rest of the article and places the epiclesis question squarely in the context of the moment of consecration question.

Perhaps the best way to sum up Salaville's position is to indicate how he confronts what he considers to be the main questions or problems involved in the epiclesis discussion. First of all, he asks, how can we reconcile the constant tradition which attributes the consecration to the words of institution with that which prays, even after the institution narrative, for the Holy Spirit to change the gifts? Salaville contends that the doctrine of appropriation partly accounts for the liturgical phenomenon called the epiclesis. Transubstantiation is a work common to all three Persons of the Trinity. In view of its analogy with the Incarnation and in the light of the general theory of sanctification we attribute or appropriate this work to the Holy Spirit.

The instantaneous character of the consecration did not impose itself on the early Church writers with the same force that it did upon later writers. It was "the Latin genius" which concluded most quickly to the instantaneous character of the consecration and to the exclusive efficacy of the words of institution. If it is a question of determining the precise moment of transubstantiation, the only solution possible is to hold with the Roman Catholic Church that the words of institution are the "form" of the Eucharist. If, however, one abstracts from the precise moment of consecration and considers the consecration as a work of the divine omnipotence common to the whole Trinity, as are all works *ad extra*, then the language of the eucharistic epiclesis and of the Fathers becomes understandable. The epiclesis stems, at least in part, from the desire to appropriate this common work of transubstantiation to the Holy Spirit.[88]

---

87. Salaville, "Epiclèse eucharistique," 194.
88. Ibid., 292–93.

But why is the epiclesis after the institution narrative and not before? Salaville meets this question with a twofold response. First of all, the position of the eucharistic epiclesis stems from the necessity of human language to enunciate successively the different aspects of something which takes place in an instant. The rituals of both East and West indicate that the Church has the custom of asking repeatedly for that which she wishes to obtain, even after the essential rite has been accomplished and God as already effected the sacrament invisibly. One finds such a phenomenon in other sacraments besides the Eucharist, especially in baptism, confirmation, and Orders. In these sacraments the minister asks that the Holy Spirit come and realize the sacrament even at a point when the words of the "form" have been pronounced and joined to the matter thus producing the effects of the sacrament.[89]

In this conjunction Salaville cites Bossuet extensively, taking pains to point out the passages which, implicitly at least, fall in line with his own thesis. There are other passages, however, which go against Salaville's view. These he tends to dismiss as inexactitudes, or lack of precision (sometimes due to the influence of Renaudot) in Bossuet's thought. For instance,

. . . do we believe that God waits for each point where we speak to him of these things before he does them? Doubtlessly not. This is all the effect of human language which can only express itself piecemeal. *And God . . . does everything at the proper time—a time which is known to him; there is no need for us to worry about the precise moment in which he does it.* It is enough that we express everything that is done by these fitting words and actions and that the whole ensemble—although done and pronounced successively—portrays for us, in a unified way, all the effects and, as it were, every facet of the divine mystery.[90]

And again:

. . . in order to say everything, one expresses successively that which is done, perhaps, all at once; one does this *without inquiring about precise moments.*[91]

---

89. Ibid., 279. Cf. also, 295–96.

90. Ibid., 281 citing Bossuet, *Explication de quelques difficultés sur les prières de la messe à un nouveau catholique* (Paris, 1710), xlvi (Italics mine).

91. Ibid., 281 citing Bossuet, ibid., xlvii (Italics mine).

And finally:

> . . . in this case what shall we do if not that which was done at Florence, in order to disquiet no one over this doctrine, and that which was done at Trent, where without determining precisely what the consecration consisted of, one simply determined what happened when it took place?[92]

These remarks by Bossuet are significant because they do raise a question in regard to this part of Salaville's thesis. How does the Church know precisely when God works if the transformation of the gifts is, as Salaville himself admits, invisibly accomplished by God? Could not the fact that the Church repeats its request for the realization of the sacrament a number of times indicate a reluctance or hesitancy, on the part of the early Church at least, about trying to pinpoint the precise moment?

The second reason that Salaville offers for the position of the epiclesis after the institution narrative is closely allied to the question of appropriation. The Fathers and even the liturgy itself tended to take cognizance of the logical order of the divine Persons between themselves and of their intervention in saving history. They did so even in the context of the anaphora itself. Thus the first part of the anaphora would usually refer to the Father, the institution narrative would refer to the Son and the epiclesis would refer to the Holy Spirit. The explanation of the location of the epiclesis within the anaphora, therefore, boils down to a question of appropriation and liturgical style.[93]

One could sum up Salaville's overall position in regard to the epiclesis as follows: the form of the Eucharist consists of the words of institution pronounced by the priest *in persona Christi*. Since transubstantiation is an instantaneous act it is not possible to say that it is begun by the words of institution and completed by the epiclesis. Nevertheless, the epiclesis is related not merely to the moral sanctification of the faithful and to Communion. It is necessary to refer it to the act of consecration itself—an act all the facets of which cannot be expressed simultaneously. One ought to consider it as an invocation of the Holy Spirit who, together with the Father and the Son, works the

---

92. Ibid., 282 citing Bossuet, ibid., 1.
93. Salaville, ibid., 295–96, 293–94. Cf. the same author's "Epiclèse . . . ," *Catholicisme*[4] (1956), 303–304.

transubstantiation at the moment that the priest pronounces the words
of the institution narrative.

The epiclesis is thus an explanation of what has already been
achieved. If placed before the institution narrative it would reduce the
latter too much to a secondary role. If placed within the institution
narrative it would interrupt the exact reproduction of the Last Supper.
Placed after the consecration it reflects the logical order of the three
Persons of the Trinity among themselves and in the economy of
salvation and also provides a natural link between the consecration
and Communion.[94]

The treatment many Roman Catholic theological manuals
give to the eucharistic epiclesis is rather meager.[95] For them the case
seems to be open and shut. In the majority of cases they preface their
treatment of the epiclesis question with statements of the magisterium
to the effect that the institution narrative alone is consecratory. Often
enough they paraphrase or quote directly the stance taken by Cardinal
Bessarion in response to Mark of Ephesus some years after the
Council of Florence:

> For it is necessary to understand these [prayers], and others of this type,
> not as in the time *in* which they are said, but as in the time *for* which they
> are said, and as if that time stood still and ceased to flow, so that now they
> would all be said in one and the same moment. . .[96]

Many of the manuals thus offer an explanation similar to
that of Salaville who, as we have just seen, offers a nuanced form of
Bessarion's basic position.

The general uniformity which one finds in regard to the
theological explanations of the epiclesis offered within the Roman
Catholic tradition, at least in so far as theological manuals are concerned, makes it unnecessary to cite other authors here. An examination

---

94. Salaville, "Epiclèse eucharistique," 296–97. Cf. also, Salaville's "L'èpiclèse d'après saint
Jean Chrysostome," 110-11, "Spiritus liturgiae . . . ," 134 ff. and "A propos de l'épiclèse," 567–68
as well Cabrol's "Epiclèse," 172–73.

95. In addition to the manuals mentioned in nn. 97, 68, and exception being made for
Heinrich-Gutberlet, we night add J. de Aldama et al. *Sacrae Theologiae Summa* IV (Matriti,
1956³) and M. Premm, *Katholische Glaubenskunde* III/1: *Allgemeine Sakramentenlehre . . .* ,
(Vienna, 1954), 284–85.

96. Bessarion, *De sacramento eucharistiae et quibus verbis Christi corpus conficiature* (PG,
161:516–17) (Italics mine).

of a number of the theological manuals published in the modern period
quickly confirms this impression of uniformity.[97] It is true that many
of the authors of these manuals make at least a terse attempt, as already
noted, to relate the epiclesis to Communion. By and large, however,
the criticism that many treatments of the epiclesis tend to isolate it
from its context within the whole eucharistic prayer and to view it too
one-sidedly from the point of view of transubstantiation [98]applies here.
The shadow of the moment of consecration is clearly in evidence. In
fact the uniformity is so great, the approach of numerous Roman
Catholic writers to the epiclesis seems at times so cramped, that it raises
an important question. Can a Roman Catholic theologian, in view of
the numerous statements of the magisterium on the exclusive consecratory role of the words of institution, even entertain the possibility
of a theological explanation that gives some consecratory value to the
epiclesis? Or have such statements closed the case and barred the way,
at least for a Roman Catholic, to such a possibility? In the next
chapter, therefore, before examining two other explanations of the
epiclesis, viz., that it is an expression of the role of the praying, believing
assembly and/or of the Holy Spirit in the Eucharist, we shall attempt
to answer this question. First, however, let us summarize this chapter.

SUMMARY

Any attempt to explain the epiclesis in terms of a "consecration
formula" runs into strong difficulties. The epiclesis as such is a prayer
and not a formula. Even those who maintain that it is consecratory,
generally do not regard it *alone* as consecratory. They tend rather to see
it as forming an indivisible consecratory unit with the institution

---

97. Cf., for instance, C. Pesch, *Compendium Theologiae Dogmaticae* IV (Freiburg i. Br., 1922²),
113 and the same author's *De Sacramentis* Pars I: *De sacramentis in genere* . . . (Freiburg i. Br.,
1914⁴), 370–71; B. J. Otten, *Institutiones Dogmaticae* V: *De sacramentis in genere* . . . (Chicago,
1923), 482–83; J. B. Heinrich and K. Gutberlet, *Dogmatische Theologie* IX: *Von den heiligen
Sakramenten* (Mainz, 1901), 729–37; E. Hugon, *Tractatus Dogmatici* III: *De Sacramentis in
Communi* . . . (Paris, 1927⁵), 406–407; J. C. Hedley, *The Holy Eucharist* (London, 1907), 79 80;
M. Scheeben-L. Atzberger, *Handbuch der Katholischen Dogmatik* IV (Freiburt i. Br., 1903—
"unveränderter Nachdruck" 1925), 619; Pohle-Gummersbach III (1960¹⁰), 284; Gutberlet, 52,
58; F. Diekamp-K. Jüssen, *Katholische Dogmatik* III (Münster, 195412), 127–29. This seems also
to be the basic position of Schmaus, 312 although he allows for the possibility of the Church's
some day declaring the epiclesis to be a necessary element of the external sign of the sacrament.
Cf. also, Brinktrine, "De Epiclesi . . . ," 159.

98. Cf. Laager, 585.

narrative. Moreover, to neglect the Communion aspect of the epiclesis is to fail to do justice to the liturgical data.

The explanation that the epiclesis expresses the necessary intention of the Church to have God realize here and now what Christ promised at the Last Supper seems to fit well into the eucharistic understanding of both East and West. Such an explanation, especially as Dinesen outlines it, seems to carry with it valuable insights for a proper understanding both of the Eucharist in general, and of the epiclesis in particular. However, this explanation, as we have seen it outlined, raises two important questions. One is, whether or not it is necessary to have an epiclesis proper to express this intention. The other is, whether or not the praying assembly really exercises a role in realizing the Eucharist.

The view that the epiclesis proper and the institution narrative form an inseparable unit within the consecratory Epiclesis underlines the tight bond between these two elements. Moreover, it seems that to deny that the whole canon with its institution narrative and/or epiclesis can play some role in the realization of the Eucharist is once again to neglect the liturgical and patristic data.

The view that through the epiclesis the already present body and blood of Christ become a *sacramentum,* i.e., an objective source of sanctification for those receiving them, raises the possibility of a fuller understanding of the term "consecration." At the same time it highlights the bond between "consecration" and Communion, as does the explanation which sees the epiclesis as the connecting link between "consecration" and Communion.

The opinion that the epiclesis was, and remains, basically an appeal for unity brings out the fact that the transformation for which the fully developed epiclesis usually appeals is not an end in itself. It is meant to lead to Christ's presence in the faithful—a presence which sanctifies them and unites them with his Father and with each other.

The position that the epiclesis is the result of the doctrine of appropriation and of the inability of human language to give voice simultaneously to all the facets of a given liturgical moment denies any consecratory value to the epiclesis and raises a question. May a Roman Catholic theologian propose an explanation which gives some consecratory value to the epiclesis? It is to this question that we now turn.

Chapter 6

The Epiclesis and the Structure of the Sacraments

Toward the end of the preceding chapter we discussed the position of some Roman Catholic theologians who do not grant any consecratory value to the eucharistic epiclesis. The uniformity and, at times, the inflexibility of such a refusal has raised the question of why so many Roman Catholic authors seem reluctant to consider even the possibility that the epiclesis might have such a consecratory value. This question, in turn, leads us to what at first glance may seem to be a digression. A treatment, however, of the notion of *substantia sacramenti* especially in relation to the epiclesis and the Roman Catholic teaching authority seems logical and necessary. It is a step toward understanding the above mentioned refusal and the position of the Roman Catholic teaching authority which may have inspired this refusal. Moreover, the insights that one gains from treating the notion of *substantia sacramenti* have important implications for the epiclesis question. These implications alone would justify the expenditure of time and energy.

Examples of Roman Catholic writers who reject the possibility that the epiclesis has consecratory worth are easy to find, especially in the early part of the twentieth century. E. Bishop, for instance, writing in 1909, remarks that theologians may differ on the fine points of whether this or that word in the institution narrative belongs to the form of the Eucharist. The basic position, however, that it is through the words of institution, ". . . at 'meum' [of 'corpus meum'] [that] the bread is transubstantiated into the Body of our Lord . . . ," remains unshaken. For Bishop this is a matter of faith: "It is this that the Roman Catholic *has* to believe; this is the position he *has* to take up, to hold, whether for theory or practice; it is therefore without any reserves mine."[1]

Bishop takes cognizance of the "passing phenomena" of those who hold that the letter of Eugenius III to the Armenians is not an infallible decision and of the suggestions that the Church's authority over matter and form may prove more extensive than previously supposed. He also mentions somewhat skeptically that Buchwald in his study of the epiclesis in the Roman Mass, "even ventures to treat the authoritative teaching as to the 'form' of the Sacrament of the Eucharist as if only a presently received 'practice' . . ." All of this, however, leaves the eminent British liturgist unmoved. "But indications such as these in no way affect the duty or position of the simple layman like myself in regard to the main question as stated above."[2]

In his dissertation on the epiclesis published in 1910, F. Varaine questions Bishop's claim that the exclusive consecratory value of the institution narrative is "of faith" or "Catholic truth." He adds, nevertheless, that although it should technically be called *sententia certa*, this is in fact what the Church believes.[3] The task, as Varaine sees it, consists mainly in reconciling the liturgical data with the Catholic belief that the institution narrative alone "consecrates."[4]

For S. Salaville in 1909 it was also a question of simply interpreting the epiclesis as found in the liturgical data in a sense favorable to the traditional doctrine of consecration by the words of institution.[5] In fact, it is this attitude which leads G. C. Smit to accuse Salaville of a certain lack of objectivity in the face of the data of tradition.[6]

M. Jugie, writing in 1943, is only one of many authors who state that, although Catholic teaching on the epiclesis is *not yet* ("nondum") a defined dogma, it is "proxima fidei."[7] In the same vein, Th. Spacil's 1929 review criticizes the position which G. Kosteljnik adopted in his book on the epiclesis published a year earlier.[8] Spacil

---

1. Bishop, "The Moment . . . ," 130 n. 1. (Italics mine)
2. Ibid.
3. Varaine, *L'épiclèse* . . . , 14.
4. Varaine, "L'épiclèse . . . ," 122.
5. Salaville, "L'épiclèse dans le canon romain de la messe," 305.
6. Smit, 102 n. 26 and 99 n. 11.
7. Jugie, *De forma* . . . , 38–39.
8. G. Kosteljnik, *Lis de epiclesi inter orientem et occidentem* (Leopoli, 1929).

complains that Kosteljnik fails to take into account statements of the magisterium which, although not solemn definitions, ". . . are authoritative decisions of the magisterium, which the Catholic theologian may not ignore."[9] J. Brinktrine makes much the same objection to Casel's theory regarding the development from the Epiclesis, i.e., the whole canon as consecratory, into the epiclesis proper.[10]

These examples should suffice to indicate that at least for Catholic authors writing in modern times there is no possibility that the epiclesis proper could make up part of the form of the Eucharist. Besides having a definite impact on attempts to work out a theology of the epiclesis, such a situation is bound to have ecumenical repercussions. Any attempt, for instance, of Rome to meet the Orthodox halfway by acknowledging that, at least in the East, the epiclesis has consecratory value would meet with stiff resistance in this atmosphere. F. Rett, for example, in an article on matter and form published in 1911 concludes that the Church has not allowed a change in the eucharistic form to include the epiclesis, although this would have had ecumenical advantages, because she *cannot* allow such a change and still be true to the principles defined by Trent.[11]

It is not surprising, then, to find among modern writers a prevailing pessimism at the prospects of finding a solution to the epiclesis question. E. Bishop, writing in 1909, reflected such a pessimism when he stated in regard to the controversy between the Roman Catholic and the Orthodox Churches:

> . . . Nor does it seem that the two contradictory assertions can be resolved into a common affirmation except by way of retractation on the one part or the other, explicit or implicit but certainly actual, such as cannot but become notorious among the people too. This it is which from the theological point of view also (it would seem) makes the case so hardly manageable.[12]

The question of immediate concern here is: What are the roots of the apparent inflexibility of some Roman Catholic authors when dealing with the epiclesis question?

---

9. Spacil, "Lis de epiclesi . . . ," 103.

10. Brinktrine, "Neue Beiträge . . . , 441 n. 33.

11. F. Rett, "Zur Frage über Materie, Form und Spender der Sakramente und die Gewalt der Kirche darüber," *Weidenauer Studien* 4 (1911), 289–98, esp. 295; cf. 274.

12. Bishop, "The Moment . . . ," 146–47. Cf. also, Höller, "Die Epiklese . . . ," 114, who cites Salaville and Alexios of Maltzew as expressing similar pessimism, and Rauschen, 126.

The Roman Catholic magisterium has exercised an important influence on these theologians.[13] Trent has defined that the Church cannot change the "substance of the sacraments."[14] Within the Scholastic framework, however, the concentration on the moment of consecration tended toward an either-or situation in regard to the consecratory value of the institution narrative and the epiclesis. To grant the epiclesis a consecratory value would seem to many to rob the institution narrative of such value. As we have seen in Chapter 2, the Roman Catholic teaching authority reflects this point of view and in regard to the epiclesis seems to reach something of a culmination in the statement of Pius X that the epiclesis cannot share in the consecration because, ". . . Ecclesiae minime competere jus circa ipsam sacramentorum substantiam quidpiam innovandi . . ." [The church does not have the right to make innovations regarding the substance of the sacraments.][15] Thus to admit that the eucharistic epiclesis could make up part of the *specific form* of the Eucharist would seem to many, including Pius X, to contradict Trent's definition regarding the *substantia sacramenti*. If such an admission does, indeed, involve a change in the substance of the sacrament the case, for a Roman Catholic theologian at any rate, is closed. It is to this question that we now turn our attention.

In the light of epiclesis, what is the *substantia sacramenti* of which Trent speaks? A brief examination of efforts to answer this question (closely related to, but not identical with, the question of the "moment of consecration") seems to be a necessary preliminary to any attempt by a Roman Catholic theologian to take another look at the epiclesis question. The conclusions of such an examination, if valid, would seem to hold for the other sacraments as well as for the Eucharist. They might also provide important insights into other facets of the eucharistic epiclesis.

THE EPICLESIS AND THE *SUBSTANTIA SACRAMENTI*

By now it should be evident that there are many ways of approaching the epiclesis and of bringing out its various facets. Fortunately for our

---

13. Cf. Rahner, "Die Gegenwart . . .," 357 ff. and SH, 309 as well as our own Chapter 2.
14. Cf. DS, 1728 (931).
15. DS, 3556 (2147a).

present purposes, E. Schillebeeckx in his *De Sacramentele Heilseconomie*
had made a penetrating analysis of the question of the *substantia
sacramenti*, in conjunction with his treatment of the epiclesis.

The Evidence of the Historical Data

As a basis for his conclusions Schillebeeckx makes a rather thorough
investigation of the historical data on the outward shape (the "matter"
and "form") of the sacraments of baptism, confirmation, and the
Eucharist.[16] We shall have to content ourselves here with a rather
broad sketch of his conclusions. We shall limit ourselves primarily to
Schillebeeckx's findings in regard to what he refers to as the liturgical
word or the "form" since this is of immediate import for the epiclesis
question. His findings in regard to the liturgical action or "matter" also
are important, however, since they at times indirectly substantiate the
evidence pertaining to the "form."

In his treatment of the development of the baptismal rite[17]
Schillebeeckx arrives at a number of interesting conclusions regarding
the liturgical word or form of this sacrament. Although we have no
absolute proof, the apparent early Christological form of the confession
of faith and the apparent later appearance of a Trinitarian confession
of faith would seem to indicate that a Christological confession of
faith served as the form of the baptismal rite in apostolic times.[18] In the
patristic period the epiclesis over the water seems to have played an
essential role in the baptismal rite. Through it the Holy Spirit made the
waters into an objective instrument of salvation. A Trinitarian profession of faith also played an essential role. Whoever in a spirit of faith
(expressed by the profession of faith) allowed himself to be immersed
in this water, now sanctified by the Holy Spirit through the epiclesis,

---

16. SH, 239–354. In *Christ the Sacrament*, 145 n. 1 Schillebeeckx lists similar studies made in
regard to the outward shape of the other sacraments. In addition to the works cited there we
might mention, Pascher, *Form und Formenwandel* . . .; B. Kleinheyer, *Die Priesterweihe im römischen
Ritus* (Trier, 1962); L. Ott, *Das Weihesakrament* (Freiburg, 1969). Of special interest is an article
by B. Fischer, "Das Gebet der Kirche als Wesenselement des Weihesakramentes," *Liturgisches
Jahrbuch* 20 (1970) 166–77. Cf. also, G. Kretschmar, "Die Geschichte des Taufgottesdienstes in
der alten Kirche," *Leiturgia* 5 (1970), 1-348 in *Leiturgia: Handbuch des evangelischen Gottesdienstes,*
ed. by K. F. Muller and J. Blankenburg (Kassel, 1952 ff.), and J.D.C. Fisher, *Christian Initiation:
Baptism in the Medieval West* (London, 1965).

17. SH, 240–83.

18. Cf. SH, 263–83.

received baptism. Thus up to the fourth century, and in some areas perhaps even up to the fifth and sixth centuries, the liturgical word or form of the sacrament was twofold. It consisted of an epiclesis over the water and a profession of faith, or, as Schillebeeckx puts it, of two epicleses since the profession of faith was also in a sense an epiclesis.[19]

In the course of time the "classical," declarative formula, which seems first to have come into use around the end of the fourth or beginning of the fifth century, took the place of the Trinitarian profession of faith at the moment of immersion. The Trinitarian profession of faith remained in the rite but in another position. From the Scholastic period on, the declarative formula of the Roman ritual took over the functions of both the epiclesis over the water and the profession of faith. Nevertheless, contends Schillebeeckx, these aspects were still in some way contained in the formula which although declarative was still appreciated as an appeal for the Holy Spirit and a testimony of the Church's Trinitarian faith. It has to be admitted, however, that the declarative formula, while it did bring out the objective instrumentality of the sacraments, also carried with it the danger that the role of the Holy Spirit and the prayer, faith character of the sacrament would be lost sight of.[20]

Having studied the historical development of the liturgical word, the *verba sacramenti* of baptism, Schillebeeckx concludes that the content, the faith-theme, is decisive. The form used to express this faith whether it be the form of an epiclesis, a detailed profession of faith or a Trinitarian formula is basically secondary.[21]

The historical data on the development of the form of confirmation seems to have followed lines similar to those found in the development of the baptismal form. Originally a simple prayer seems to have served as the *verba sacramenti*. Later one encounters a twofold form which consisted of an epiclesis and a formula. The original prayer had in the meantime been shifted forward and was no longer considered part of the *verba sacramenti*. The resemblance between the development of the consecration of the myron or chrism and that of the consecration of the baptismal water is striking. The oil like the water had, according to the Fathers, its consecratory force only through the

---

19. SH, 252. Cf. 240–53.
20. SH, 252–53; cf. SH, 248–62 for the treatment of the general development of the "form."
21. SH, 267.

epiclesis which was prayed over it. In the East this consecration of the myron was regarded almost as a sacrament in itself.[22]

Unlike the consecration of the water, however, the consecration of the chrism retained much of its force in the eyes of theologians. Saint Thomas and in general the theologians of his day considered this latter consecration as a condition for the validity of confirmation. There is nothing, however, in Church documents to indicate that it is *now* seen as a condition for validity. Thus we have a phenomenon similar to that in baptism. In the patristic period the constitution of the *sacramentum*, the sacrament as an objective instrument of salvation, consisted of two moments: the epiclesis and the confirmation formula. Whether or not the formula eventually took both functions upon itself as was the case in baptism, is less clear in the case of confirmation.[23]

Schillebeeckx's conclusions from his study of the data on the form of confirmation parallel his conclusions on the form of baptism and the matter of confirmation. Despite the fact that the substantial sacramental meaning of the rite remained the same there have been radical changes in the form of this sacrament.[24]

We have already seen various aspects of Schillebeeckx's interpretation of the data in regard to the eucharistic "form."[25] It should suffice here to recall some of these briefly. The Fathers considered the whole eucharistic prayer as a consecratory, Trinitarian Epiclesis, which Schillebeeckx considers essential to any Christian sacrament although it may lie hidden in a declarative formula.[26] Because different facets of the Trinitarian Epiclesis in this sense appear in different sacraments this Epiclesis must be more closely determined in each sacrament, much the same as light reflected through a prism can take on different shades. Thus it seems that Fathers regarded the entire canon as a single Trinitarian Epiclesis which the institution narrative specified as a *eucharistic* Epiclesis in the broad sense. Since on the other hand the words of institution are basically narrative in form and since all the sacraments draw their form and effective power from a *verbum fidei* which informs the sacrament ("een informerend 'verbum

---

22. SH, 304–306.
23. Cf. ibid.
24. SH, 306.
25. Cf. above, chapter 5.
26. SH, 343–44.

fidei'") a brief epiclesis proper calling the Holy Spirit down upon the offerings was added.

With the growing precision of the consecratory epiclesis arose the problem of the relationship between the institution narrative and the epiclesis proper within the consecratory canon as a whole. The East tended to lay stress on the epiclesis; the West on the institution narrative. In the early centuries, however, neither did so to the exclusion of the other element. Only later, as we have seen in Chapter 2, was attention focused on a moment of consecration. Since this development it has become the constant tradition of the Roman Catholic teaching authority to affirm with a strong degree of exclusivity the words of institution as the Eucharistic form. The Orthodox have on the other hand, and at times with similar exclusivity, stressed the role of the epiclesis.[27]

Schillebeeckx's conclusions regarding the historical data on the Eucharist may be summed up as follows: For the Fathers the eucharistic prayer as a whole was consecratory. There was a twofold central moment of "forma eucharistica" which consisted of institution narrative and epiclesis.[28] Whether this twofold moment was a *"forma transsubstantiationis"* or a *"forma sacramenti"* (in the patristic sense of *sacramentum*, an objective source of salvation) remains an open question. What is clear is this: there has been an evident change in the concrete form (the *subjectum significationis*) of the Eucharist while the signification expressed in words and gestures, the *substantia sacramenti* has remained unchanged.[29] Schillebeeckx sums up well the general conclusion of his study of confirmation and the Eucharist as well as similar investigations of the other sacraments when he states:

> . . . The positive data provided by an investigation of this kind show clearly that there has been enormous variation in the shape of the liturgical word and the liturgical action (the so-called form and matter) but that, even so, the general direction of the sense manifested in each sacrament has remained constant.[30]

---

27. Cf. SH, 329–54, esp. 342–44 for the stages of this development as Schillebeeckx sees it.

28. Cf. Botte, "L'épiclèse . . . syriennes orientales," 69.

29. Cf. SH, 353–54.

30. Schillebeeckx, *Christ the Sacrament*, 145–46; cf. 157–58. Cf. also, Pascher, *Form* . . . , esp. 31–32, 68–69; Pourrat, 76–77 n. 2; Lebreton, 430.

Specific *Form* Not *Substance of Sacrament*

The situation that confronts one, then, is this: Trent has defined that the Church cannot change the substance of the sacraments as instituted by Christ. This historical data reveals, however, that the specific form of the sacraments has undergone change, at times even radical change. The logical conclusion, for a Roman Catholic theologian at least, would seem to be that the specific form is not to be identified with the *substantia sacramenti*. If one grants that the eucharistic epiclesis was once also considered an essential part of a twofold consecratory moment (of "form"), however one explains this twofold moment of "form," the same conclusion would seem to hold true for the Eucharist. The specific "form" has undergone change without, however, modifying the substance of the sacrament.

Some would deny this. In a work published in 1960, A. M. Roguet, for instance, in examining statements that the Roman teaching authority has made concerning the "form" of the Eucharist, admits that the form has varied in other sacraments. The Church has in fact altered them. He contends, however, that for the Eucharist the case is different. The words of institution were established by Christ himself and are, therefore, necessary for the Eucharist.[31]

The historical data, however, although by no means absolute, seems to indicate that the epiclesis did at one time constitute part of the consecratory form of the Eucharist.[32] This would tend to favor the stand that Schillebeeckx takes on the question. He acknowledges that the institution narrative has a real consecratory value and that although this is not a solemn dogma we can consider it as a datum of our faith. Nevertheless, he contends that neither official Church documents in general, nor the Councils of Florence and Trent, nor such statements as contained in the decree of the Holy Office on May 23, 1957,[33] support a *de fide* argument that the essential sacramental significance belongs exclusively to the words of institution. None of

---

31. Roguet, *L'Eucharistie* I, 389. The possibility that another element (e.g., the epiclesis) could *also* be considered necessary without making the words of institution unnecessary does not seem to have presented itself as a serious consideration either in Roguet's own thought or in the documents he is citing.

32. Cf. Botte, "L'épiclèse . . . syriennes orientales," 69; Cabrol, "Epiclèse," 173–74; Betz, 328; Gouillard in Salaville, *Nicolas Cabasilas*, 32; Smit, 128–29; Lebreto, 430.

33. DS, 3928.

these documents exclude the possibility that the epiclesis could still have a consecratory value in liturgies where in fact such a sacramental significance is given to it.[34]

Schillebeeckx's stance raises two questions which may help shed light on the eucharistic epiclesis. First, how does one explain, in the light of Schillebeeckx's position, statements such as that of Pius X in regard to the epiclesis? Secondly, what is the *substantia sacramenti?*

In regard to the first question, it is clear that, despite all the weaknesses in the Council of Florence discussion of the epiclesis and in the *Decree for the Armenians,* the Roman Catholic Church, while not defining it, has taught officially that the institution narrative alone has consecratory value.[35] The question is why did the official magisterium take such a stand? In a day and age when the hermeneutical principles of *form criticism* are generally accepted as applied to the Bible, there seems to be no reason why one cannot apply a certain form criticism to papal and conciliar statements.[36]

In fact Schillebeeckx has done just that in regard to the question of the eucharistic presence, and the doctrine of transubstantiation.[37] His study is a good example of both the method and its fruits. Schillebeeckx lays the groundwork for his later conclusions by examining the origin, growth, and final draft of canons 1 and 2 of the Council of Trent on the sacrament of the Eucharist.[38] The genesis of these canons leads to the conclusion that there are three different levels in the Tridentine dogma. First of all, we have the core of the dogma which lies in the affirmation of a specific and distinctive *eucharistic* presence, namely, the real presence of Christ's body and blood under the sacramental species of bread and wine (canon 1). The insistence on the *lasting* character of this presence underlines its special and distinctive quality and thus distinguishes it from the presence in

---

34. Cf. SH, 333–35 and *Christ the Sacrament,* 158–59; cf. also, SH, 388–91. Schmaus, 312 seems to take a similar stand when he states that the Church could declare the epiclesis proper a necessary element of the external sign.

35. Cf. Chapter 2.

36. Cf. Schillebeeckx, *The Eucharist,* 25–29.

37. Ibid.

38. Ibid., 29–39; cf. DS, 1651–52 (883–84). Schillebeeckx's approach here seems superior to that of Rahner, "Die Gegenwart . . . ," 362 who states: "It should be noted here that the history of the discussion on this point at the Council is not very instructive and helpful. Therefore, it will not be specifically treated." The results of Schillebeeckx's investigation seem to belie this statement.

the other sacraments. Secondly, we have the expression of the distinctive mode of Christ's presence in the Eucharist. Schillebeeckx contends that, given the historical circumstances, the fathers of the Council of Trent *could not* establish or express the eucharistic real presence unless they insisted on the acceptance of a change of the substance of bread and wine into the substance of Christ's body and blood (canon 2). Finally, we have the terminology. The change of bread and wine was very suitably (*aptissime*) called transubstantiation (final sentence of canon 2). This final level is the most relative of the three.[39]

The reasoning of both Bonaventure and Thomas followed a similar pattern. They began with the indisputable fact of faith, a distinctive real presence in the Eucharist. Because of what this implied for them they concluded—on the basis of theological reasoning—to a change of the substance of the bread.[40]

> . . . For Thomas especially, the "change of the substance" of the bread and the wine was a theological conclusion drawn *from* the datum of faith of the unique eucharistic presence. It was only then—in the *third* place as it were—that Thomas appealed to the Aristotelian doctrine of the substance and its accidents.[41]

What is most significant for our study is Schillebeeckx's contention that within the historical, and especially philosophical, framework in which they found themselves the fathers of the Council of Trent had to affirm a change in the substance of bread and wine. Within the prevailing Aristotelian framework of thought, "it was impossible to safeguard the distinctively Catholic character of Christ's real presence in the Eucharist without affirming transubstantiation."[42] One can raise the question today, as Schillebeeckx himself does, whether it is not possible to have a *real*, ontological change in the bread and wine without necessarily having to appeal to a "trans-substantiation," in the Aristotelian sense. Within this framework, then, the Roman teaching authority seems to have seen only one way to protect a vital truth. This way consisted in proclaiming the *exclusive* consecratory value of the

---

39. Schillebeeckx, ibid., 39–53. Cf. also, Powers, 34–40, esp. 38–40 and Thurian *L'Eucharistie*, 261 and the same author's *Le pain unique*, 58–61.

40. Schillebeeckx, ibid., 48–51.

41. Ibid., 50–51.

42. Ibid., 59; cf. 53–63.

words of institution. While one may be able today to envisage, from within another philosophical framework, a different solution to the epiclesis question, to demand this of theologians and magisterium from another era would be to demand too much.[43]

Schillebeeckx's conclusions in regard to Trent are significant for the present study because they suggest similar conclusions regarding the magisterium and the epiclesis. At the end of Chapter 2 the question was raised whether the Roman teaching authority, situated as it was in the either-or framework of instantaneous transubstantiation, could have taken another stand on the epiclesis without, in its eyes, denying any consecratory value to the institution narrative. In light of Schillebeeckx's conclusions regarding the real presence and in view of the historical evidence on the question of the epiclesis, the answer would seem to be, "No." The truth which the magisterium was trying to protect, the datum of faith as it were, was that the words of institution have received a certain consecratory value or power from God. In the framework of instantaneous transubstantiation it seems to have appeared that to affirm a consecratory value for the epiclesis would be to deny consecratory value to the words of institution.

The comparison between the question of the real presence and the question of the eucharistic epiclesis does not, it is true, represent an exact parallel. Nor have we been able here to analyze the official documents on the epiclesis question as thoroughly as Schillebeeckx has analyzed Trent's statements on the real presence. Nevertheless, the evidence seems sufficient to suggest that Schillebeeckx's study of the real presence holds valuable insights for the investigation of the epiclesis. Not only has he underlined the relativity of certain aspects in the doctrine of transubstantiation, that is, the terminology; he has also provided us with a clue to a plausible explanation of the differences between his position on *substantia sacramenti* and official statements, such as that of Pius X, regarding the epiclesis. These statements were drawn up by men convinced that the only way to preserve *any* consecratory value for the institution words was to proclaim that these words, and these words *alone,* formed the moment of consecration and were therefore exclusively consecratory.

---

43. Cf. ibid., 53–58, 62–75. Cf. Powers, 40 and C. Davis, 173.

The Meaning of *Substantia Sacramenti*

This leads to the second question which Schillebeeckx's position on the substance of the sacrament has raised. What is the meaning of *substantia sacramenti*? Since the shape of both liturgical action and liturgical word (matter and form) has undergone such far-reaching changes, the action and word in themselves cannot be the substance of the sacraments.[44] If they were, the Council of Trent's *salva substantia*[45] would stand in direct contradiction to the historical data. On the other hand, according to the common usage of the day the word *substance* does seem to have had for Trent some reference to matter and form.[46] In what sense, then, are the liturgical action and the liturgical word intrinsic, essential components of the *outward sacramental sign*?

To understand Schillebeeckx's theory on the substance of a sacrament one has to understand his notion of symbolic activity, here understood as an action which gives a meaning to matter and through which the properly spiritual activity of the person becomes visible or expresses itself. In the concrete, moreover, there is no such thing as a symbol without an act of the mind. It is the human spirit which gives new meaning to matter, which draws upon the latent capacity of matter to signify something other than itself. It is the human spirit, for instance, which takes ordinary food and drink and makes them a sign of solidarity, of interpersonal intimacy, of the sealing of a friendship in a meal. It is, then, the human mind which establishes a link between the sign and the thing signified. Gestures and words play an important role in this symbolic activity since they externalize the intention of the person; they give this intention a sensible form. Thus the entirety of the symbolic activity consists in the intention—the movement of the mind creating the symbol—and the sign—the externalizing of the intention by a gesture and/or words. The combination of these two elements results in the *signification*.[47]

---

44. Crehan, "Epiklesis," 226, notwithstanding.

45. DS, 1728 (931).

46. Schillebeeckx, *Christ the Sacrament*, 115–16; cf. SH, 422.

47. For the various aspects of Schillebeeckx's understanding of symbolic activity, cf. SH, 394–403, *Christ the Sacrament*, 76–78 and *The Eucharist*, 99–101, 130–51. Cf. also, Smit, 131–32, who gives a good summary of Schillebeeckx's thought in this area, and K. Rahner, "Zur Theologie des Symbols," 275–311.

In the sacraments this signification stems from Christ. It is
the externalized (incarnated) intention of Christ. This intention,
however, can only be perceived fully through faith and this is where
the Church enters in. It is the Church's faith which perceives what
Christ intended to have expressed by words and gestures. In the
context of the sacraments, therefore, signification means the intention
of Christ as perceived by the Church and manifested by liturgical
actions and words.[48]

It is this signification in its fullest sense that makes up the
essence of the outward sign of the sacrament. It is this which forms
the *substantia sacramenti*. The substance of the sacrament (i.e., of the
outward sign) is not simply the spiritual meaning (*significatum*)
intended by Christ. Nor is it the liturgical action and word (matter
and form) considered in themselves. It is rather the combination of
these joined together by the faith of the Church.

> . . . The essence of a sacrament, explicitly or implicitly instituted by
> Christ, is the signification within a sevenfold orientation as it is externally
> manifested in a visible act of the Church, and hence in a (liturgical) action
> accompanied by a prayer of faith or an indicative formula of faith (in
> which the special direction of the signification is made manifest).[49]

This, then, is what must remain unchanged despite historical,
ecclesiastical alterations in the sacraments. In this light, Trent's "salva
substantia illorum" could best be understood as: "except for the sacramental signification, manifested by *some* word(s) (form) and *some*
gesture (matter) which according to the—(we would add here, faith)—
judgment of the Church is suited for the expression of this sacramental
signification."[50]

Within this view the Church could change the *specific* form of
the sacraments and still leave the substance of the sacrament untouched.
Within such a view it is conceivable, for instance, that the Church

---

48. Cf. SH, 403–408 and *Christ the Sacrament*, 116–17. Cf. also, Smit, 132–33.

49. Schillebeeckx, *Christ the Sacrament*, 155; cf. SH, 429. Cf. also, Smit, 134–35.

50. SH, 426. Once again it is important to note that Schillebeeckx is not equating substance
with the signification (in the sense of the simply spiritual meaning) intended by Christ. Rather,
for him the substance of the sacrament equals the signification incarnated in *some* word and some
gesture. Cf. SH, 425 and Smit, 133–135 n. 137.

could declare that the epiclesis, *in addition* to the words of institution would henceforth belong to what is called the form of the Eucharist.[51]

The Role of Faith in the Structure of the Sacraments

Besides giving us an explanation which enables us to reconcile Trent's definition with the historical data, Schillebeeckx's treatment of *substantia sacramenti* touches upon the importance of faith in the twofold structure of the sacramental sign. A close examination of the role that faith plays in this twofold structure may bring with it insights which are valuable for a proper understanding of the Eucharist in general, and of the eucharistic epiclesis in particular. Once again we turn to Schillebeeckx, this time for his treatment of the twofold structure of the *outward sign* of the sacraments.

Schillebeeckx begins by noting that in Scripture the liturgical action (e.g., washing with water, the laying on of hands, the breaking and sharing of the Eucharist) was always coupled with a prayer or a *word*. For the Fathers, too, the bringing together of an earthly and a heavenly element in the sacraments found its expression in a liturgical action and a *word* or epiclesis through which the *pneuma* of the *Logos* came down upon the material element. For the Fathers this word or prayer was a word of faith, the community's confession of faith in the sacramental event.

> . . . It is, that is to say, Christ's own proclamation of the word, made known by means of the Gospel, accepted through the faith of the Church, and confessed with regard to the sacramental action in a *verbum fidei*, a word of faith. Unquestionably the Fathers attributed a value to the word of faith above that of the element in the sacraments.[52]

Thus the Fathers were concerned directly with a mystical bringing together of an earthly element and the divine power invoked by a praying, believing community.

In contrast, the Scholastics, at least after the period of Hugh of St. Victor and Peter Lombard, concentrated more on the outward sacramental sign. They looked upon the word and the element as

---

51. The often cited case of the ordination rite offers a possible analogy for such a hypothesis. Cf. Pascher, *Form . . .* , 20–22, 68–69; SH, 429–41, esp. 434–41 and B. Fischer, "Das Gebet der Kirche als Wesenselement des Weihesakramentes," in *Liturgisches Jahrbuch* 20 (1970) 166–77.

52. Schillebeeckx, *Christ the Sacrament*, 111–12; cf. SH, 358–63. Cf. also Smit, 106–107.

constitutive parts without which the *outward sign* cannot be present. The terms *matter* and *form* used to describe these parts gradually took on Aristotelian overtones and precisions. Eventually the liturgical word was seen as fulfilling the function of *forma* in the strict Aristotelian sense of the principle of determination for the sacramental sign. In effect the great Scholastics were saying,

> . . . In the course of time the theory even came to be used as a principle from which conclusions could be drawn, and the original, merely comparative, character of its terminology was forgotten.[53]

One danger in the later Scholastic approach, a danger to which we shall return shortly, is that in focusing so much attention on the makeup of the outward sign it can give the impression that this is the whole of the sacramental event. It can thus allow the divine action to slip too far into the background.

To be fair to the writers of modern books within the Roman Catholic tradition, they do seem to have taken pains to point out that they are only speaking of the external rite of the sacraments when dealing with matter and form.[54] They are far less clear, however, on the role that the Church's faith plays in the formation of this same external rite. Here Schillebeeckx provides a healthy counterbalance. He points out that the Church's faith has to play an essential role in constituting the outward sacramental sign because it is only through faith that the Church can grasp the significance of what Christ intended and communicate this significance to those partaking:

> . . . Because a sacrament is a symbolic act of Christ in his Church, it is only through faith in Christ that the Church is able to make this spiritual signification manifest in her sacraments, and so the faith of the Church is necessary for the constitution of an outward sacramental sign.[55]

It is only in their signifying, in manifesting the Church's act of believing that the liturgical action and words belong to the essence of

---

53. Schillebeeckx, *Christ the Sacrament,* 113–14; cf. 111–14 for the outline of the whole development. Cf. also, E. Masure, *Le Signe* (Paris, 1953), 199–213.

54. Cf., for instance, M. Scheeben-L. Atzberger, *Handbuch der katholischen Dogmatik* IV (Freiburg i. Br., 1903), 480–82; J. B. Franzelin, *De Sacramentis in genere* (Rome, 1905[5]), 33–34, 69–70; C. Pesch, *De Sacramentis* Pars I (Freiburg i. Br., 1914[4]), 47; J. B. Heinrich-K. Gutberlet, *Dogmatische Theologie* IX (Mainz, 1901), 60; Pohle (Gummersbach) (1960[10]), 47–50; F. Diekamp-K. Jüssen, *Katholische Dogmatik* III (Münster, 1953[12]), 9–12.

55. Schillebeeckx, *Christ the Sacrament,* 117.

a sacrament. Simply putting together matter and form, words and gestures, does not constitute a sacrament *or even* the outward sign of a sacrament. The structure of the outward sign of the sacrament is indeed twofold, consisting of action and word. But the word is the *verbum fidei*. It involves faith. Otherwise it is insufficient. To overlook this is to stand on the brink of sacramental physicism.[56]

To sum up this section briefly: To constitute the outward sacramental sign there must be a liturgical action plus a liturgical word *plus* the faith of the Church. Or, in other words, the actions and words express the Church's faith. The awareness of the crucial importance of the Church's faith in the composition of even the outward sign of the sacrament leads to the next major consideration.

THE EPICLESIS AND THE PRAYING, BELIEVING ASSEMBLY

The relationship between the epiclesis and the role of the praying, believing assembly is the next object of discussion. It is hoped an examination of the various aspects of this relationship may provide some valuable perspectives for the proper understanding of both these elements in the eucharistic action.

E. Schillebeeckx, for instance, reflects some characteristics of the Roman Catholic approach to both the epiclesis and the role of the praying, believing assembly. First of all, he maintains that the Church or the assembly plays an unmistakable role in the realization of, in the causality of the sacraments.

> . . . it is the Church's sacramental word of faith that actually brings about the saving manifestation of Christ's redemptive act in the sacrament. Through an *epiclesis*, that is, through a word or prayer by which God is "called down," Christ's act of redemption comes into the Church's act.[57]

However real this causality might be, it is an instrumental and subordinate causality and has to be understood within the context of the Church's role as the visible prolongation of Christ on earth. The basis for the Church's firm belief that the sacraments will cause what

---

56. Cf. ibid., 114 (Cf. also 117–122).
57. Ibid., 121.

they symbolize, that they will certainly sanctify whoever opens himself up to them, lies in the belief that Christ is here and that he is praying with the assembly or, rather, that the assembly is praying with him. This is the basis for the proper understanding of *ex opere operato* as well as for the proper understanding of a declarative formula when such is used in the sacraments.[58]

Despite its role in realizing the sacraments and its assurance that God will act, the assembly must always approach the sacraments as a praying, pleading assembly. Even when the rites no longer reveal it, this "epiclesis attitude" must always be present.

> This twofold aspect of the sacraments (first Christ's own ritual prayer for grace, in which the Church prayerfully joins and with it gives ritual expression to her prayer, and second the effective bestowal of the prayed-for grace) helps us the better to grasp that the substance of a sacrament always includes a twofold element: an *epiclesis* in the form of a request (*in forma deprecativa*), that is to say, a prayer in which we plead with the Father by the power of the Spirit and together with Christ; and a definitive bestowal (*in forma indicativa*). Both elements are always present, even when they no longer appear, as was formerly the case, in two separate ritual moments in the Liturgy. Moreover, the one essential moment (whether it be an expression in the form of an epiclesis or an exclusively indicative formula) has in any case the twofold significance.[59]

It is also characteristic of the Roman Catholic tradition and in line with Schillebeeckx's position on the substance of the sacraments to regard the epiclesis *proper* as not absolutely necessary for the realization of the sacrament.[60] Schillebeeckx acknowledges, however, that the absence of a clear-cut epiclesis can lead to unfortunate misunderstandings. One can get *and give* the impression that the effectiveness of the sacrament rests to a great extent on the mere juxtaposition of words and gestures. This juridical interpretation of the sacraments, though unjustifiable, can more readily slip in when the epiclesis aspect of the sacraments is lost sight of.[61] An explicit epiclesis could help underline both the divine action and the faith of the community.

---

58. Cf. ibid., 55–109.
59. Ibid., 87.
60. Cf. Smit, 135.
61. Schillebeeckx, *Christ the Sacrament*, 87.

L. Bouyer in his *Eucharistie*, while refusing to be drawn into the polemic over the consecratory value of the epiclesis proper, also affirms the interplay between the divine action and the praying assembly in realizing the Eucharist:

> In other words, the consecrator of all of these eucharists is always Christ alone, the Word made flesh, insofar as he is ever the dispenser of the Spirit because he handed himself over to death and then rose from the dead by the power of this same Spirit. *But in the indivisible totality of the Eucharist, this Word, evoked by the Church, and her own prayer calling for the fulfillment of the Word through the power of the Spirit come together for the mysterious fulfillment of the divine promises.*[62]

Bouyer thus seems to see no dichotomy between the divine action and human action in the realization of the Eucharist.

In a study which first appeared in 1921, M. de la Taille also acknowledges a role to the Church's faith in the realization of the sacraments. He does so, moreover, in a manner that might be said to be characteristically Roman Catholic in that it gives strong emphasis to the role of the ordained minister. De la Taille suggests that a priest consecrates only as manifesting the faith of the Church. He must have the intention of doing what Christ intended to be done. In other words, he must intend to signify what the Church's faith has perceived to be the signification which Christ intended for this sacrament.[63] If he does this, "then his action will be effective and he will consecrate."[64]

De la Taille also acknowledges the need for an implicit invocation or an "epiclesis attitude." To begin with, in order to be effective the institution narrative must either be interwoven with or preceded by some form of prayer in which God is addressed. Otherwise one would simply have a historical narrative. Moreover, there can be no consecration without at least an implicit appeal for transformation. Referring to statements of Gregory Nyssa and John Chrysostom he remarks:

> . . . It is quite true that these and many other Greek Fathers, as well as not a few Latin Fathers, did say that the consecration was effected by some kind of invocation of God. . . but such a view is in no way repugnant to

---

62. Bouyer, *Eucharistie*, 433–34 (467) (Italics mine).

63. De la Taille, 393–98, esp. 395 n. 1 and 398. Cf. Gallagher, 241–42.

64. De la Taille, 396.

our thesis, for as we shall see later, there can be no consecrative narrative of the Supper which does not contain an implicit petition for transmutation.[65]

He contends that such a petition for transformation is contained, in a "pragmatic" way, in the word of institution as recited in the Mass. The basis for this claim is the view that every offering of a victim implicitly contains an appeal for its acceptance, and acceptance in the case of the Eucharist involves a transformation of the gifts into the body and blood of Christ.[66] De la Taille's conclusion in regard to the epiclesis proper places him squarely within the Roman Catholic tradition. For him the epiclesis proper, while it is appropriate, is neither necessary nor efficacious.[67]

P. Dinesen would also object to giving the epiclesis proper a causal character but would do so on entirely different grounds. As noted in the preceding chapter, Dinesen succeeds very well in bringing out the prayer character of the epiclesis and its function as an expression of the faith of the assembly. For him the assembly in praying the epiclesis expresses its faith in the former wonderful deeds of God—deeds which include the Last Supper—and at the same time manifests its belief that God will realize the eucharistic wonder *here and now* in its midst. Dinesen balks, however, at the thought that through the epiclesis the praying, believing assembly exercises any role, however subordinate, in realizing or causing the wonder of the Eucharist. His objection stems not, as was the case with de la Taille, simply from the refusal to grant the epiclesis proper any efficacy. In Dinesen's case it seems to be rather a question of refusing the assembly itself any efficacy, through any prayer or formula whatsoever.[68]

Perhaps J. J. von Allmen's position on the epiclesis holds the key to understanding the reserve which Dinesen and others show in regard to the role of the praying, believing assembly in realizing the Eucharist. Von Allmen notes that the form of the epiclesis is less important than the attitude which it imposes on the Church. The form is, nevertheless, important. It provides a corrective to the "magical interpretation" of

---

65. Ibid., 413 n. 1; cf. 464–73.

66. Cf. ibid., 437–39, 422–25 and 471. Cf. also, F. J. Wengier, *The Eucharist-Sacrifice* (Milwaukee, 1945), 184–85.

67. Cf. de la Taille, 419–37.

68. Cf. above, Chapter 5.

the Eucharist which sees the words of institution as practically coercing God. The immediate context of the epiclesis is that of the presence of Christ in worship. And the Church, the assembly, is totally dependent on God for this presence. ". . . it cannot be induced, it can only be besought. *Maranatha!*"[69] The epiclesis serves as a reminder that the Church is essentially praying, and not reigning, in the Eucharist. The epiclesis makes the assembly clearly dependent in its *Maranatha*.[70]

Von Allmen makes it clear, however, that it is not a question of doubting. Those assembled believe that God will certainly keep his promise, but freely and sovereignly as their Lord. The assembly waits in hope and expectation. It is ". . . open to the free and sovereign action of its Lord: it does not seek to manipulate it. In this sense, it is the antithesis of magic."[71] It is this desire to avoid any possibility of a magical, mechanistic interpretation which explains the reserve which some show in regard to the assembly's role in the Eucharist. This same desire leads von Allmen to prefer, contrary to P. Brunner, the epiclesis *after* the institution narrative as the Orthodox have it.[72]

Not only does von Allmen regard the epiclesis as a corrective to a magical interpretation because it rings out the dependence of the praying assembly upon God; he also sees the epiclesis as a corrective to an over-clericalization of the Eucharist. It brings out the fact that it is the *whole* Assembly which, through the mouth of the priest, calls upon God to make his presence felt *here and now*. Thus, a proper understanding of the eucharistic epiclesis would be a step toward de-clericalizing our understanding of the Eucharist.[73]

From within the Orthodox tradition we find C. Kern, in conjunction with his treatment of the epiclesis which appeared in *Irenikon* in 1951, expressing similar reservations in regard to the special role of the priest or minister of the sacrament. The celebrant is only an image, a symbol of Christ. He acts in the name of the assembly by

---

69. Von Allmen, *Worship* . . . , 28.

70. Von Allmen, *Essai* . . . , 31–33. Cf. MacLean, 407.

71. Von Allmen, *Worship* . . . , 29; cf. 162–63, 244. Cf. along the same lines Brunner, "Zur Lehre . . . ," 352–53. Cf. also, Hahn, 18, and Meyendorff, "Notes . . . ," 28.

72. Von Allmen, ibid., 30–32 and Essai . . . , 33–34. Cf. also, Schmidt-Lauber, 167 referring to Brunner, "Zur Lehre . . . ," 360, 356 ff.

73. Von Allmen, *Essai* . . . , 35–36. Cf. also, F. Heiler, "Ein liturgischer Brüchenschlag zwischen Ost und West," *Eine Heilige Kirche* 21 (1939) 251, 253–54; W. C. Bishop, "The Primitive Form . . . ," 393 and Thurian, *Le pain unique*, 75–77, 92, 99 and esp. 96.

praying for the Holy Spirit and not by pronouncing a "consecration formula" and thereby manifesting his own power.[74] Moreover, it is the Holy Spirit alone who consecrates, and distinctions such as *minister secundus et instrumentalis* and *minister primus et principalis* are subtleties not found in the Fathers and lost on the oriental mind.[75]

N. Nissiotis, Orthodox professor and Director of the Ecumenical Institute of the World Council of Churches in Chateau de Bossey, Switzerland, also refuses to see the priest's role, while unique and important as it may be, apart from the role of the whole assembly. The Catholic Church does see a difference between the priesthood of the baptized and the ministerial priesthood. He develops the point more positively than Kern, however, and therefore seems to strike a better balance. Writing in 1963, Nissiotis notes that liturgical prayer is not merely an individual, subjective petition. It involves the encounter between God present in space and time and the praying, worshipping community gathered together to receive the coming Lord and to express this coming in earthly symbols. The whole concept of prayer, then, is a reciprocal one, involving God's presence as well as our attempt to respond to that presence. This is the reason that the key moment of the Eucharist is the invocation of the Holy Spirit who acts not only upon the elements but also upon the faithful. This invocation, which helps unite, in the Body of Christ, the invisible world with the visible world, the celestial with the earthly, belongs to, is the "reserved 'right' " of the *whole* assembly.[76] It is:

> . . . an act which can be performed not by a cleric who repeats the words of institution of Jesus as his vicar, but only by the members of His Body gathered with one accord in one place. The Eucharist is the manifestation of the People of God called to be priests as they gather to offer the eucharistic sacrifice, with their λειτουργοσ in their midst represented by the person specially elected by the community of believers for this function, to voice this invocation (always in the first person plural).[77]

The priest indeed leads the worshipping community and acts on behalf of the bishop. He personifies the priestly character of all the

---

74. Kern, 185 n. 1. cf. 182–84. Cf. also, Maltzew, 428 and esp. Evdokimov, *L'Orthodoxie*, 250.

75. Kern, 185 n. 1; cf. 182–83.

76. Nissiotis, "Worship, Eucharist and Intercommunion," 193–95, 207–209.

77. Ibid., 214.

faithful present and at the same time symbolically represents Christ *the* Priest. Nevertheless, it is the *whole* praying, believing assembly in union with its head and through the power of the Holy Spirit which "shows forth and reactualizes" the Last Supper here and now.[78] When the priest prays the epiclesis it is in reality, ". . . the universal sacerdotal Body of all believers voicing these words through *their* celebrant."[79] Thus the epiclesis becomes an expression of the fact that the praying, believing assembly shares in the realization of the Eucharist and that it is the *whole* assembly, not just one ordained member of this assembly, that has such a share.

Writing in 1962, B. Bobrinskoy, Professor for Orthodox Theology in St. Serge Institute, Paris, analyzing the place of the praying assembly in the Eucharist, also places the role of the minister squarely within the context of the praying assembly. The whole Eucharist is a thanksgiving and a proclaiming of the wonderful deeds of God; the whole eucharist is, nonetheless, an epiclesis, an ardent prayer of the eucharistic assembly. It is because the dual presence of Christ and the Holy Spirit is not automatic that such an ardent supplication is necessary. The object of this prayer is twofold: it asks that the Holy Spirit consecrate the gifts, making them the body and blood of Christ and that the Father be pleased with the sacrifice and pour the fullness of his grace upon the faithful.[80]

It is the *whole* praying, believing assembly which realizes the presence of Christ and which unites with the same Christ in giving thanks, offering, invoking and receiving Communion— in the Holy Spirit.

> . . . for the president of the eucharistic assembly does not consecrate alone, *ex sese,* and before a congregation present but passive; the Eucharist is liturgical, that is to say, a communal action of the whole assembly, in the name of which, and together with which, the minister acts.[81]

---

78. Ibid., 214–15; cf. 198–99, 209 and the same author's "Pneumatologie orthodoxe," 91, 94–97, 100–101. Cf. also, S. Bulgakov, *The Orthodox Church,* trans. by E. Cram (London, 1935), 130–31 where the author acknowledges the special role of the ordained priest and Paquier, 62–70 who seems to maintain a good balance in this area. Cf. also, Meyendorff, 28 and Gore, 213–14.

79. Nissiotis, "Worship, Eucharist, and Intercommunion," 209 (italics his); cf. also the same author's "Pneumatologie orthodoxe," 99–101.

80. Cf. Bobrinskoy, "Le Saint Esprit . . . ," 52, 55.

81. Ibid., 55; cf. 56.

In the preceding section an examination of the "substance of the sacrament" in the light of the epiclesis brought out the need to include faith in our understanding of the dual structure of the outward sacramental sign. In the present section even a brief glance at the relationship between the epiclesis and the role of the praying, believing assembly in modern writings has revealed various shades of interpretation. Some theologians stress the causal role of the assembly while others emphasize the assembly's absolute dependence upon God for the realization of the Eucharist. Some, perhaps in reaction to exaggerations in this area, strongly object to granting the priest or minister a special role in the realization of the sacrament whereas others content themselves with situating this role squarely within the context of the assembly and with underlining the fact that it is the assembly as a *whole* which acts.

The various shades of interpretation should underline once again the richness and complexity of the epiclesis question and make one wary of either-or solutions. They should also alert one to a number of possible extremes in this area. It is possible, for instance, to deny any consecratory role to the assembled faithful either in favor of the ordained minister alone or in favor of divine intervention alone. It is also possible to favor the role of the assembled faithful to the exclusion of the ordained minister or at times, seemingly at least, even to the exclusion of the need for divine intervention. Some of the theologians examined have already touched upon the last mentioned extreme in their efforts to emphasize the absolute dependence of the praying assembly upon the intervention of God. They have pointed to the epiclesis not only as an expression of the role of the praying, believing assembly in the Eucharist but also as a possible corrective to a tendency to overemphasize this role at the expense of the divine action. In addition to the authors already mentioned, Schillebeeckx is a good case in point. With all his efforts to bring out the role of the believing community in the sacraments, he still strives to put this role in the context of, and to subordinate it to, the divine action.

The sacraments as ecclesial symbolic activity express the Church's belief that God, the *Kyrios*, is personally acting here and now.

. . . Sacramental symbolic activity, although performed through the Church by the mediation of the minister, is fundamentally a personal act of the *Kyrios*, who is the actual High Priest throughout the action. Therefore that which ecclesiastical symbolic activity expresses first of all is the *fides Ecclesiae,* the faith of the Church in the (eternally-actual) redemptive act of the Saviour. . . [82]

Thus the sacraments reflect both the human and the divine involved in their realization. Both elements are essential and both find embodiment in the sacramental ceremony as a whole. The ancient Church and the Eastern church today by using a deprecatory form in the sacraments underline the conviction that God alone is the giver of grace. The Western Church, "convinced of the Church's role as the sacramental Christ," generally highlights this aspect by means of a declarative formula. Both aspects are true and, despite the tension at times, have to be maintained because the fact is that, ". . . through the sacramental confession of faith human symbolic action becomes the visible prolongation and presence of the invisible saving act of the risen Christ."[83] It is to the relationship of the epiclesis to the divine action of the Holy Spirit, as seen through the eyes of some modern theologians, that we now turn.

THE EPICLESIS AND THE HOLY SPIRIT

There is a tendency at times to stress the role of the praying assembly at the expense of the divine action in the sacraments. There is also at times the tendency to exaggerate the role played by the external rite to the detriment of the same divine action. Perhaps P. Batiffol represents one of the most blatant examples of such exaggeration during the period with which we are dealing. Writing in 1908, he rejects three proposed explanations of the epiclesis with what seems to be an almost exclusive, mechanistic stress on the words of institution:

> . . . For the words of the institution narrative are for us theologians the form which consecrates: They are necessary and they suffice to work the change . . . the form works by itself to such a degree that it is complete.[84]

Thus according to Batiffol, the epiclesis has nothing to add to the institution narrative. Moreover, the idea that the whole eucharistic prayer is in some way consecratory has no foundation.

---

82. Schillebeeckx, *Christ the Sacrament,* 119.

83. Ibid., 119–120.

84. Batiffol, "Nouvelles Etudes . . . (1)," 524–25.

Even more striking is Batiffol's attempt to contrast Cyprian and Firmilian's claim that the Holy Spirit realizes the sacrament of baptism with the "Roman position" represented by Pope Stephen which, according to Batiffol, rightly sees the words of the baptismal formula *alone* as realizing the sacrament.[85]

Statements such as these seem at times to leave Roman Catholic sacramental theology open to the accusation of magical tendencies. Such statements also indicate the need for a healthy awareness of the role of the Holy Spirit in the sacraments. It is just such a need that a number of authors see the epiclesis filling.

The Epiclesis: Expression of the Holy Spirit's Role in the Eucharist

A number of modern theologians hold that the basic function of the epiclesis is to express the role of the Holy Spirit in the Eucharist.

C. Kern, for instance, contends that one must view the epiclesis in its context. This context is the "realistic symbolism" (Symbolisme réaliste) of worship. The whole ecclesial worship is, moreover, a revelation of Christian dogma and Christian philosophy.[86] In this context it becomes clear that the epiclesis is a symbolic expression of the *how* of the eucharistic "consecration." It symbolizes the fact that this "consecration" is the work of the Holy Spirit, not of humans.[87] From this point of view the epiclesis proper is not merely a ritual detail of more or less ancient origin. It is rather a manifestation of belief in the Holy Spirit as Lord and Life-giver, Divine Power and Source of

---

85. Ibid., 526. Cf. also, Batiffol's "La question de l'épiclèse eucharistique," 641–62, esp. 657–61. For a very different interpretation of Augustine's words, see Schillebeeckx, *Christ the Sacrament*, 111. Cf. also Cabrol, "Le canon romain et la messe," 515–17.

That Batiffol's case is not a unique one is witnessed to by E. Hugon, *La causalité instrumentale en théologie* (Paris, 1924), 130 who sees a major weakness in the moral causality explanations in the fact that such explanations seem to have the sacraments move the Holy Spirit rather than having the Holy Spirit moving and applying the sacraments; and by Schillebeeckx who in *Christ the Sacrament*, 107–109 also acknowledges the fact that some theologians have treated the question of the *ex opera operato* efficacy of the sacraments apart from their Christological (and, we would add, pneumatological) context and thus have unwittingly given the impression of a purely materialistic, juridical approach to the sacraments. Cf. also, Semmelroth "Personalismus . . . ," 202–207.

86. Kern, 167.

87. Ibid., 193 citing Salaville, "Epiclèse eucharistique," 298.

Sanctification.[88] Consequently, since all agree on the presence and activity of the Holy Spirit in the Eucharist, the epiclesis proper should help unite rather than divide.[89]

P. Evdokimov, in his *L'Orthodoxie*, published in 1959, echoes the viewpoint that the epiclesis proper is the expression of the Holy Spirit's work in the Eucharist. For him the epiclesis is a "eucharistic Pentecost" which invokes and expresses the Spirit's activity not only in the eucharistic elements but, even more important, in the faithful themselves. It is not, he contends, simply the epiclesis proper as a liturgical fact which separates the East and the West but, rather, the epiclesis as the expression of the theology of the Holy Spirit.[90]

E. Schillebeeckx in his turn stresses the relationship between epiclesis and the special role of the Holy Spirit. He notes that the Greeks attribute works *ad extra* to the three Persons of the Trinity. Unlike most of the Latin authors, however, they still maintain the inner Trinitarian structure in describing these works. Transubstantiation, for instance, as *opus ad extra* is seen as accomplished by the Father ("a Patre") through the Son ("per filium"), but perfected in (by the power of) the Holy Spirit ("in Spiritu Sancto") who is the *"vivens operatio filii."* According to Schillebeeckx, every divine activity *ad extra* thus culminates in the operation of the Holy Spirit. In this way the "consecration" is achieved by and through the intervention of the Holy Spirit. To Schillebeeckx, the epiclesis gives expression to this intervention of the Holy Spirit.[91]

Basis for this Interpretation in Saving History

What is the basis in the events of saving history for seeing the epiclesis as an expression of the role of the Holy Spirit in the Eucharist? The answer to this question is extremely varied. One of the most outspoken proponents of a parallel between the Incarnation and the eucharistic epiclesis is J. Betz. As we have seen already, Betz contends that the Fathers saw the Eucharist as the making present of the Incarnation ("die Vergegenwärtigung der Inkarnation"). This patristic point of view

---

88. Kern, 168.

89. Ibid., 193-94 citing Salaville, "Epiclèse eucharistique," 298.

90. Evdokimov, *L'Orthodoxie*, 249–51.

91. SH, 336. Cf. Tillard, *The Eucharist: Pasch* . . . , 89–90, 94–95.

Betz terms the "eucharistic Incarnation principle."[92] The epiclesis is the liturgical expression of this eucharistic Incarnation principle. It expresses the parallel between the action of the Holy Spirit in the Incarnation and his action in the eucharistic transubstantiation.[93]

S. Salaville also notes this parallel between the activity ascribed to the Holy Spirit in the Incarnation and the activity which the epiclesis ascribes to the Spirit in the Eucharist. He points out that particularly the Syrian texts of the epiclesis employ terms to describe the Spirit's action in the Eucharist which correspond to the terms the Bible uses to describe the Spirit's activity in the Incarnation.[94] Moreover, in conjunction with a quote from a mozarabic *Post Pridie* for Pentecost which speaks of the analogy between the Holy Spirit in the Incarnation in the transformation in the Eucharist Salaville states that, ". . . one cannot ignore the fact that this second analogy (Incarnation-transubstantiation) is commonplace in the eucharistic theology of the East, and that one encounters it very often in the epiclesis formulas."[95]

On the basis of some of the most important anaphora texts *alone*, P. Dinesen, as we have seen, rejects the attempt to explain the epiclesis as a new Incarnation. He finds neither in the context (with its narration of God's wonderful deeds, its institution narrative, and its Communion section) nor in the wording of the epiclesis itself anything that allows us to see the Incarnation as the key to understanding the epiclesis.[96]

The fact is that the bond between the epiclesis and the Incarnation seems to find its strongest support not in the liturgical texts but in the writings of the Fathers. A number of authors admit, for instance, that Justin saw the analogy between the Incarnation and the Eucharist although they maintain that he probably attributed both to the intervention of the Logos.[97] E. Atchley cites a number of patristic writers who connect either the eucharistic or baptismal epiclesis, or both, with the Incarnation. Among these we find Chrysostom, Ambrose,

---

92. Betz, 261, 299.

93. Ibid., 327. Cf. Wetter, 79 and Jugie, *Theologia Dogmatica* . . . V, 716.

94. Salaville, "Epiclèse eucharistique," 224.

95. Salaville, "L'épiclèse d'après saint Jean Chrysostome . . . ," 103.

96. Dinesen, 82–87.

97. Cf., for instance, Bishop, "The Moment . . . ," 158–63 and Salaville, "La liturgie decrite par saint Justin et l'epiclese," 226–27.

and Gregory the Great.[98] Betz, too, supports his position primarily
with his analysis of patristic texts.[99]

Whereas some see the similarity between the epiclesis and the
Incarnation, others stress the parallel between the epiclesis and the
Resurrection. J. Lècuyer, for instance, in an article published in 1961
remarks that Theodore of Mopsuestia saw the epiclesis as signifying
a "sacramental resurrection" in the offerings by making the risen Christ
present in them. In addition, the epiclesis was aimed at realizing
a communication of the life of the risen Christ to the faithful, thus
uniting them more deeply with Christ and with one another. This
then is the sense of the epiclesis as Lècuyer finds it in the writings of
Theodore and also of John Chrysostom. It is a sign of the invisible
action of the Holy Spirit, of the presence in heaven and upon the altar
of the risen Christ and a pledge of our participation in the grace of
this risen Lord.[100]

We have already seen that J. P. de Jong also views the eucharistic epiclesis in the context of the Resurrection.[101] Through the
epiclesis and the action of the Holy Spirit a "transfiguration" takes
place. The eucharistic action moves from the figure of the sacrificial
death of Christ, his body and blood given for us, to the figure of
Christ's glorified body and blood given to us as divine nourishment.[102]

J. H. Crehan, although reluctant to tie the epiclesis too closely
to the rite of commixture, as de Jong does, also links the epiclesis to
the Resurrection. He contends that if one wishes to find a remembrance of the Resurrection in the Mass the epiclesis would be a likely
candidate. A petition that the Holy Spirit be sent to ratify what has
been done in the Eucharist is in liturgical terms the equivalent of the
Resurrection of Christ which was God's acceptance or ratification of
the sacrifice of his Son.[103]

---

98. Atchley, *On the Epiclesis . . .* , 69, 74, 183; cf. also, 138–39.

99. Betz, 268–300. Cf. Dinesen, 87 n. 45 for a sharp critique of Betz's method and conclusions.

100. Lécuyer, "La théologie . . . ," 410; 408–409. Cf. also, Jugie, *Theologia Dogmatica . . .* V,
308–309; Sage, 265 and Schmidt-Lauber, 159. Dix, *The Shape . . .* , 284 remarks that the actual
terms of the invocation as Theodore reports it contain no trace whatever of this idea.

101. Cf. Chapter 5.

102. de Jong, "Le rite . . . ," 258–268.

103. J. H. Crehan, "Theological Trends," in *Theology in Transition*, ed. by E. O'Brien (New
York, 1965), 24. Cf. also the same author's "Epiklesis," 226.

The Ascension also comes up for consideration in conjunction with the eucharistic epiclesis but usually only in conjunction with Pentecost. B. Bobrinskoy, for instance, in two articles published in *Studia Liturgica* in the early 1960's has developed well the relationship between these two events of saving history and the epiclesis. The life of the Church is a continuing Pentecost which was only *begun* nineteen hundred years ago. In her daily life and especially in the Eucharist, the Church lives in an attitude of invocation and expectation of the Holy Spirit which characterizes the period after the Ascension. But she also lives in a posture of receiving the "real presence" of the Holy Spirit which characterizes Pentecost.[104] The epiclesis with its invocation of the Holy Spirit and the expectation of his coming parallels the ten days between the Ascension and Pentecost during which the disciples gathered together in the Temple and in the upper room and joyfully awaited the Paraclete which Christ had promised them. Thus in the eucharistic epiclesis the Church joins Christ's priestly intercession in heaven, praying to God to bestow his Spirit on the gifts and upon the faithful.[105] A true Pentecost is accomplished when in answer to this invocation the Holy Spirit descends upon the gifts and—this is important and often overlooked—upon the assembly. This coming of the Holy Spirit upon both is a "tangible pledge that the offerings of the Church have been accepted upon the celestial altar."[106]

Writing in 1915, K. J. Merk even uses Pentecost as the core of his theory on the origin and development of the epiclesis. He holds that the epiclesis arose from the joining of a Pentecost notion originally found in the anamnesis to an offertory prayer which originally preceded the anaphora. The two were joined and first placed between the Sanctus and the institution narrative. Later the resulting prayer was tacked on to the anamnesis after the institution narrative and became an epiclesis in the strict sense.[107]

It is one thing, however, to draw an analogy between the epiclesis and Pentecost and quite another to trace the epiclesis back to an ancient mention of Pentecost in the anamnesis. J. Brinktrine makes

---

104. Bobrinskoy, "Le Saint Esprit . . . ," 47–49, 52. Cf. also, Evdokimov, "Eucharistie . . . ," 61.

105. Bobrinskoy, "Worship and the Ascension," 114.

106. Ibid., 120, Cf. Thurian, *Le pain unique*, 41–46. Fortescue, 403 also links the epiclesis to both the Ascension and Pentecost. Cf. p. 346.

107. Merk, *Der Konsekrationstext* . . . , 110–35. Cf. Cabrol, "Anamnèse," 1895.

this quite clear in rejecting Merk's theory three years after its publication. Brinktrine gives the following reasons for his opposition to Merk's view: None of the ancient liturgies, all of which have an epiclesis, contain such a mention of Pentecost in the anamnesis. *The Apostolic Constitutions* and the Eastern liturgies in general mention the death, Resurrection, Ascension, and Second Coming of Christ, *then* comes the appeal for the Holy Spirit. Moreover, the baptismal epiclesis has no mention of Pentecost before its appeal for the Holy Spirit unless one postulates that it originally stemmed from the alleged mention of Pentecost in the anamnesis. And Brinktrine rejects that possibility decisively.[108]

We have included a brief description of the saving history basis offered for the interpretation that the epiclesis is an expression of the role of the Holy Spirit in the Eucharist for two reasons. First of all, such a description helps underline the activity of the Holy Spirit which is an element common to these saving events and the Eucharist.[109] Secondly, and more important, such a description makes one aware of the need to view the epiclesis against the backdrop of saving history as Schillebeeckx has done so masterfully for the sacraments in general.[110] This awareness may, in turn, hold the key to solving the apparent dilemma of the interpretation now under consideration.

The Apparent Dilemma in this Interpretation

From the very start the view that sees the epiclesis as an expression of the role of the Holy Spirit in the Eucharist runs up against a dilemma of seemingly major proportions. How does one reconcile the position that Christ is the High Priest who consecrates the Eucharist with the claim that the "consecration" takes place through the activity of the Holy Spirit?

In 1933 A. G. Hebert tackled the problem of the epiclesis raised in conjunction with the Church of England's proposed Canon of 1928. In his article Hebert rightly remarks that to solve the practical difficulty of where to put the epiclesis and how to work it, one

---

108. Brinktrine, "Zur Entstehung . . . ," 490–91. Cf. also Baumstark, "Zu den Problemen . . . ," 347.

109. Cf. M. J. Scheeben-A. Rademacher, *Die Mysterien des Christentums* (Freiburg i. Br., 19123), 436–37, 452–54.

110. Cf. Schillebeeckx, *Christ the Sacrament*, 18–47.

must first seek the meaning of both the epiclesis and the eucharistic action itself. He points out that one factor which makes the epiclesis question a thorny one is the necessity of doing justice both to the activity of Christ and that of the Holy Spirit. Both are present and acting; we must take both into account and express the role of both. The West has tended to stress the fact that Christ, the High Priest, is Celebrant. The East has tended to underline the action of the Holy Spirit. Neither seems to have done justice to the other aspect.[111]

Herbert proposes a practical solution of the epiclesis question: try to bring out the simultaneity of the presence and activity of Christ, the High Priest, and of the Holy Spirit. "We need some form of Epiclesis which shall preserve the consecratory character of the Dominical Words."[112] It should also try to avoid too exclusive an emphasis on the "act of consecration and the Real Presence in the elements." Rather, here it should underline the Church's offering of herself with Christ in the Holy Spirit. Hebert sees a divided Epiclesis as most capable of uniting these aspects.[113]

J. Armitage Robinson, writing in 1924 suggested quite a different approach. He regards the difficulty as a matter of two fundamentally distinct points of view. The West regards Christ as consecrating the Eucharist. The East, on the other hand, regards the Holy Spirit as consecrating. Robinson urges that the two ideas be kept distinct and that nothing be done by Western authorities which might even seem to depart from the Western point of view.[114] Responding to Robinson's article F. E. Brightman rejects Robinson's claim that the ideas of East and West are "profoundly different" in that the one regards the Spirit, the other Christ, as consecrating. Brightman insists, rather, that both ideas are true and should be harmonized as well as possible.[115]

In 1934, G. Dix, on his way to maintaining that the "Western tradition" which holds that it is the Word who consecrates the Eucharist is primitive, was to make some interesting observations in this regard. He contends that the "very combination of the two ideas only emphasizes the essential duality. Each theologian holds both

111. Hebert, "The Meaning . . . ," 198–99, 201–206.
112. Ibid., 209.
113. Ibid., 208–10.
114. Robinson, "Invocation in the Holy Eucharist," 99–100.
115. Brightman (Correspondence: Invocation . . .), 37–38.

doctrines, but each frames his own explanation only in terms of one of them." Moreover, ". . . The duality and also the balance of these two ideas (Christ present and acting, the Holy Spirit present and acting) seem to us now of the utmost importance to eucharistic theology."[116] For although some of the great theologians of the fourth century were conscious of a dual operation in the Eucharist, they were, in a sense, innovators and taught it, as it were, confusedly, making no attempt to reconcile the two aspects of this operation. The task of reconciliation remains and a simple appeal to patristic texts does not suffice for the accomplishment of this task.[117]

O. Casel, among others, has attempted to underline the fact that where the Spirit is present, Christ is present. There is no opposition. In the sacraments it is the Spirit of Christ or, perhaps better, the "pneumatic Christ" who is present (". . . der pneumatische Herr ist in den Mysterien gegenwärtig").[118]

Finally, some remarks of B. Bobrinskoy in this area are significant. They help to draw together some of the aspects which must be kept in mind in any attempt to reconcile the activity of Christ and of the Holy Spirit in the Eucharist. Bobrinskoy points out that the Holy Spirit is present "in person" ("en personne"), His presence is invisible and non-corporeal (in contrast to the presence of the "body-person" Christ in the sacramental signs). Nevertheless, although the Spirit is present in a different manner from Christ, he is no less *really* present and in no way subordinate to Christ. There is a reciprocity and not a subordination between Christ present and the Holy Spirit present.[119]

The views recorded in this section by no means represent an exhaustive listing. They should suffice, however, to drive home once again the fact that to cope with the epiclesis question one must cope with the apparent contradiction between the claim that Christ consecrates and the claim that the Holy Spirit consecrates. This is especially true of any explanation which regards the epiclesis as an expression of the role of the Holy Spirit in realizing the Eucharist. The views we

---

116. Dix "The Origins . . . ," 127. Cf. also Robinson, (Correspondence: Response to Brightman), 176–77.

117. Dix. Ibid.

118. O. Casel, "Mystereiengegenwart," JLW 8 (1928), 161–63. Cf. J. J. von Allmen, *Prophétisme sacramental*, 291–93.

119. Bobrinskoy, "Le Saint-Esprit dans la liturgie," 58, 56, 48.

have just examined, in addition to putting the problem into focus, should also provide some clues to its solution.

SUMMARY

The inflexibility and pessimism of certain Roman Catholic writers in regard to the epiclesis question seem to stem from statements of the magisterium which link the epiclesis to the question of the *substantia sacramenti*.

     The historical data indicates, however, that while the sense manifested in each sacrament has remained constant the *specific* "form" has at times undergone radical change and therefore should not be identified with the unchangeable *substantia sacramenti*. The data also seems to indicate that the eucharistic epiclesis was once, and therefore possibly could again be, considered to have a consecratory value *together with* the institution words. Magisterium statements to the contrary can be explained by the philosophical, theological framework in which they were made. The *substantia sacramenti* is the signification intended by Christ as this signification is perceived by the faith of the Church and expressed by gestures and words which the Church's faith judges suitable for this purpose.

     The importance of the Church's faith in the sacraments raises the possibility of viewing the epiclesis as an expression of the role of the praying, believing assembly in the Eucharist. In such a view an epiclesis proper could help protect the role of the praying, believing assembly from an overemphasis on the material rites as well as from an overemphasis on the role of the ordained minister. At the same time, such an epiclesis could serve as a reminder that the assembly is always *praying*, i.e., dependent on God for the realization of the Eucharist. The view that sees the epiclesis as an expression of the role of the Holy Spirit in the Eucharist follows similar lines. Inherent in this view is the need to reconcile the activity of Christ with that of the Holy Spirit in the Eucharist.

Part III

A Synthesis

In his study of the relationship between the epiclesis and sacramental theology, G. C. Smit remarks that the amount of recent literature on the epiclesis question bears witness to the lively interest this question holds for Western theologians. Smit hastens to add, however, that a complete accord has never been realized on this subject. Perhaps this is asking too much. To expect complete accord on a question as complex and as many-faceted as that of the epiclesis is to expect the impossible. Perhaps this is just the weakness of many attempts to solve the epiclesis question. Too often they may have been looking for a single, all-embracing solution.

Be that as it may, it is not our purpose in the pages that follow to propose such an all-embracing solution. Rather, we simply hope to draw on the data seen so far, especially the interpretations modern writers have given to the epiclesis, in order to put the problems that accompany the various facets of the epiclesis into proper perspective. Once this has been done, the directions in which one should look for a solution to these problems may already suggest themselves.

Chapter 7

The Epiclesis and the Moment of Consecration Question Re-examined

One might be tempted to pass over the moment of consecration question in silence since, as we have seen, it has already received more than its share of attention in attempts to solve the epiclesis question. The moment of consecration still looms large in any attempt to appreciate the importance of the eucharistic epiclesis. Therefore, we shall examine this problem against the broader context of the real presence in the Eucharist. Hopefully, this will open up new possibilities for a satisfying solution to the moment of consecration question itself and to the question of the epiclesis in relationship to this problem.

WITHIN A SCHOLASTIC FRAMEWORK

Within a Scholastic framework the real presence of Christ in the Eucharist receives its explanation in terms of *transubstantiation*. Briefly, transubstantiation, as it is understood in Scholastic circles at any rate, is the explanation in which the substance of the body and blood of Christ replaces the substance of the bread and wine. According to this view, the appearances or *accidents* of the bread and wine remain and are supported by the substance of Christ's body and blood.

Complexities Within This Framework

Within the Scholastic framework of transubstantiation one can still employ various explanations of the epiclesis proper as it appears in liturgical documents. One can, for instance, see in the epiclesis an expression of the role of the Holy Spirit in the Eucharist. One can see the epiclesis as an expression of the intention of the Church, an intention which Trent has defined as necessary for the realization of the sacrament.[1] Within this framework one can also see the epiclesis as a phenomenon of human language which cannot say everything at once. It seems, however, that within the Scholastic framework one is almost constrained to interpret this last explanation of the epiclesis— true enough in itself—in such a way as to deprive the epiclesis of any *consecratory* value, a value indicated by early liturgical texts and attested to by a number of the Fathers.[2]

Why is this so? Because the Scholastic explanation of transubstantiation tends to focus attention on the change in the physical elements[3] and at the same time to insist upon the instantaneous character of this change. Once this is done, an either-or tension between the role of the institution narrative and that of the epiclesis is almost bound to arise.

For, once one allows attention to center on the change of the elements, this change inevitably takes on increasing, not to say supreme, importance in the minds of many.[4] And when, in addition, one maintains that this change by the very nature of things is instantaneous,[5] a conflict is almost equally inevitable. Those favoring the consecratory value of the institution narrative are bound to compete with those favoring the consecratory value of the eucharistic epiclesis. Each side seeks to win *the* moment for its candidate, whether that candidate be the institution narrative or the epiclesis.

---

1. Cf. R. de Salvo, *The Dogmatic Theology on the Intention of the Minister in the Confection of the Sacraments* (Washington, 1949), 20 and DS, 1611 (854); cf. also, DS, 1312 (695) and 1262 (672).

2. Cf. Botte, "L'épiclèse . . . syriennes orientales," 69; Betz, 328; J. Gouillard in Salaville, *Nicolas Cabasilas,* 32 and Cabrol, 173–74. Cabrol remarks that theologians rightly shrink from the radical step of accusing the Fathers and the early liturgies of having erred in this matter.

3. Cf. Schillebeeckx, *Christ the Sacrament,* 112–14 and the same author's *Eucharist,* 90–91, 97; Davis, "Understanding . . . ," 174. Bulgakov, "Das eucharistische Dogma," 35–36 puts the critique of this tendency in particularly sharp focus. Cf. also, Rahner, "Die Gegenwart . . . ," 383–84 and "Uber die Dauer . . . ," 387–97.

4. Cf. Casel, *Das christliche Opfermysterium,* 533 in this regard.

5. Cf. S. T. III, q. 75, a. 7.

Possible Alternatives

One can, of course, deny the instantaneous character of the change. One can even admit the instantaneous character of the change but either refuse to ask the question of precisely when this change takes place or acknowledge that we simply do not know the answer to this question. In practice, however, as long as one remains in the Scholastic transubstantiation context there is a tendency to underline the instantaneous character of the change and to seek to pinpoint the precise moment of this change.[6] And this attempt to pinpoint the *moment of consecration* leads to an either-or situation which immeasurably compounds the difficulty of the epiclesis question. To try to answer the question whether it is the institution narrative or the epiclesis which consecrates, i.e., which is (subordinate to the divine action, of course) responsible for the change in the elements, is not only to try to answer a difficult question. It is in our opinion to try to answer the wrong question.

As long as the epiclesis question remains in the Scholastic framework of transubstantiation, it seems doomed to remain in the shadow of the moment of consecration question. As long as it remains in the shadow of the moment of consecration question, a satisfactory treatment of this same epiclesis question is hard to envisage.

What is the solution, then? How can one alleviate, if not completely eradicate, the either-or dilemma which for so long has plagued the epiclesis question? One possibility is to change the framework in which the epiclesis until now has generally been regarded.

In recent years the Scholastic doctrine of transubstantiation has come under increasing fire as a satisfactory explanation for the real presence in the Eucharist.[7] It is not a question here of denying a distinctive, objective, eucharistic presence.[8] Nor is it even a question of denying that a real, ontological change takes place in the bread and wine in realizing this presence of Christ in the Eucharist.[9] Rather,

---

6. Cf., for instance, Salaville, "Epiclèse eucharistique," 201–202. Cf. also, SH, 348–54. Cf. also, on the part of the Orthodox, L'Huillier, 317 who, appealing to the realism of the Eucharist, also insists on an instantaneous transformation.

7. Cf. Bulgakov, 34–44; Schillebeeckx, *The Eucharist*, 90–96; Davis, 160, 173–74, 176; Powers, 145–47. For much of what follows, cf. John H. McKenna, "Eucharistic Presence . . . ." *Theological Studies* 60 (1999) 294–317.

8. Cf., for instance, Schillebeeckx, ibid., 39–76; Davis, 170–72; Powers, 38–40.

9. Cf. Schillebeeckx, ibid., esp. 63–76; Davis, 172–73 and Powers, 40.

critics of the Scholastic approach are basically challenging the ability of an explanation which rests primarily on an Aristotelian natural philosophy to do justice to the reality of the eucharistic presence. In attempting to explain the real presence exclusively in impersonal terms and in using the Aristotelian theory of a distinction *in a physical thing* between its substance and its accidents as its basic analogy, Scholasticism runs the very real risk of distorting or at least impoverishing the meaning of this real presence.[10]

The use of such an analogy today meets with a number of objections. First of all, the Scholastic understanding of quantity which plays a key role in the Scholastic explanation of transubstantiation is hardly reconcilable with the findings of modern science. Secondly, on the level of physical reality at which the Aristotelian philosophy of nature applies, bread and wine are no longer considered to be substances. The term *substance* has increasingly come to be reserved for personal beings. Finally, and this objection seems to us the most telling, the Scholastic explanation focuses too much attention on the change which takes place in the elements. It fails to refer this change sufficiently to the interpersonal, sacramental context of an encounter between Christ and the faithful. And it is only in this context that such a change finds its purpose and meaning.[11]

It is this dissatisfaction with the Scholastic approach to the question of the real presence and the development of an anthropology of the symbolic act based on a view of man which is not dualistic, among other things,[12] which have led a number of modern theologians to suggest a new, more personalistic framework for understanding the real presence.

For similar reasons, one could suggest that we are no longer seeking to understand the eucharistic epiclesis from within the Scholastic framework of transubstantiation but, rather, against the background of a more personalistic understanding of the real presence.

---

10. Cf. Davis, 160; Nissiotis, "Worship . . . ," 209, 211–12.

11. Cf. Davis, 160, 173–74; Schillebeeckx, ibid., 94–95; Powers, 146–46; Bulgakov, 34–44 and esp. 40, 43, 87; and Rahner, "Die Gegenwart . . . ," 381–84. Cf. also Cummings, *Eucharistic Doctors* . . . , 137 who notes that in colloquial language today "substance," and "substantially" are not understood in the metaphysical sense of Thomas Aquinas. Today they mean what is physical and material.

12. Cf. Schillebeeckx, ibid., 96–107.

Within a Personalistic Framework

The approach to the question of the real presence which we have
termed "personalistic" has for its basic analogy an interpersonal
encounter, that is, the presence of one person, as a person, to another
person, as a person. Two aspects of this personalistic approach are of
special significance for our study of the eucharistic epiclesis. The first
of these is the allowance which this approach makes for degrees of
presence. The second is the role which the personalistic approach gives
to bodily presence in an interpersonal encounter.

The Basic Analogy

To begin with, this approach allows for, in fact even calls for, a distinction between different types or degrees of presence. For instance, one
person can be present to another with a purely physical, spatial, or
local presence the way water is present to a glass or a corpse to a coffin.
An example of purely local presence would be the case of two persons
standing next to one another in a crowded bus, each one oblivious of
the other. Despite the physical juxtaposition of their bodies these two
persons remain basically unaware of one another. Even when one of
them unknowingly jostles the other the situation may not advance
much beyond this local presence. The person jostled may now be
aware of the other person but not as a person but rather as a thing, an
object, namely, in this case, an elbow sticking in his ribs. They still
remain on the most primitive level of presence, namely, that of purely
physical or local presence.

      There is, however, a deeper, more personal level of presence.
This takes place when one person seeks to communicate with another
person. This communication may begin with a smile or a friendly
greeting. It may also end there. Or the person wishing to communicate
may seek to go further. He may in the course of time offer himself to
be known and loved by the other. In order to do this he must to a
certain extent reveal himself for what he is—in the hope that the other
person will come to know and love him, as a person, and accept him
for what he is. In this attempt at self-communication, in this attempt
to reveal himself to the other, this person is in a sense offering himself
to the other and thus establishing a presence far deeper than that of

a purely local presence. But this is still not the deepest form of presence. It is still not a fully personal presence.

For a fully personal presence a response on the part of the other person is necessary. Presence in its deepest sense is a mutual, *inter*personal presence. Thus it is not enough for the one person to offer himself to be known and loved. It is also necessary that the other person, to some extent at least, try to reciprocate by accepting the offer and by offering himself to be known and loved for what he is. Such a presence can find many different expressions and many different qualitative changes or intensities. But on this level presence is always mutual. It involves a mutual knowledge not just about, but of one another as persons. It also involves mutual love because it would seem that only in a climate of love can a person really reveal himself for what he is. Such a presence in which two persons offer themselves to each other, open themselves to one another and thus enter into each other's life is no less real than the purely local presence we have described. In fact, it is this level or degree of presence, this interpersonal encounter, which is most real. For only in the context of mutual, reciprocal giving of persons to each other is there real presence in its fullest sense.[13] The allowance for degrees of presence which the personalistic approach to the real presence makes is, then, one aspect which seems to be of special significance for our study of the epiclesis.

The second significant aspect is the understanding which the personalistic approach gives to the role of bodily presence in an interpersonal encounter. As we have already noted, within this approach *purely* physical, local presence is the most primitive level or degree of presence between persons. Yet within the personalistic framework bodily presence, while it remains secondary to interpersonal presence, is nonetheless necessary for the development of this fuller presence. This corresponds to what we know of human nature. Every human exchange, every attempt of one person to communicate with another takes place in and through our bodiliness.[14] There is no way of

---

13. On the question of the degrees of personal presence cf. Schillebeeckx, *The Eucharist*, 104, 117–19 who is basically summarizing some of the main points in P. Schoonenberg, "Christus' tegenwoordigheid voor ons," *Verbum* 31 [1964], 406–407. In addition to the articles in Dutch which Schillebeeckx cites, cf. Schoonenberg, "The Real Presence . . . ," 7–8. Cf. also, Powers, 121–25, 133–36 and Davis, 160–61.

14. Schillebeeckx, *Christ the Sacrament*, 15–16; cf. also xvi, 9, 50–51. Cf. also, Powers, 160–61 and Davis, 166.

getting around this, given the present human condition. An interpersonal encounter, for instance, may have had for its starting point a smile or a friendly greeting. Having advanced through words and bodily gestures beyond the most primitive level of local presence, a deep friendship may develop in which there is a mutual giving and accepting in knowledge and love of one another as persons. This mutual, personal—and therefore quite real—presence not only owed its origin and establishment to bodily presence of one kind or another. It also finds its expression through bodily words and gestures. And this expression of an already existing personal presence in its turn often tends to intensify this presence.[15]

Moreover, the personalistic approach generally tends to situate this bodily or local presence within an anthropology of the symbolic act based on a view of human beings which is not dualistic. A sign or "symbolic representation" as such always refers to something else which is absent. On the other hand, our bodiliness, together with its modes of expression, are real symbols or "symbolic realities" and therefore contain the reality which they express. A kiss, for instance, is not a sign of something else, of someone hidden behind it. Rather, it is, or at least can and should be, that person expressing his love for another person. In addition, we can in a sense extend our own bodiliness or bodily presence by using material objects as expressions of ourselves. A wedding ring, for instance, is no longer simply a piece of metal for the woman who has received it or for the man who has given it. Although it has undergone no physical change, the ring has indeed been transformed. It now possesses a new reality. It personifies the one who has given it. It is this man expressing in a concrete way, his gift of himself to the woman he loves.[16]

The personalistic approach does not, then, deny the necessity or even the importance of bodily presence for a full interpersonal presence. What it does try to do, however, is to put this bodily presence into perspective. This presence is always subordinate to the deeper personal presence to which it can lead and which it can express and intensify. Moreover, there are times when our bodiliness can even

---

15. Cf. Rahner, "Personale und sakramentale Frömmigkeit," in *Schriften zur Theologie* IV (Einsiedeln, 1955), 136–38 and Ledogar, "Faith, Feeling . . . ," 13–14, 19–21.

16. Cf. Rahner, "Zur Theologie des Symbols," 275–311, esp., for instance, 279, 303, 310–11; Powers, 81–86, 166–67; Schillebeeckx, *The Eucharist*, 99–101, Davis, 166–67.

hinder the deeper personal presence which we seek. There are times when our bodily limitations make it difficult, if not impossible, to express our *free* gift of ourselves to another. There are times, for instance, when a blush, a change in our breathing or in our facial expression force us to reveal ourselves in a way or at a time in which we did not wish to reveal ourselves. There are times, too, when our very bodiliness makes it possible for others to pin us down, to make us an objectifiable "thing" to be gazed at, for instance, or pitied, against our will. At all these times our bodiliness deprives us of a certain freedom—a freedom which is an important element in the self-giving necessary for a fully personal presence.[17]

The understanding which the personalistic approach gives to the role of bodily presence in an interpersonal encounter has, then, a twofold significance for our understanding of the Eucharist and the eucharistic epiclesis. For not only does this approach highlight the importance and indeed the necessity of bodily presence for such an encounter; it also underlines the limitations and the subordinate character of this level of presence in relation to the fully personal, mutual presence of which we have spoken.

Application to the Eucharist

The next step in the attempt to situate the epiclesis in a new framework is to see how the basic analogy of an interpersonal encounter applies to the Eucharist and, in particular, to the question of the real presence.[18] Every analogy, of course, limps. This is even truer in the case at hand. Added to the complexity and mysteriousness of human personal relationships is the complex and mysterious character of God's dealings with us. Moreover, trying to understand the real presence in the light of human personal encounter involves a number of related questions which we can only touch on here.

---

17. Cf. Powers, 105–106, 121–22.

18. Schillebeeckx, among others, has attempted to apply this analogy to the sacraments in general as well as to the question of the "real presence." Cf. *Christ the Sacrament*, 1–3. Powers, 111–54 has given a good summary of the steps leading up to the application of the analogy of interpersonal encounter to the question of the "real presence." For reservations on the application of "encounter" to the sacraments, cf. E. O'Brien, "Theology in Transition," in the book of the same title edited by O'Brien (New York, 1965), 237–38.

It involves, for instance, an appreciation of Christ's glorified body in view of his Resurrection and Ascension. Here we might simply note that this body, while it somehow retains its identity with Christ's body during his earthly life, has nevertheless been "Spiritized," filled with the Holy Spirit. It is now a "spiritual (πνευματικόν) body" such as that of which Paul speaks in his letter to the Corinthians (1 Corinthians 15:44). In consequence, Christ's bodiliness no longer hinders his efforts to establish the deepest personal presence possible with man. His bodiliness no longer enables others to pin him down, to make him an objectifiable thing. Rather, his bodiliness has become the perfect vehicle of his self expression. He can now give himself with a sovereign and absolute freedom and with an intimacy and intensity impossible before his glorification. Closely related to this point is Christ's presence to his Church. As a result of his glorification Christ is able to join himself to his Church more intimately than the human person is joined to his own body, so that the Church becomes "the Body of the Lord."[19]

The union of Christ with his Church in turn is closely related to another question important for the understanding of the real presence, namely, the question of grace. In opening himself up in love to us and in loving obedience to the Father and in having received the Father's acceptance of this loving obedience in the form of his own glorification through the Holy Spirit, Christ is now able to do more than merely unite the Church with himself. Through this union with himself he introduces his faithful into the life of grace, uniting them with himself and with the Father in the bond of unity, the Holy Spirit. In other words, he introduces his faithful into an interpersonal encounter with the entire Trinity. It is this life of grace which the Eucharist, in general, and the *real presence*, in particular, is meant to embody and express and, in so doing, to intensify.[20]

This leads to another question related to the proper understanding of the *real presence*, namely, that of the manifold presence of Christ in the Eucharist. Christ is present, first of all, in anyone living

---

19. For an excellent study of Christ's bodily existence before and after the Resurrection and the Ascension, seen in relation to the Eucharist, cf. Bulgakov, "Das eucharistische Dogma," 47–57, 79 and esp. 87. Cf. also, Powers, 103–11; Tillard, *The Eucharist: Pasch* . . . , 116 ff. and *S. T.* III, 54, 1 ad 2. Cf. also McKenna, "The Eucharist, Resurrection, and the Future," 144–65.

20. Cf. Davis, 160–66.

the life of grace. He is personally present in the whole believing community and in a special way when the faithful gather together in his name. He is present in the priest or president of the liturgical assembly and in the reading of the Sacred Scriptures in this assembly. In each of these cases he is *really*, personally, present and active although in different modes and in a different intensity. To understand the real presence of Christ in the gifts of bread and wine it is imperative that we situate this presence in the context of these other modes of his presence.[21]

The question of the real presence thus involves a number of related questions. It can only be understood properly against the background of an appreciation of Christ's glorified body, his personal presence to his Church and to the individual faithful and his manifold presence within the eucharistic celebration itself.

It is only within this larger context that the distinctive presence of Christ in the gifts—the presence usually referred to as the real presence—has its place and its meaning. This real presence is a substantial, lasting presence, lasting as long as the appearance of bread and wine are still food and drink. To refer to this presence as "substantial" presence is not to deny that the whole Christ is present in the other modes of his presence in the Eucharist. It is rather to affirm the distinctive character of Christ's presence in the gifts. Christ takes hold of the bread and wine and makes use of their bodiliness to offer himself in a "bodily presence" to the faithful. The bread and wine are not merely signs or tokens of Christ, pointing to him and reminding us of him. Rather, with the sovereignty and freedom that now belongs to his glorified bodily existence he identifies himself with the bread and wine using them to embody and express his eternal giving of himself to his Father and to the faithful. While remaining unchanged on the physical level, the bread and wine have indeed undergone a substantial change, a change which does not depend on the faith of the *individual* Christian. On the sacramental, ontological level they are no longer bread and wine; they *are* Jesus Christ, "body and blood, soul and divinity," offering to unite his faithful to himself in his sacrifice

---

21. Cf. Davis, 170–71, 176 and Schillebeeckx, *The Eucharist*, 103–104 as well as the *Constitution de Sacra Liturgia* (December 4, 1963), art. 7 in AAS 56 (1964), 100–101 and *Instructio de cultu mysterii eucharistici* (May 25, 1967) art. 9 in AAS 59 (1967), 547.

and thus to unite them with the Father and with each other in the Holy Spirit.[22]

The change in the bread and wine is, then, a real, substantial change—no less real than had it taken place on the merely physical level of reality. In fact, this change is more real, more substantial, than a merely physical change. The "bodily presence" of Christ in the bread and wine is also real—but no more real than the mutual presence of Christ and his faithful in the life of grace. In fact, it is this mutual, personal presence, this unity between Christ and his faithful and their unity with each other in Christ that the "bodily presence" of Christ in the gifts is to embody and express and, in so doing, to intensify. It is this personal unity of the faithful with Christ, and through Christ with the Father and with each other in the Holy Spirit, which is *the* real presence. It is this presence that is the *raison d'être* of the "bodily presence" of Christ in the Eucharist and of the change in the bread and wine. And this presence is a personal, and therefore, a reciprocal or mutual presence.[23]

From all this, two points should emerge. First of all, the "bodily presence" of Christ and the change which accompanies it, while important and even necessary, are always subordinate to the deeper, personal presence which they are intended to express and intensify. They should not, therefore, be allowed to occupy the center of the stage in any discussion of the Eucharist in general, and the epiclesis in particular. Secondly, even the personal presence of Christ offering himself to his Father and to his faithful does not constitute presence in the fullest sense since, as we have seen in examining the basic analogy, presence to be fully personal must be mutual, reciprocal. In the Eucharist, then, the Church[24] must also respond by opening up to Christ's gift of himself; otherwise we do not have presence in its fullest sense. The sacramental sign becomes, therefore, at the same

---

22. Cf. Davis, 171–73 and Schillebeeckx, ibid., 144–51, 42–53. Cf. also, Brunner, "Zur Lehre . . . ," 232–38; Schoonenberg, "The Real Presence . . . ," 9.

23. Cf. Davis, 160, 169, 176–77; Schillebeeckx, ibid., 140–41; Casel, *Das christliche Opfermysterium,* 464–65; Rahner, "Die Dauer . . . ," 395.

24. We presume here the Father's acceptance of Christ. In fact, this seems to underlie Christ's glorification. He is as man eternally in the act of giving himself to the Father in loving obedience (this includes giving himself to and for us) *and* of being accepted in his humanity by the Father in the full outpouring of the Holy Spirit. This giving and accepting represents the fullest, mutual presence envisionable and the paradigm for all other forms of personal presence.

time an embodiment of the mutual, personal presence of Christ and his Church and an invitation to every believer to participate personally in this presence. As Schillebeeckx puts it:

> . . . The presence offered by Christ in the Eucharist naturally precedes the individual's acceptance of this presence and is not the result of it. It there-fore remains an offered *reality*, even if I do not respond to it. My disbelief cannot nullify the reality of Christ's real offer and the reality of the Church's remaining in Christ. But, on the other hand, the eucharistic real presence also includes, in its sacramentality itself, reciprocity and is therefore completely realized only when consent is given in faith to the eucharistic event and when this event is at the same time accomplished personally, that is, when this reciprocity takes place, in accordance with the true meaning of the sign, in the sacramental meal.[25]

THE IMPLICATIONS OF PERSONALISTIC APPROACH FOR EPICLESIS/INSTITUTION QUESTION

The application of the personal encounter analogy to the question of the real presence has important implications for the notion of eucha-ristic "consecration" and, consequently, for the *moment of consecration* problem. Both these questions, in turn, have had a great impact on the understanding of the eucharistic epiclesis.

Consecration

Within the Scholastic framework of transubstantiation, *consecration* referred to the realization of the eucharistic presence. Following the analogy basic to this framework, however, this presence was conceived in physical terms. Thus the real presence was the *bodily presence* of Christ or the presence of Christ in the gifts of bread and wine. The consecration, consequently, was the changing or transformation of the bread and wine. The moment *this* change took place became, as we have already noted, the almost all important moment of consecration.

Within the personalistic framework , consecration might still be regarded as the realization of the eucharistic presence. Within this framework, however, presence has taken on a much broader meaning. Following the personal-encounter analogy basic to this framework, the

---

25. Schillebeeckx, *The Eucharist*, 141.

bodily presence of Christ and the change which takes place in the gifts become *means* toward the realization of a fuller, and more important, mutual presence.[26] This broader understanding of presence would, in turn, seem to call for a broader understanding of *consecration* in the Eucharist. Consecration, like presence, would then be seen not simply in light of the change in the material gifts but also in light of the change in those partaking. Their ability to respond to Christ's bodily presence and their share in the formation of a mutual, personal presence would thus become an integral part of the *consecration*.

The implications of such a wider notion of consecration for the epiclesis question would be numerous. To begin with, such a notion would seem to correspond with the liturgical data on the epiclesis. The early texts indicate that the epiclesis rarely, if ever, referred to a change in the gifts apart from a change in those partaking of the gifts. In addition, a broader notion of consecration would allow certain theological explanations of the epiclesis to take on greater significance and force. This would be especially true of those theological explanations which we have summed up under the heading, "The Epiclesis as Realizing the *Sacramentum*." [27] These explanations have in common the fact that they stress the function of the epiclesis in the adaptation of the gifts—already transformed into the body and blood of Christ—in view of their reception by the faithful.

In binding together the transformation of the gifts and the transformation of the faithful, the broader notion of consecration would also boost those explanations which see the epiclesis as the bond between consecration, in the narrower sense, and Communion, as well as those which see the epiclesis as an appeal for unity. For in this context the Communion would in a sense become as important as the change in the bread and wine since this Communion would be a sacramental expression of the reciprocity necessary to full, personal presence.[28] As N. Nissiotis puts it:

---

26. Once again, to affirm that the *bodily presence* of Christ and the change in the gifts are *means* is not to deny their importance or even their necessity. It is simply to subordinate these aspects of the Eucharist to the end for which they are intended; Cf. Casel, *Das christlich Opfermysterium*, 464–65.

27. Cf. above, Chapter 5.

28. Cf. Schillebeeckx, *The Eucharist*, 141. Interesting in this regard is the statement in the Faith and Order Studies 1964–1967, 61–62: "Anamnesis and epiklesis, being unitive acts, cannot be conceived apart form communion."

. . . The bread and the wine do not have value in themselves; it is given to them by the fact that they are consumed by and in the Body of Christ. In the East, the bread and the wine are described as a foretaste of the full communion of the Parousia, thus emphasizing that the fact that those who are already members of Christ's Body communicate, is just as important as the consecration of the material elements.[29]

Moreover, the broader notion of consecration brings out the purpose both of the change of the gifts and the Communion, namely, the sanctification of the faithful or, to be more specific, the union through Christ of the faithful with the Father and with each other in the bond of unity, the Holy Spirit.

The Moment of Consecration

Not only does the personalistic framework shed new light on the notion of consecration but in so doing it also seems to shed new light on the *moment of consecration* question which for so long has plagued the epiclesis question. Within the Scholastic transubstantiation framework the basic analogy is a physical one. Now, this basic physical analogy, at least as it has been employed in Scholastic circles, hardly seems to allow for degrees of presence. A *thing* is physically either there or not there.[30] In such a framework it is natural that the moment which marks the passage from physical absence to physical presence would become important. In fact, in such a framework there is the tendency to make this moment almost all-important and, as we have already remarked, this tendency seems to have made itself felt in the Scholastic treatment of the eucharistic presence.

Moreover, in the Scholastic framework the moment of presence, physical presence, not only became more important; it also became more determinable. At least, on the basis of a physical analogy in which one physical substance instantaneously replaces another, it might have seemed easier to determine the precise moment of this replacement.

If within the Scholastic framework the *moment of consecration* became more important and, seemingly at least, more determinable, it also became more problematic. For instance, when the patristic texts are brought to bear on the epiclesis question they often seem terribly

---

29. Nissiotis, "Pneumatologie orthodoxe," 99.

30. Cf. Mascall, 74–75; Powers, 122. Cf. also *S. T.* III, q. 75, a. 7 and Cummings, 137.

ambiguous. Perhaps it is the concern with, and the polemics over, the *moment of consecration* that have contributed to making them so. Perhaps it is because these texts have been uprooted from their native soil that they seem so obscure, their meaning so elusive. They stem from an environment where the question of a precise, exclusive *moment of consecration* made little sense and seems, in fact, never to have been posed. We have transplanted these same texts into an almost totally alien environment where the precise *moment of consecration* receives much, far too much attention. And it is in this alien environment that we have sought clear-cut answers to our questions about the epiclesis. It is little wonder that we rarely find in the patristic texts answers clear-cut and unambiguous enough to satisfy us.

The concentration on the *moment of consecration* has, however, raised problems not only in the interpretation of patristic texts. It seems also to have been at least partially responsible for producing or fostering attitudes toward the Eucharist in general, and Communion in particular, which could hardly be considered the most healthy.[31] The concentration on the *moment of consecration* has, to say the very least, proven to be far from an unmixed blessing, Salaville's statement that this concentration is a boon stemming from the "Latin genius"[32] notwithstanding.

In contrast to the Scholastic transubstantiation framework, the personalistic framework seems to make the moment of "bodily presence" less important, the moment of full presence less determinable and, consequently, the whole question of a *moment of consecration* less problematic. In the context of an analogy based upon an interpersonal encounter, "bodily presence" is less important than the fuller, mutual presence to which it can lead. In the same context, the change which brings about this "bodily presence" in the Eucharist and the moment in which this change takes place also are correspondingly less important.

Moreover, in the personalistic framework not only is the mutual, interpersonal presence more important, it is also more difficult to determine precisely. As long as one speaks of the eucharistic presence in terms of a purely physical change, it would seem easier to hold for a particular moment of change[33] and perhaps even seem easier to

---

31. Cf. Jungmann, *Missarum Sollemnia* I, 158 ff., II, 252 ff.; Smit, 120 and Powers, 28–31.

32. Salaville, "Epiclèse eucharistique," 292.

33. Cf. Mascall, 74–75 and Powers, 122.

pinpoint this moment. Once one begins to speak of this eucharistic presence in terms of personal encounter and intersubjective relationships, however, it would seem to follow that one cannot pinpoint the moment when full presence, full intersubjectivity is reached. A personal encounter between two persons is so complex, so mysterious that it would seem presumptuous to say at what precise moment this encounter reached its highpoint.

Within this personalistic context, then, it should become increasingly apparent that the question of a precise *moment of consecration* in the Eucharist is a question better left unasked or at least unanswered. This is not to say that there is no moment in which a mutual presence reaches its highpoint. Nor is it to say that it is anthropologically unsound or that Church authorities have no right to set temporal highpoints in the *ritual expression* of this mutual presence. It is normal and acceptable, it seems, to wish to set aside a certain *space of time* as distinct from another, e.g., a time when the assembly can continue to regard the gifts as bread and wine and a time when that same assembly can receive those gifts with the firm belief that they are no longer mere bread and wine but Jesus Christ offering himself to the faithful.[34] It also seems normal and acceptable to wish to set up practical norms for a space of time or even a particular point in the sacramental rite after which the gifts, for instance, are to be treated with a special reverence.

An attempt, however, to fix theologically an exact moment of consecration, while perhaps reflecting a normal human tendency, hardly seems acceptable. To attempt such a precision seems to be, in effect, to attempt to pinpoint God's sovereign action. And this would be to run the risk of making God, or at least God's free activity, an objectifiable "thing" to be gazed at, examined, etc. It is one thing, for instance, to say that the institution narrative expresses the necessary intention of the Church to do what Christ commanded and her faith that God will realize God's promises here and now and, thus, that the institution narrative has a consecratory value. It is quite another thing to pinpoint the exact moment when God joins the divine action to

---

34. This is the point that H. B. Meyer is making in his review of the German translation of Thurian's *L'Eucharistie* (cf. *ZKT* 86 [1964] 457).

this intention and faith of the Church.[35] This pinpointing is hardly acceptable even on the basis of a physical analogy. It becomes even more unacceptable on the basis of an interpersonal analogy.

The attitude most in keeping with the personalistic approach to the Eucharist would seem, then, to be the following: There is a moment in the Eucharist when Christ makes himself "bodily present" to his faithful. There is also a moment when the fuller, mutual presence, for which it is subordinate, reaches a highpoint. It is possible to indicate ritual expressions of these moments or highpoints, even to make these ritual expressions essential to the sacramental rite and the basis of practical norms of reverence. Beyond that, however, one ought to admit that one does not know precisely when such mysterious moments take place. Nor is it important that we know. That is God's work. The assembly's task is to celebrate these mysteries and to partake of the gifts with the firm belief that God is at work here and now and that what it is receiving is no longer merely bread and wine but Jesus Christ himself.[36]

This seems to have been the attitude of the early Fathers who saw the whole eucharistic prayer as consecratory. There were highpoints in this eucharistic prayer, to be sure, but for the Fathers the question of a precise *moment of consecration* remained basically unasked. Moreover, there seems to be a trend inside as well as outside the Roman Catholic tradition which reflects this same attitude in the treatment of the epiclesis question. Perhaps O. Casel was somewhat prophetic in this regard. He maintained that the solution of the epiclesis controversy lies in the West's ridding itself of the juridical, formalistic view that the institution narrative alone rather than the entire eucharistic prayer is consecratory and the East's returning to the ancient understanding of the effective power of the institution narrative. In a letter to Professor (late Bishop) W. Stählin dated March 13, 1939, Casel admitted that his view on the epiclesis question had not found general acceptance even among his Catholic colleagues. He was convinced, however, that this view, namely, that the whole canon is consecratory, would in the long run win the recognition because it

---

35. We presume here that such a pinpointing is not necessary to preserve the consecratory value of the institution narrative.

36. Cf. Dinesen, 105–106, 101, 103.

rested on a factual basis.[37] From within the Roman Catholic tradition,
A. Kavanagh reflected not only Casel's viewpoint and what seems
to have been that of the early Fathers but also some of the aspects we
have seen in examining the personalistic approach to the Eucharist.
"More is involved in 'consecration' than the transformation of bread
and wine into the sacramental body and blood of Christ. Considering
liturgically, in terms of the whole eucharistic prayer, 'consecration'
is a processive offering to the Father of the whole assembly—Christ's
body which is the church."[38]

Within the Orthodox tradition, too, there seems to be a
general reluctance today to speak of a *moment of consecration*.[39] Perhaps
more significant for current trends in regard to the *moment of consecration* is a statement contained in the *Resumé of the Emerging Ecumenical
Consensus on the Eucharist* prepared for the World Council of
Churches' Commission on Faith and Order and dated May, 1968:

> . . . The consecration cannot be limited to a particular moment in the
> liturgy. Nor is the location of the epiklesis in relation to the words of
> institution of decisive importance. In the early liturgies the whole "prayer
> action" was thought of as bringing about the reality promised by Christ.
> A recovery of such an understanding may help to overcome our differences
> concerning a special moment of consecration.[40]

It is perhaps in conjunction with this view, namely, that the
whole eucharistic prayer is consecratory, that the personalistic approach
carries the greatest implications for the epiclesis question. For the
personalistic approach, with its degrees of presence and its subordination
of physical presence to a fuller, mutual presence, provides a congenial
environment for seeing the whole eucharistic prayer as consecratory.
This is especially true when one combines the view that the whole

---

37. Casel, *Das christliche* . . . , 555.

38. Kavanagh, "Thoughts on the Roman Anaphora," 6–7.

39. Cf. P. Verghese, Syrian Orthodox priest and Associate General Secretary of the World
Council of Churches in his book, *The Joy of Freedom: Eastern Worship and Modern Man* (London,
1967), 50–51.

40. *The Resume of the Emerging Ecumenical Consensus on the Eucharist* (May, 1968) was very
kindly supplied to me in mimeograph form by Rev. Reinhard Groscurth of the World Council of
Churches' Secretariat on Faith and Order. The text we have cited is based on paragraphs produced
by the Faith and Order Commission at Bristol in 1967 and has appeared in a booklet entitled
Faith and Order Studies 1964–1967 (Lausanne, 1968), 62. Cf. also, Thurian, *L'Eucharistie*, 274–75;
Atchley, "The Epiclesis: A Criticism," 35; Hebert, "The Meaning of the Epiclesis," 208–209.

eucharistic prayer is consecratory with the broader notion of consecration reflected in the explanations summed up under the heading, "The Epiclesis as Realizing the *Sacramentum*." Admittedly, the personalistic framework may not succeed in banishing the moment of consecration question entirely. It should, however, alleviate this question considerably. And this would be a great boon to the question of the eucharistic epiclesis. For it would then be possible to concentrate on more important aspects of the epiclesis, namely, its relationship to the praying, believing assembly and to the Holy Spirit.

Chapter 8

The Epiclesis and the Realization of the Eucharist

The preceding chapter suggested possibilities for alleviating the "moment of consecration" question—an issue which has clouded the epiclesis question. This chapter will attempt to indicate how the eucharistic epiclesis[1] can shed light on various aspects involved in the realization of the Eucharist.

THE EPICLESIS AND THE PRAYING, BELIEVING ASSEMBLY

The epiclesis proper can serve as a reminder that God realizes the Eucharist *for* the assembly and, in particular for the partaking assembly. The epiclesis proper can also bring out the fact that God realizes the Eucharist *through* the believing assembly. Finally, the epiclesis proper can underscore the fact that it can only be as a *praying* assembly that the assembly has a share in the realization of the Eucharist.

Realization for the Partaking Assembly

To begin with, an epiclesis proper, similar to the more fully developed epiclesis of the early anaphoras, can underscore the fact that the transformation of the gifts has for its aim the benefit or transformation of the assembled faithful. In the earliest anaphoras, e.g., that of the *Apostolic Tradition* and that of Addai and Mari, the epiclesis seeks the sanctification of the assembled faithful. The transformation of the gifts

---

1. Unless otherwise indicated, we shall be speaking throughout this chapter of epiclesis proper, i.e., the developed epiclesis as found in the early anaphoras.

goes unmentioned. Even later, when the epiclesis did come to appeal for a transformation of the bread and wine into Christ's body and blood, the epiclesis made it clear that this transformation was in view of the assembly's sanctification. Almost invariably one reads of a transformation of the gifts *so that* the faithful might receive such benefits as unity, forgiveness, and life in the present and/or in the eschatological future.[2] It would be hard to find a clearer statement of the relationship between the transformation of the gifts and the transformation of the assembled faithful. Such a relationship, moreover, reflects the thought of such classical writers as Thomas Aquinas[3] and Nicholas Cabasilas[4] as well as modern personalistic thought which sees Christ's bodily presence in the Eucharist as a means to a fuller presence of Christ in his faithful and, in this sense, a transformation of the faithful. As B. Bobrinskoy puts it: "The purpose of sanctifying the material gifts lies outside themselves, in their utilization by man and in his edification."[5]

Not only, however, can an epiclesis proper bring out the fact that the transformation of the gifts finds its meaning and purpose in the sanctification of the assembled faithful; it also highlights the fact that this sanctification should take place through the *reception* of the gifts. In other words, the eucharistic epiclesis can underscore the unity of "consecration," in the narrower sense, and Communion. It is no

---

2. Cf. Chapter 1. Note the questions raised regarding the authenticity and dating of the *Apostolic Tradition* (Chapter 1,note 25). Cf. also Tillard, "L'Eucharistie . . . ," 369–74. In this connection it is interesting to note that the eschatological aspect seems to have been neglected in twentieth-century treatment of the epiclesis. Despite the fact that in the epicleses we have examined eternal life or some other eschatological benefit occurs more consistently than any of the other desired benefits, few twentieth-century authors seem to bring out the eschatological side of the epiclesis. Bouyer, *Eucharistie,* 176 (177), 182 (183), 301 (311) contends that the original epiclesis reflected the eschatological character of its *berakah* basis and Nissiotis, "The Importance of the Doctrine of the Trinity for Church Life and Theology," in *The Orthodox Ethos* edited by A. J. Philippou (Oxford, 1964), 69 states that: ". . . In invoking the Father to send the Spirit, the Church recapitulates and enacts the whole of the divine economy and effects the continuity and unity between cross, resurrection, Pentecost and the final Parousia . . . The epiclesis of the Spirit points [to] the moment of eternity already present in time and unites history with its source and purpose: the last things." Bobrinskoy, "Le Saint-Esprit, vie de l'église," 190 suggests a link between the Logos of "christological" epiclesis and Christ's second coming. He sees this type of epiclesis complementing the Spirit epiclesis. In general, however, the eschatological aspect of the epiclesis has received surprisingly little attention from twentieth-century students of the eucharistic epiclesis.

3. Cf. S. T. III, q. 73, a. 3.

4. Cf. Cabasilas, 25.

5. Bobrinskoy, "Présence réelle . . . ," 408.

accident that by far the majority of the epicleses examined ask that the gifts be transformed so that those *partaking* of these gifts ("accipientibus," "qui in fide vera ederit . . . et biberit," "μεταλαβόντες" "μετέχοντας" etc.) may benefit. The epiclesis texts take it for granted that those who have come together to celebrate the eucharistic meal will partake of that meal. In a modern context in which some theologians stress the meal character of the Eucharist and in which it is important not to separate the real presence of Christ in the bread and wine from the acceptance of this real presence in those partaking in Communion, this aspect of the epiclesis becomes increasingly important.

It is true that the "real (or "bodily") presence" of Christ in the Eucharist does not depend on the individual's belief or acceptance. Christ's offer of himself remains real even when it does not find personal acceptance on the part of the individual member of the assembly. Nevertheless, it is in view of this personal acceptance that Christ makes his offer. Whatever may be said for minimalist interpretations regarding the "validity" of the Eucharist,[6] one fact remains. Christ's *sacramental* offer of himself finds its complete realization only in the *sacramental* acceptance of this offer by the faithful.[7]

The eucharistic epiclesis is admirably suited to drive home this unity between the "consecration" or the realization of Christ's "bodily presence" and Communion or the sacramental acceptance of this "bodily presence."[8] An epiclesis proper can thus serve as a reminder that God realizes the "bodily presence" of Christ in the Eucharist *for* the assembly and, more specifically, for the communicating assembly.

Realization through the Assembly

Not only, however, can an epiclesis proper call to mind the fact that God realizes the Eucharist *for* the assembly; it can also indicate that

---

6. Cf. Ledogar, "Faith, Feeling . . . ," 15. Cf. also, Schillebeeckx, *Christ the Sacrament*, 123–27.

7. Schillebeeckx, *The Eucharist*, 141. Cf. also, Bobrinskoy, "Présence réelle . . . ,"405–412, esp. 408–409; Nissiotis, "Pneumatologie orthodoxe," 10.

8. In this regard we might simply mention in passing Kavanagh's criticism of a "split epiclesis," i.e., placing the appeal of the epiclesis for the transformation of the gifts before the institution narrative and the appeal for the sanctification of the faithful after the institution narrative. Cf. Kavanagh, "Thoughts on the New Eucharistic Prayers," 6, 9–12. Besides the other reservations that Kavanagh has in regard to this "split epiclesis," it would seem that it does run the risk of obscuring the basic unity of "consecration" and Communion. Cf. also, John H. McKenna, "Eucharistic Prayer: Epiclesis," in *Gratias Agamus; Studien zum eucharistischen Hochgebet*, edited by Andreas Heinz and Heinrich Rennings (Vienna 1992) 287–90.

God realizes the Eucharist *through* the assembly. This latter proposition is admittedly a delicate one. Yet we should investigate this proposition carefully. One danger in the later Scholastic approach lay in focusing too much attention on the material elements of the outward sacramental sign. One could thereby get, and give, the impression that the realization of the sacrament rests to a great extent on the mere juxtaposition of words and gestures. One would thus leave oneself wide open the accusation of championing a sacramental physicism or magic. There are also some who, perhaps in reaction to such a sacramental physicism, emphasize that it is God alone who realizes the Eucharist. For these people, the proposition that the assembly plays a role in the realization of the sacraments can be particularly touchy.

Both the aforementioned positions, when carried too far, seem to jeopardize a balanced understanding of the Eucharist. For, to deny the role that the believing assembly plays in the realization of the Eucharist—whether one makes this denial in favor of the external rite or even in favor of the divine intervention—is to deny a very real aspect of the eucharistic encounter.

It is especially within a personalistic approach to the sacraments that this becomes clear. Once one admits that a full, personal encounter must by its very nature be mutual, the believing response of the Church becomes a necessary element in the realization of the sacramental encounter. For the sacramental sign of the Eucharist is not merely a symbol of Christ's "bodily presence" to his Church. It is at the same time a symbol of the presence of the Church, believing and responsive, to Christ.[9] Christ's presence in the Eucharist is not realized out of a clear blue sky. It is in the context of a believing assembly, an assembly which celebrates the memorial of Christ's Passion, death, Resurrection, and Ascension, that God intervenes.[10] It is in this context, a context which presupposes not only God's intervention but also the Church's faith, that the presence of Christ to his Church *and* of his Church to

---

9. Schillebeeckx, *The Eucharist*, 141–42: "The eucharistic presence is therefore not dependent on the faith of the individual, but the sacramental offer cannot be thought of as separate from the community of the Church. It is, after all, a real presence of Christ *and of his Church*." (Italics his). Cf. also, Kavanagh, "Thoughts on the Roman Anaphora," 6–7.

10. Cf. Thurian, *Le pain unique*, 39–47 where he brings out this context well in relating the anamnesis and the epiclesis.

Christ takes place. And it is in this context that the individual is invited to become personally involved in this mutual presence.[11]

Thus, both the human and the divine elements belong to, are necessary for, the full symbolic reality. That it is God who takes the initiative, that God is absolutely free and sovereign in realizing the Eucharist, is undeniable. Without the divine intervention there is simply no sacrament, no sacramental encounter. It is, nevertheless, also undeniable that the Church plays a role, however subordinate, in the realization of the sacrament. Without the Church's faith there is also no sacrament and no sacramental encounter. As Rahner, speaking of the sacrament as an "efficacious word,"[12] puts it:

> . . . In this relationship of efficacious word of God and the effective hearing of the word, which is also effected by God himself, both realities are so interrelated that one can safely say: if one was not there, the other could not exist either or, at least, it could not be what it is. . . [but] what was said in the Reformation teaching about the act of faith constituting the presence of the Lord, although it was false and heretical when applied to the individual, can have a good Catholic sense when said of the Church as a whole.[13]

That the faith of the Church is necessary for the realization of a sacrament is hardly something new. Augustine, for instance, clearly recognized this. He acknowledged the power of the word in realizing a sacrament: "Accedit verbum ad elementum, et fit sacramentum."[14] He hastened to add, however, that the power of this word hinges not on the fact that it is spoken but on the fact that it is believed: *"Unde ista tanta virtus aquae, ut corpus tangat et cor abluat, nisi faciente verbo, non quia dicitur, sed quia creditur?"* ("Where then does the water get such power that it touches the body and cleanses the heart, unless it is the action of the word, not because it is spoken, but because it is believed?")[15] Thomas Aquinas cited and seconded Augustine on the

---

11. Schillebeeckx, *The Eucharist*, 143–44.

12. Rahner, "Wort und Eucharistie," *Schriften* . . . IV, 330.

13. Rahner, ibid.; 353. Cf. Bouyer, *Eucharistie*, 433-34 (467) and Brunner, "Zur Lehre . . . ," 217 as well as above, chapter 6. The balanced approach of these authors seems to underscore the one-sidedness of positions such as that of Salaville, "Epiclèse eucharistique," 201-202 who insists that the words of "consecration" must be pronounced *in persona Christi* and not *in nomine Ecclesiae*. Both dimensions, divine and ecclesial have to be represented or present in some way for a really complete eucharistic presence.

14. *Tractatus in Johannis evangelium* 80:3 (CCL 36:529).

15. Ibid., (Italics mine). Cf. Ledogar, "Faith, Feeling . . . ," 14–15.

necessity of faith for the realization of the sacrament.[16] In addition, Thomas pointed out that this is why the intention of the minister to do what the Church intends is a *minimul* requirement for the realization of a sacrament. This intention supplies, at least minimally, a necessary component, namely, the faith of the Church.[17] Bonaventure was no less clear on this point.[18]

As already seen, the Orthodox tradition, following the lead of such men as Nicholas Cabasilas also recognizes the need for the Church to express her belief and apply the words of Christ here and now to the realization of the Eucharist. It goes without saying that the Reformation tradition has affirmed, perhaps at times with too individualistic a bent,[19] the necessity of faith for the sacraments.

Even Trent, for all its opposition to the proposition that the sacraments confer grace through faith *alone*,[20] insisted on the necessity of the intention of the minister for the realization of a sacrament.[21] And as we have just seen, both Thomas and Bonaventure viewed this intention in terms of the Church's faith. Unfortunately, since Trent's rejection of the position that faith *alone* was sufficient, sacramental theology, within the Roman Catholic tradition at least, "has spent most of its time *minimizing* the role of faith in sacramental action."[22] Vatican II happily reasserted the necessity of faith as a presupposition for the realization of the sacraments.[23]

In view of all this it seems hard not only to deny that the Church's faith is necessary for the realization of a sacrament but also,

---

16. S. T. III, q. 60, a. 6 and 7 ad 1. Cf. Ledogar, ibid., 15.

17. Cf. S. T. III, q. 64, a. 9. Cf. also Schillebeeckx, *The Eucharist,* 142; Ledogar, ibid.

18. Bonaventure, *In IV Sententiarum* d. 6, p. 2, a. 2, q. 1 ad 2 (*Opera Omnia,* Quaracchi edition, IV [1889], 153) and *Breviloquium* Paris VI, ch. 7 (*Opera Omnia,* Quaracchi edition, V [1891], 271–72). Cf. Fransen, 16 and Schillebeeckx, ibid., 142 n. 55 who offers an additional reminder that the statements of both Thomas and Bonaventure in this regard have to be considered within the context of the medieval understanding of the Eucharistic presence.

19. Cf. Rahner, "Wort und Eucharistie," 353.

20. DS 1608 (851).

21. DS, 1611 (854); cf. DS, 1312 (695), 1262 (672) and R. de Salvo, *The Dogmatic Theology on the Intention of the Minister in the Confection of the Sacraments* (Washington, 1949), 20. In this context Ledogar, "Faith, Feeling . . . ," 15 remarks that Trent also acknowledged that no one was ever justified without faith. Cf. DS, 1529–31 (799–800).

22. Ledogar, ibid. (Italics his).

23. Cf. *Constitutio de Sacra Liturgia* (December 4, 1963), art. 59 in AAS 56 (1964), 116. Cf. also, E. J. Lengeling, *Die Konstitution des zweiten vatikanischen Konzils über die Heilige Liturgie* (Münster, 1964), 134 in his commentary on this article.

in consequence of this, to deny that the Church plays a very real role in the realization of the sacraments.[24] Moreover, it is important to keep two things in mind. First, it is a question here of realizing not simply the so-called fruits of the real presence, although the Church's faith certainly plays a role in realizing these as well.[25] Rather, it is a question here of realizing the real presence itself. Secondly, it is normally, ideally, the faith of the Church here and now present, i.e., the local assembly, which shares in this realization. It may be true that, in the absence of a believing assembly here and now, the intention of the minister may supply the *minimum* required for a sacrament, namely, the faith of the church at large. This remains, however, the bare minimum,[26] and one should build one's theology not on the minimum but rather upon the ideal or normal. As R. Ledogar puts it, ". . . normally speaking, it is the faith of those *present* (i.e., the faith of the church which they have made their own) that accomplishes the marvelous change and transformation that our Roman tradition calls 'Transubstantiation.'"[27]

Thus, God freely and sovereignly effects a real presence in the Eucharist. God does so, however, through the faith of the Church, since this presence involves both Christ present and offering himself to his Church and the Church accepting and responding to this offer in faith. Moreover, involved in this mutual presence is an invitation to

---

24. This does not, of course, preclude disagreement over the terms used to describe the Church's part in the sacramental encounter, e.g., "to cause," "to effect," "to share in the realization of," "to play a role," etc. All too often these terms have nuances or, even more regrettably, in the course of polemics have taken on connotations which make them unacceptable to one party or another.

25. Besides its prayer, issuing from faith, that the Holy Spirit open the recipient to God's saving presence, the assembly by manifesting its own faith can help, *at least* on the psychological plane, to stir up the faith of the recipient. Cf. Ledogar, "Faith, Feeling . . . ," 19–23.

26. Nissiotis, "Worship, Eucharist . . . ," 214–15, if one takes his words literally, would seem to go one step further. He declares that, "It is, therefore, impossible for one priest to celebrate alone a service of Holy Communion as 'his mass', and no Communion service can be *valid* with only one communicant." (Italics mine). While acknowledging all the dangers to the essentially communal nature of the Eucharist, and even the abuses, that the so-called private mass could lead to, one would also have to admit that it would not be possible for the Roman Catholic tradition to accept the claim that such Masses were invalid. Schillebeeckx, *The Eucharist*, 142 n. 54 reflects what seems to be a more realistic position in this regard: "On the basis of the presence of both Christ and his Church, the *liturgical* form of the Eucharist requires the presence of a believing community. The *dogmatic* form of the 'real presence' of the people of God is undoubtedly preserved in the so-called 'private mass,' namely in the consecrated signs (which 'we are,' as Augustine said), but, if there is no real community celebrating mass together with the priest, the possibility of a liturgical experience of this reciprocal real presence is reduced to a minimum!" (Italics his).

27. Ledogar, "Faith, Feeling . . . ," 23.

each individual in the assembly to personally share in this presence and thus have it attain the goal for which it was intended.

We have dwelt on the role that the Church's faith plays in the realization of a sacrament because of the implications this role has for an understanding of the Eucharist and, in particular, of the eucharistic epiclesis. For if the Church's faith is indeed necessary for the realization of the Eucharist, those explanations which regard the epiclesis proper as an expression of the Church's intention and/or the Church's faith take on increased significance. For these explanations would in effect be saying that the epiclesis proper expresses an element which is absolutely necessary for the realization of Eucharist. In other words, they would be saying that the epiclesis proper can express the fact that God realizes the Eucharist *through* the assembly.[28] The fully developed eucharistic epiclesis could thus help counteract any tendency to deny the role that the believing assembly plays in the realization of the Eucharist. This holds true whether such a denial stems from an exaggerated emphasis on the external rite in the sacrament or an isolated stress on the divine intervention.

Moreover, an epiclesis proper could also help counteract any tendency to exaggerate the role of the ordained minister, as important as that is, at the expense of the whole assembly. The stress on the exclusive consecratory value of the institution narrative, coupled with the insistence that the ordained minister pronounces the words of consecration *in persona Christi* and not *in nomine ecclesiae*,[29] can tend to play down the role of the whole assembly in the realization of the Eucharist. The roles of both should be balanced. The attention given to the "intention of the minister" within a Scholastic framework,[30] while understandable in the context, could tend in a similar direction. The epiclesis proper could do much to underscore the fact that normally it is through the *whole* assembly, not merely through the ordained minister, that God acts here and now. The ordained minister does indeed have a special and necessary function. One might even regard him as a sort of symbolic point of convergence where Christ's offer of himself and the assembly's believing response to this offer find expression. Nevertheless, it is the whole assembly which, through the

---

28. Meyendorff, "Notes . . . ," 28 has expressed this aspect of the epiclesis well.

29. Cf., for instance, Salaville, "Epiclèse eucharistique," 201.

30. Cf. Schillebeeckx, *Christ the Sacrament*, 122–31.

mouth of the ordained minister, calls upon God to make his presence felt here and now. It is through the *whole* assembly that God realizes the Eucharist.

The eucharistic epiclesis can underline the fact that God realizes the Eucharist *for* the believing assembly. It can also express the fact that God realizes the Eucharist *through* the assembly and through the *whole* assembly. It is important to note, however, that it, in the final analysis, is always God who does the realizing. It is to this final point and its relationship to the epiclesis that we now turn.

Realization through the Praying Assembly

Some authors shy away from the thought that the assembly plays a role in the realization of the Eucharist. They do so, it seems, precisely because of their desire to underline the absolute sovereignty of God in effecting the sacraments. Admittedly, an exaggerated concentration on the rite or the assembly's role in the Eucharist can detract from a healthy understanding of this divine sovereignty in realizing the sacraments. For instance, a juridical, mechanistic presentation of the doctrine of *ex opere operato*, cannot only exaggerate by giving the impression that the physical rites are "magical"; such a presentation can also exaggerate by giving the impression that the Church or the assembly has a certain control over God in regard to the sacraments.

In the preceding section, however, we were concerned with avoiding another extreme, namely, the denial of any role to the assembly in the realization of the Eucharist. Once one acknowledges this role and admits that the epiclesis can express this role, the way is clear to examine a more obvious and more important facet of the eucharistic epiclesis. This is the facet which reflects the assembly's basic dependence in the realization of the Eucharist. In the eucharistic prayer the assembly gratefully acknowledges the wonderful deeds of God (the *mirabilia Dei*) in creation and in the events of redemption, one of the highpoints of which is the institution of the Lord's Supper. The assembly sees in the renewed celebration of the Lord's Supper a memorial of all God's wonders but especially of the greatest wonder of all, Jesus Christ, and his "passover" through death to a new life. Moreover, the assembly proclaims that in celebrating Christ's paschal mystery in the Eucharist it does so in grateful obedience to his command to, "Do this as a memory of me."

At the same time, the assembly is aware that what it is now doing is a memorial in the fullest, biblical sense of that word. For the community not only recalls Christ and his paschal mystery; it firmly believes that, on the basis of his promises, God will act here and now and will transform the gifts of bread and wine. God will make Christ present in his eternally actual offering of himself to his Father and to his fellow men. Despite its confidence that God will act here and now, however, the assembly is aware of its limitations. It cannot induce the divine action. It cannot force God's hand. It can only acknowledge God's wonders and *pray*, pray that God will make these wonders present here and now for this assembly. There is no question of the assembly's doubting that God will act. Its confidence, however, rests not on its own power. This confidence rests rather on the promises of God and on the awareness that the prayer of the assembly is united to that of Christ.

As long as one remains conscious of this basic dependence of the community upon God for the realization of the Eucharist, as long as one keeps in mind that the assembly always stands before God as a *praying* assembly, there is little danger of ignoring God's absolute sovereignty in one's understanding of the Eucharist. One of the greatest values of an epiclesis proper lies, moreover, in its ability to drive home the fact that the believing assembly must pray for the realization of the Eucharist. The fully developed epiclesis, whatever else it may be, is always a prayer. Even the view that the primitive meaning of epiclesis was the naming of a name must include this prayer aspect or face the accusation of magical tendencies.

In the epiclesis, the assembly, having recalled the events of saving history and having made grateful acknowledgment of these events, confesses its own helplessness. It appeals to God to act upon the bread and wine in view of those about to partake of them. In other words, the assembly appeals to God to transform both the gifts and the assembled faithful so that this celebration of the Eucharist may bring about a mutual, eucharistic presence. The assembly asks God to intervene here and now so that this celebration may express and deepen the unity between Christ and his faithful and the unity of the faithful with each other and with the Father in Christ. All of this it asks for through the action of the Holy Spirit. How and when this action is to take place is God's concern. The believing community's concern is to partake of the gifts with the firm assurance, springing from faith, that God has answered its prayer. One major contribution of the epiclesis proper to a healthy understanding the Eucharist lies precisely in its ability to express the helplessness and dependence and, at the same time, the prayerful confidence of the assembly.

Thus, the epiclesis serves various functions. It can bring out the fact that God realizes the Eucharist *for* the assembly and that he does so *through* the *whole* assembly. It can also bring out the fact that this assembly is a *praying* assembly, totally dependent upon God for the initiative in realizing the eucharistic encounter. We have seen all these facets of the epiclesis before. Our purpose here is to show that it is not a question of exclusivity but rather one of complementarity and that an epiclesis proper is well suited to voice these various facets simultaneously.

Furthermore, there is still another facet of the epiclesis proper which deserves our attention. With rare exceptions the fully developed epiclesis of the early anaphoras is an appeal for the Holy Spirit. This aspect of the epiclesis question must also be considered.

THE EPICLESIS AND THE HOLY SPIRIT

It would be presumptuous to think that one could propose all-embracing, definitive solutions to the complex questions surrounding the epiclesis. The relationship of the epiclesis to the Holy Spirit's role in the Eucharist is a case in point. A proper grasp of the Spirit's activity in the Eucharist would involve a study in itself. Even the decrees of Vatican II leave much to be desired here.[31] Nevertheless, it is necessary to broaden the horizons on the epiclesis question to include the role of the Holy Spirit both in saving history and in the Eucharist. The need to reconcile the activity of Christ with that of the Holy Spirit in the Eucharist is inherent in the view which sees the epiclesis

---

31. Cf. Tillard, "L'Eucharistie et le Saint-Esprit," 363–64 who notes that the *Decree on the Ministry and Life of Priests* (December 7, 1965) AAS 58 [1966], 991–1024), art. 5 and the *Instruction on Eucharistic Worship* (May 25, 1967) (AAS 59 [1967], 539–73), art. 3, 6, 8, 38, 50 have made a more conscious effort here. Cf. Bobrinskoy, "Le Saint-Esprit vie de l'église," 195 who quotes a Catholic expert at Vatican II as referring to the Holy Spirit as still "ce grand méconnu." " Celui dont on ne savait comment parler et où les paroles sonnaient creux." Cf. also, Verheul, 51.

as an expression of the Spirit's role in the Eucharist. This became
evident when dealing with that theological explanation of the epiclesis.
To reconcile the activity of Christ and the Holy Spirit in the
Eucharist, however, it is first necessary to reconcile this activity in the
broader context of the saving economy. Consequently, a brief sketch of
the interaction of Christ and the Spirit in saving history and in the
Eucharist will precede the application of insights in these two areas
to the epiclesis question.

The Holy Spirit and Saving History

If Christ is the sacrament of encounter between God and ourselves,[32]
it is because he bears within his "body-person" the fullness of the Holy
Spirit. One may speak of a Johannine-Alexandrian approach which
stresses the Incarnation or the descendant, Logos-Flesh movement. In
this approach the emphasis is on the fact that the Logos became one
of us and by so doing divinized us.[33] One may also speak of the
Pauline-Antiochene approach which stresses the death-resurrection
(glorification) or the ascendant, Human-Divine movement. Here the
emphasis is on the fact that the Son of God, become one of us, is
made *Kyrios* or Lord only at the moment of his Resurrection.[34]

Nevertheless, here as elsewhere it is a question not of exclusivity
but of complementarity. Incarnation is not simply the fact that the
Logos or Second Person of the Trinity took on human flesh through
birth. Incarnation, in its fullest sense, is a life-time process of becoming
human, fully human. For Christ it involved a progressive opening up
in loving obedience to his Father and in love to us. Corresponding to
this opening up on the part of Christ was his progressively being filled
with the Holy Spirit or, to put it another way, the fullness of the Holy
Spirit, which he possessed from the beginning, was gradually being
unveiled in him. The culmination of this dynamic process took place
in his death, Resurrection, and glorification.[35]

Thus, whether one looks upon the redemptive process as a
gradual filling up of Christ with the Spirit or as a gradual unveiling of

---

32. Cf. Schillebeeckx, *Christ the Sacrament,* esp. 5–54.

33. Cf. Tillard, *The Eucharist: Pasch* . . . , 71–102.

34. Ibid., 102–12.

35. Schillebeeckx, *Christ the Sacrament,* 20–27. Cf. also, Verheul, 52–58 who outlines very
well the Spirit's role in the various stages of Christ's saving mission.

the fullness of the Holy Spirit which Christ possessed from the first moment of the Incarnation, a number of common factors emerge. First, a progressive "transformation" of the human Christ is involved. Secondly, the whole process involves an interaction between Christ and the Spirit. It is not a question of an either-or here. This becomes especially clear when one views the activity of Christ and the Spirit in relationship to the sanctification of humankind. We have here a double presence, a double service and mediation, a double action of Christ in the Spirit and the Spirit in Christ serving as "the two hands of the Father" in drawing man into a new life.[36] Moreover, it is no question of a watered down notion of "appropriation" in which the distinctive divine personalities become lost in the common, *ad extra* activity of the Trinity. Rather, it is "appropriation" in the strong sense which the Greek tradition and writers like Thomas Aquinas within the Latin tradition have given this notion.[37] Drawing us up into the Trinitarian life is indeed a common work. In achieving it, however, each Person keeps his own characteristics; the operation comes from the Father, through the Son and is accomplished in the Holy Spirit. Finally, both approaches to the redemptive process agree in seeing the Resurrection, or perhaps more exactly, the paschal mystery, as the event which enables Christ to dispense to us the Spirit with which he is filled, the Spirit of new life. It is the Holy Spirit who accomplishes our sanctification, who carries the work of Christ to its fulfillment. Or, to put it another way, it is Christ, filled with the Holy Spirit, who, through his own Resurrection and exaltation as Lord (*Kyrios*), is now able freely to communicate this life-giving Spirit to us.

One can regard the paschal mystery as the event which enables Christ to radiate the fullness of the Spirit which he possessed from the very first moment of the Incarnation.[38] Or one can see this paschal mystery as the event through which Christ is transformed and *receives* the fullness of the Spirit which he, as *Kyrios*, shares with us.[39] It seems, however, to be basically a case of different emphases.[40] In both

---

36. Cf. Bobrinskoy, "Le Saint-Esprit vie de l'église," 186–87, 191.

37. Cf. Tillard, *The Eucharist: Pasch* . . . , 89–90, 94–95; P. H. Dondaine, *La Trinité* II (Paris, 1950), 409–23.

38. Tillard, ibid., 72–73.

39. Ibid., esp. 104–105.

40. Ibid., 111–12, 120. Cf. Verheul, 57.

approaches, moreover, it is clear that Christ, as *Kyrios*, as triumphant Lord, exercises his saving activity only in the Spirit ("en pneumati"). Thus in the saving economy, while each one has a distinct role, the activity of Christ and the Holy Spirit are inseparably entwined. This "symbiosis" holds true for any saving activity but especially for that of the glorified Lord. As J. M. Tillard puts it: "One sees then that for Paul, when it is necessary to designate the agents, the names *Kyrios* and *Pneuma* are interchangeable. Jesus is Lord in the Holy Spirit."[41] This "pneumatological Christology," as Nissiotis calls it,[42] has important implications for the Eucharist and for the eucharistic epiclesis as well.

The Holy Spirit and the Eucharist

The first implication of the relationship of Christ and the Spirit in the saving economy, flows from the fact that the Eucharist is an activity of the triumphant Lord, the glorified *Kyrios*. To say that the glorified Lord is at work is automatically to say that the Holy Spirit is at work since the glorified Lord is the Spirit-filled Lord, the "pneumatic Christ."[43] It is the penetration of Christ by the Spirit which has brought about Christ's glorification and it belongs to the Holy Spirit to bring the work of Christ to its fulfillment. It belongs to the Holy Spirit to take the historic and objective work of Christ, the summit of which is the paschal mystery, and to actualize it in the lives and destinies of the faithful and of all humankind.[44]

In the Eucharist he does this not only by realizing the so-called fruits of the Eucharist in the faithful; he is also intimately bound up with the transformation of the bread and wine into the body and blood of the Lord. The testimony that it is the Holy Spirit who realizes this transformation, apart from any question about the moment in which he does so, is unimpeachable. Theodore of Mopsuestia, Cyril of Jerusalem, John Chrysostom, Augustine, Paschase Radbert, and

41. Tillard, "L'Eucharistie et le Saint-Esprit," 367; cf. 376. Brunner "Zur Lehre . . . ," 355–56 speaks of the "dynamischer Identifikation" of Christ and the Holy Spirit since Christ's resurrection and glorification.

42. Cf. Nissiotis, "Pneumatological Christology . . . ," 241. Cf. also, Clément, "Après Vatican II . . . ," 46–47.

43. Cf. Tillard, "L'Eucharistie . . . ," 366–69. Cf. also O. Casel, "Mysteriengegenwart," JLW 8 (1928), 161–63.

44. Cf. Tillard, *The Eucharist: Pasch* . . . , 120 and the same author's "L'Eucharistie . . . ," 367.

Thomas Aquinas,[45] not to mention many of the early epicleses, are among the numerous witnesses to this fact.

The bread and wine have become "spiritual" nourishment in the fullest sense of that word. They are filled with the Holy Spirit. For they are no longer ordinary bread and wine but the body and blood of the glorified Christ who has become "Spirit-ized," filled with the Holy Spirit. They are radically different just as Christ after his resurrection and ascension is radically different, since the bread and wine, as he, have been impregnated with the Holy Spirit. The bread and wine *are* the "pneumatic Lord, the *Kyrios*." As Tillard puts it, "Everything becomes clear when one discovers, with the great Tradition, that the Body and Blood thus present are the Body and Blood of the Risen Lord, therefore the *Spirit-ized ("pneumatiques")* Body and Blood."[46] Moreover, since after the Ascension it is only in and by the Holy Spirit that Christ is present to his Church, the intervention of the Holy Spirit is indispensable for the accomplishment of this "eucharistic wonder."[47]

The real wonder, however, has yet to take place. The whole purpose of the "humanization" of the Logos is the "divinization" of us. Evdokimov sums it up well when he says, "God became incarnated in man and man became Spiritualized in God. To the Incarnation, the humanization of God corresponds to the pneumatization, the divinization of man."[48] The purpose of Christ's Resurrection and Ascension was similarly not to take Christ away from his disciples; it was to make him present to them in a new way. His presence was to be interiorized. No longer was he to stand before them; he was to live on within them. This is the goal of the Eucharist. It is precisely this interiorization and divinization, moreover, that is the task of the Holy Spirit in the Eucharist. He is there not simply to "Spirit-ize" the bread and wine by making the glorified body and blood of Christ present in them. Even

45. Cf. Salaville, "Epiclèse eucharistique," 235–47; Tillard, L'Eucharistie . . . ," 378–83; Cabrol, "Le canon romain et la messe," 515–17; Smit, 118–19.

46. Tillard, "L'Eucharistie . . . ," 376.

47. Cf. Tillard, *The Eucharist: Pasch* . . . , 112–27. It is, however, especially from the Orthodox theologians that one receives, if not a grasp at least a glimpse of, the richness of the relationship of Christ's glorified body, the Holy Spirit and the Eucharist in the light of the Resurrection and Ascension. Cf. esp. Bulgakov, "Das eucharistische Dogma," 47–55 and Evdokimov, "Eucharistie . . . ," 59–62.

48. Evdokimov, *L'Orthodoxie*, 251.

more he is there to "Spirit-ize" those who partake of the bread and wine by making the glorified Lord present in *them*.

This "Spirit-izing" of those partaking involves two aspects. First, the Holy Spirit makes the body and blood of Christ, in a sense, capable of achieving its saving effects in the faithful. Secondly, the Holy Spirit works in the hearts of the faithful to open them to the action of the sacramental body and blood of the Lord. As we have pointed out a number of times already, if either the presence of Christ offering himself *or* the acceptance of the assembled faithful is lacking, a full sacramental encounter does not take place. Now, it is the Holy Spirit who makes possible not only the offer and the attitude of acceptance *but also* the joining of the two here and now in the celebration of the Eucharist.[49]

Finally, before closing this section we should emphasize once more that it is in no way a question of the Holy Spirit replacing Christ in the Eucharist. It is permissible, even necessary at times, to concentrate on one or the other for the purpose of obtaining a better theological grasp of their distinct roles in the Eucharist. One should, however, never lose sight of the fact that the Eucharist is inseparably an action of the *Kyrios*, glorified Lord, and of the *Pneuma tou Kyriou*, the Spirit of the Lord. It is the Risen Lord exercising his Lordship in the Spirit or, to put it another way, it is the Spirit of the Lord at work.[50]

The Holy Spirit and the Epiclesis

The effort to view the epiclesis against the broader context of the Holy Spirit's activity in saving history and in the Eucharist has a number of important consequences for the epiclesis question. First of all, a glance at the Spirit's activity in saving history indicates the value of attempts to parallel the epiclesis with the Incarnation, the Resurrection, the Ascension, and Pentecost. As long as such attempts do not lose sight of the basic unity of the Spirit's activity in saving history, as long as they avoid an either-or exclusivity in regard to the Spirit's role in the Incarnation, Resurrection, etc., they can shed much light on the

---

49. Cf. Tillard, "L'Eucharistie . . . ," 378. Cf. also, Bobrinskoy, "Présence Réeli . . . ," 414.

50. Cf. Tillard, ibid., 369, 373–77. Cf. also, Bobrinskoy, "Le Saint-Esprit dans la Liturgie," 58, 56, Davies, *The Spirit* . . . , 136–40 and Craig, 22, 25–28 who points out that Nicholas Cabasilas took this complementarity into account. Cf. also, von Allmen, *Prophétisme sacramentel*, 291–93, 299–300 and Verheul, 58–59.

Spirit's role in the Eucharist by situating this role in the broader
perspective of saving history. For the Holy Spirit forms a unifying
thread between the Incarnation, as we have explained it above, the
death, Resurrection, Ascension and the crown of all these, Pentecost.
He does so by "Spirit-izing" Christ, by transforming Christ into
a "life-giving Spirit"[51] for us and by carrying this life-giving function
of Christ to its fulfillment.

It is, moreover, the epiclesis proper which gives voice to the
Spirit's role in the accomplishment of Christ's life-giving function in
the Eucharist. It is the epiclesis proper which makes it clear that
without the Holy Spirit the eucharistic, "pneumatic"[52] body and blood
of Christ are not present. It is the epiclesis proper which underscores
the Holy Spirit's role in "Spirit-izing" the bread and wine and making
them objective means of salvation for those who properly partake of
them. Furthermore, it is the epiclesis proper, especially the Antiochene
type, which invokes and expresses the Spirit's activity not only upon
the eucharistic gifts but also upon the assembled faithful. The eucharistic epiclesis thus makes it clear that the Eucharist is there so that
the Holy Spirit may fill, may "Spirit-ize" the faithful as he has already
"Spirit-ized" Christ and the gifts. In fact, it would be hard to find
a better expression of the Spirit's role in the Eucharist than a fully
developed epiclesis proper.

To raise the objection that such a stress on the role of the
Holy Spirit downgrades Christ's role in the Eucharist is to miss the
interplay of Christ and the Holy Spirit in the saving economy. To ask
"Is it Christ or is it the Holy Spirit who consecrates?" is to ask a false
question. The very fact, however, that this question has been asked in
conjunction with the epiclesis indicates the need to place the epiclesis
in the context of a "pneumatological Christology."[53] It also indicates
the truth of Evdokimov's contention that what separates the East and
the West in this area is not the fact of the epiclesis but rather the
theology of the Holy Spirit to which the epiclesis gives voice.[54]

51. Cf. Romans 1:4 and the accompanying footnote (d) in *The Bible of Jerusalem;* cf. also,
Romans 8:11, Acts 2:32–36, 2 Corinthians 3:18.

52. Cf. Tillard, *The Eucharist: Pasch* . . . , 105 ff.

53. Nissiotis, "Pneumatological Christology . . . ," sp. 235–36, 239, 240–44.

54. Evdokimov, *L'Orthodoxie,* 250.

Is an Epiclesis Proper Necessary?

In the course of this chapter we have pointed to the epiclesis as an expression of the fact that God realizes the Eucharist *for* the assembly, *through* the *whole* assembly and through the actions of the priest and the *praying* assembly. We have also treated the epiclesis as an expression of the Holy Spirit's role in the realization of the Eucharist. In view of all this, the question of the need for an epiclesis proper is bound to arise.

As is so often the case, much depends upon how one poses the question. One may ask: "Is an epiclesis proper *absolutely* necessary for the realization of the Eucharist?" The intervention of the Holy Spirit is absolutely necessary. Of this there can be no question. Nor can there be any question that the assembly, while playing a necessary role in the realization of this sacramental encounter, must always approach the Eucharist as a *praying* assembly, acknowledging its own helplessness, appealing for the realization of God's promises here and now and believing firmly that God will answer its appeal. In other words, the "epiclesis attitude" is also absolutely necessary in the realization of the Eucharist, even when it is not made explicit.[55] But the question is whether it is *absolutely* necessary to make *explicit* the intervention of the Holy Spirit and the total dependence of the assembly.

On the basis of our study we would be reluctant to answer, "Yes," to such a question. This reluctance stems from two sources. The first source is the historical data. If one understands "epiclesis proper" as a Spirit epiclesis, one would have to admit that the evidence in favor of such an epiclesis being primitive and universal is far from certain. If one understands "epiclesis proper" as *some* form of appeal for the sanctification of the gifts and/or the faithful, then the evidence for its primitive and universal character is much more favorable. One must admit, however, that this is not the ordinary understanding of the term *epiclesis proper.* Moreover, although this admittedly does not prove the point, one must take into consideration the fact that even an epiclesis so understood was not considered absolutely necessary by some of the major Christian traditions. The Roman Catholic tradition is a case in point. The second source of this reluctance is simpler but perhaps more important. It is the fear of making a god out of any formula, be it the institution narrative *or* the epiclesis.

---

55. Cf. Schillebeeckx, *Christ the Sacrament*, 87.

To pose the question in terms of absolute necessity, however, is to chance tending in the direction of a sacramental minimalism. Moreover, one should build one's theology and practice too, for that matter, not on the minimum required but rather upon the ideal or, at least, the normal. Perhaps, then, one should pose the question of the epiclesis' necessity in another form, namely, "Is an epiclesis proper a *practical* necessity in the realization of the Eucharist?" In the face of such a formulation the reluctance to give an affirmative answer vanishes.

For it belongs to human beings to give some expression to their deepest beliefs and feelings or to risk having them stagnate. It is not enough simply to believe or intend something. It is necessary to express this belief or intention in some word or gesture. The wife, for instance, who demands: "If you really love me then why don't you ever show it and say it?" may be doing more than simply nagging. She may, quite legitimately, be questioning whether a deep feeling or conviction which never finds expression is still there at all. A statement of the United States Bishops' Committee on the Liturgy seems apropos here:

> People in love make signs of love and celebrate their love for the dual purpose of expressing and deepening that love. We too must express in signs our faith in Christ and each other, our love for Christ and for each other, or they will die . . . From this it is clear that the manner in which the Church celebrates the liturgy has an effect on the faith of men. Good celebrations foster and nourish faith. Poor celebrations weaken and destroy faith.[56]

Similarly it is a practical necessity for the eucharistic assembly to express its awareness, for instance, of the necessary intervention of the Holy Spirit and of its own need for a praying or "epiclesis" attitude. If it fails to do so, the assembly runs the risk of having this awareness stagnate or fall into the oblivion of forgetfulness. It pertains, moreover, to symbolic activity to express and deepen our, and in this case the assembly's, beliefs and feelings. And within this symbolic activity it is usually the spoken word which possesses a value superior to the sign or action in giving voice to these beliefs.[57]

---

56. Statement on "The Place of Music in Eucharistic Celebrations" made by the United Sates Bishops' Committee on the Liturgy and appearing in the Committee's *Newsletter* 4 (Jan./Feb., 1968), 1-2. Cf. also, Ledogar, "Faith, Feeling . . . ," 13–14, 19–22 and Schillebeeckx, *Christ the Sacrament*, 92–95 and McKenna, "Eucharistic Prayer: Epiclesis," 287–90.

57. Schillebeeckx, ibid., 117–22.

It is in view of all this that we would maintain that an epiclesis proper is a *practical* necessity in the realization of the Eucharist. The epiclesis is not the only means of expressing the role of the Holy Spirit in the Eucharist, the total dependence of the praying assembly, the unity between consecration and Communion, etc. It is, however, a preeminent means of expressing these important aspects of the eucharistic celebration.[58]

Before closing this chapter it would be well to touch on a question that is allied to the need for an epiclesis proper in the eucharistic prayer. This is the question of the position one should give to such an epiclesis in relation to the institution narrative. It goes without saying that when one views the entire eucharistic prayer as consecratory the positioning of the epiclesis automatically becomes less problematic. In any case, the position of an epiclesis proper is not essential to the epiclesis question as a whole.

It is possible to opt for a position before the institution narrative, at least for the portion of the epiclesis which appeals for the transformation of the gifts into Christ's body and blood. This is the course which the Roman Catholic tradition has chosen for the eucharistic prayers introduced in 1968.[59] In favor of this position one can point out that such a position parallels to some extent the events of saving history. The invocation of the Holy Spirit on the bread and wine recalls his descent upon Mary in the Incarnation. The Holy Spirit first brought about Christ's presence in the world and made Christ into a saving instrument capable of sanctifying those who come into contact with him. Only then did he sanctify the faithful through contact with Christ.[60] In addition, one can argue that a "consecratory" epiclesis before the institution narrative corresponds to the Western theology on the consecratory value of the institution narrative[61] and that there is some ancient precedent for such an arrangement.[62]

Once again, there is no question here of an either-or situation. One cannot exclude the possibility of placing the whole epiclesis before

---

58. Cf. von Allmen, *Worship: Its Theology* . . . , 242–44, 288 and Vischer, 302 ff.

59. Cf. *Notitiae* 40 (1968), 156 ff.

60. Cf. Thurian, *Le pain unique*, 50–53.

61. Cf., for instance, Brunner, "Zur Lehre . . . ," 356–57; Thurian, ibid., 48–49 and the same author's "La théologie des nouvelles priers eucharistiques," MD 94 (1965), 82–83, 91.

62. Cf. Thurian, *Le pain unique*, 50–51 and Vagaggini, *The Canon* . . . , 67–69, 92, 140.

the institution narrative. Nevertheless, on the basis of our study we would tend to side with those preferring a position after the institution narrative. A number of arguments seem to favor such an arrangement. It would certainly seem to reflect the stronger of the ancient traditions. Such an arrangement would also reflect the Trinitarian and saving economy—Father, Son, Holy Spirit; Pentecost and the gift of the Holy Spirit as the seal of the paschal mystery.[63] Moreover, the arrangement which places the epiclesis or a part of it *before* the institution narrative interrupts the narration of God's wonder-deeds, among which belongs the Last Supper.[64]

Two arguments appear particularly forceful in favor of an arrangement which places the entire epiclesis after the institution narrative. First, such an arrangement would seem to stress better the basic helplessness of the assembly in the realization of the Eucharist and thus help avoid any "magical" understanding of the words of institution. Secondly, such an arrangement would avoid a "split epiclesis," i.e., one in which the appeal for the transformation of he gifts is separated from the appeal for the sanctification and unification of those partaking in those gifts. Since one of the advantages of an epiclesis proper in the traditional sense lies in its ability to underscore the unity of consecration and Communion such a "split epiclesis" hardly seems desirable.[65]

For all these reasons it would seem that placing the entire epiclesis *after* the institution, while it is not the only solution, is the preferable one.

---

63. Cf. Salaville, "Epiclése eucharistique," 293–95.

64. Cf. Kavanagh, "Thoughts on the New Eucharistic Prayers," 9.

65. Cf. Kavanagh, "Thoughts on the New Eucharistic Prayers," 6, 9–12. Cf. also, Bobrinskoy, "Le Saint-Esprit, vie de l'Eglise," 189 and McKenna, "Eucharistic Prayer: Epiclesis 289–90. For a comparison of the epiclesis in more recent eucharistic prayers, cf. McKenna, "The Epiclesis Revisited" in *New Eucharistic Prayers* edited by Frank Senn. New York, 1987, 169–94.

Chapter 9

The Epiclesis Revisited

With the advent of liturgical renewal, a great number of eucharistic prayers have appeared in the various Christian churches.[1] The purpose of this chapter is to compare the epicleses within those eucharistic prayers. See Table 9.1 at the end of this chapter for a useful summary. As you will see, the epiclesis is only one element in the eucharistic prayers and to isolate it, as we have done in this chapter, is to risk one-sidedness. The comparisons reveal that the epicleses of the other traditions are closer to the Greek Orthodox epiclesis. A presupposition of the comparison is that a fully developed epiclesis generally contains three elements:

1. an appeal for the Holy Spirit

2. to transform or sanctify the bread and wine

3. so that they may benefit those who partake of them worthily.[2]

ANGLICAN: THE *BOOK OF COMMON PRAYER*

The first set of eucharistic prayers to occupy our attention is that of the *Book of Common Prayer*. Eucharistic Prayer I has been retained without change from the 1928 book.[3] The text of the epiclesis reads:

---

1. A version of this chapter has appeared in *Ephemerides Liturgicae* 99 (Nos. 4–5, 1985) 314–336.

2. Cf. This volume, Chapter 3, Summary and "Eucharistic Epiclesis: Myopia or Microcosm?" *Theological Studies* 36 (June 1975) 265. See also J. H. McKenna, 'The Eucharistic Epiclesis in Twentieth Century Theology (1900–1966)," *Ephemerides Liturgicae* 90 (1976) 289–328 and 446–482.

3. Cf. R. H. Miller, *Study Guide for the Holy Eucharist* (proposed *Book of Common Prayer*) (Wilton, Conn.: Morehouse-Barlow, 1977) 24.

And we most humbly beseech thee, O merciful Father, to hear us; and, of thy almighty goodness, vouchsafe to bless and sanctify, with thy Word and Holy Spirit, these thy gifts and creatures of bread and wine; that we, receiving them according to thy Son our Savior Jesus Christ's holy institution, in remembrance of his death and passion, may be partakers of his most blessed Body and Blood.[4]

The First Person of the Trinity as addressee is asked to bless and sanctify "the bread and wine" with the Word and Holy Spirit. By retaining the first Standard Book's (1793) capitalization of the "Word" the prayer seems to refer to the incarnate Word and not, as Cranmer had intended, to the institution narrative.[5] There is no epiclesis upon the people and no eschatological reference in the epiclesis or elsewhere.[6] The desired benefit is that those receiving might be partakers of Christ's body and blood.

The text of the epiclesis in Eucharistic Prayer II is:

And we most humbly beseech thee, O merciful Father, to hear us, and with thy Word and Holy Spirit, to bless and sanctify these thy gifts of bread and wine, that they may be unto us the Body and Blood of thy dearly-beloved Son Jesus Christ.[7]

Once again the First Person of the Trinity is the addressee, as throughout this set of eucharistic prayers, even though the terms may vary. Again the request is to bless and sanctify the gifts that they "may be unto us" the body and blood of Jesus Christ.

Eucharistic Prayer A has some variations. It reads:

Sanctify them by your Holy Spirit to be for your people the Body and Blood of your Son, the holy food and drink of new and unending life in him. Sanctify us also that we may faithfully receive this holy Sacrament, and serve you in unity, constancy, and peace; and at the last day bring us with all your saints into the joy of your eternal kingdom.[8]

Here we have a petition to sanctify the gifts by the Holy Spirit "to be for your people" Christ's body and blood. There is an epiclesis

4. Ibid., 335.

5. M. J. Hatchett, *Commentary on the American Prayer Book* (New York: Seabury, 1980) 369–71.

6. Cf. ibid., 307.

7. Miller, 342.

8. Ibid., 363.

upon the people[9] that they might partake "faithfully" and serve in unity, constancy, and peace. There is also an eschatological reference.

Eucharistic Prayer B has a lengthier epiclesis:

> We pray you, gracious God, to send your Holy Spirit upon these gifts that they may be the Sacrament of the Body of Christ and his Blood of the new Covenant. Unite us to your Son in his sacrifice, that we may be acceptable through him, being sanctified by the Holy Spirit. In the fullness of time, put all things in subjection under your Christ, and bring us to that heavenly country where, with (_____and) all your saints, we may enter the everlasting heritage of your sons and daughters; through Jesus Christ our Lord, the firstborn of all creation, the head of the Church, and the author of our salvation.[10]

The First Person of the Trinity ("gracious God") is asked to send the Holy Spirit upon the gifts that they "may be the sacrament" of Christ's body and blood. There is also an epiclesis on the people that they may be united to Christ's sacrifice, be acceptable and be sanctified. There is no mention of partaking but the eschatological dimension is once again prominent.

Eucharistic Prayer C is much more terse:

> And so, Father, we who have been redeemed by him, and made a new people by water and the Spirit, now bring before you these gifts. Sanctify them by your Holy Spirit to be the Body and Blood of Jesus Christ our Lord.[11]

Linking Eucharist with Baptism, it simply asks the First Person of the Trinity to sanctify the gifts "to be" Christ's body and blood. There is no epiclesis on the people, no further benefits requested and no eschatological reference.

Eucharistic Prayer D does contain some of these elements:

> Lord, we pray that in your goodness and mercy your Holy Spirit may descend upon us, and upon these gifts, sanctifying them and showing them to be the holy gifts for your holy people, the bread of life and the cup of salvation, the Body and Blood of your Son Jesus Christ.

---

9. Cf. Hatchett, 371.
10. Miller, 369.
11. Ibid., 371.

Grant that all who share this bread and cup may become one body and one spirit, a living sacrifice in Christ, to the praise of your name.[12]

The petition is for the Holy Spirit to descend upon people and gifts "sanctifying and showing" the gifts to be the body and blood of Jesus Christ. The prayer also asks that those partaking become united and "a living sacrifice of praise." It is significant that, although this eucharistic prayer is practically identical with the *Roman Missal*'s Eucharistic Prayer IV, here the epiclesis follows the institution narrative. The Roman version opts to split the epiclesis, placing the invocation over the gifts before the institution narrative.

LUTHERAN BOOK OF WORSHIP

Here we will treat the epiclesis in the full eucharistic prayer, although other options are offered.[13] The epiclesis in Eucharistic Prayer I reads:

> Send now, we pray, your Holy Spirit, the spirit of our Lord and of his resurrection, that we who receive the Lord's body and blood may live to the praise of your glory and receive our inheritance with all your saints in light.[14]

The addressee is the First Person of the Trinity, as it is throughout this set of eucharistic prayers. The request is for the sending of the Holy Spirit. The "spirit of our Lord and of his resurrection" is deliberately ambiguous to include a sense of "the essential meaning, mood, and disposition."[15] No mention is made of the Spirit coming upon the gifts or upon the people, although this may be implied. The transformation of the gifts receives no attention. Rather, the focus is on the effect of partaking in the Lord's body and blood, viz., that those who do may live to the praise of God's glory and receive their "eschatological" inheritance.

The epiclesis text in Eucharistic Prayer II is similar:

> Send now, we pray, your Holy Spirit, that we and all who share in this bread and cup may be united in the fellowship of the Holy Spirit, may

---

12. Ibid., 375.

13. Cf. P.H. Pfatteicher and C.R. Messerli, *Manual on the Liturgy* (Lutheran Book of Worship) (Minneapolis, Minn.: Augsburg Publishing House,1979) 241–43.

14. *Lutheran Book of Worship* (Ministers Desk Edition) (Minneapolis, Minn.: Augsburg Publishing House, 1978) 223. Henceforth LBW.

15. Cf. Pfatteicher, 238.

enter the fullness of the kingdom of heaven, and may receive our inheritance with all your saints in light.[16]

Again there is no mention of the effect of the Spirit's sending on the gifts but rather on the desired effect of receiving them, viz., unity, entering into the heavenly kingdom and the inheritance of the saints.

Eucharistic Prayer III has a lengthier epiclesis:

. . . we implore you mercifully to accept our praise and thanksgiving, and, with your Word and Holy Spirit, to bless us, your servants, and these your own gifts of bread and wine; that we and all who share in the body and blood of your Son may be filled with heavenly peace and joy, and, receiving the forgiveness of sin, may be sanctified in soul and body, and have our portion with all your saints.[17]

This time the petition is for Word and Spirit "to bless" both gifts and people. Once again the emphasis is not on the changing of the gifts but the benefits for those partaking, viz., peace, joy, forgiveness, sanctified souls and bodies. The eschatological dimension again appears.

Eucharistic Prayer IV is Gordon Lathrop's translation of Hippolytus.[18] The epiclesis reads:

Send your Spirit upon these gifts of your Church; gather into one all who share this bread and wine; fill us with your Holy Spirit to establish our faith in truth, that we may praise and glorify you through your Son Jesus Christ.[19]

Now the request is for the sending of the Spirit upon the gifts and the filling of the people with the same Holy Spirit. Unity, establishing of faith in truth are asked for those who share in the bread and wine that they may give praise and glory to God.

METHODIST: *AT THE LORD'S TABLE*

The epiclesis in Great Thanksgiving 1 reads:

Send the power of your Holy Spirit on us, gathered here out of love for you, and on these gifts. May the Spirit help us know in the breaking of this bread and the drinking of this wine the presence of Christ who gave

16. LBW, 223.
17. LBW, 225.
18. Pfatteicher, 241.
19. LBW, 226.

his body and blood for all. And may the Spirit make us one with Christ, one with each other, and one in service to all the world.[20]

The request is for the "power" of the Holy Spirit on gifts and people that the breaking of bread and drinking of wine may lead to knowing the presence of Christ. Unity will become another benefit.

Great Thanksgiving 2 does not really have an epiclesis as such. Rather it has a prayer that those receiving may be partakers of the divine nature. This appears before the institution narrative.[21]After the narrative there comes a prayer for the acceptance of the people's sacrifice of praise and thanksgiving, for forgiveness and other benefits of Christ's passion.[22]

Great Thanksgiving 3 has the following epiclesis:

And we beseech thee, O merciful Father, to bless and sanctify with thy Holy Spirit both us and these thy gifts of bread and wine, that the bread which we break may be the communion of the body of Christ and the cup of blessing which we bless, the communion of his blood.[23]

The prayer asks simply that the First Person of the Trinity bless and sanctify both gifts and people with his Holy Spirit. This will have the effect that the bread and cup may be the communion of the body and blood of Christ.

Great Thanksgiving 4 is the same as Eucharistic Prayer II from *Word/Bread/Cup* by the Consultation on Church Union.[24] The epiclesis reads:

Loving God, pour out your Holy Spirit upon us and upon these gifts, that they may be for us the body and blood of our Savior Jesus Christ. Grant that we may be for the world the body of Christ, redeemed through his blood, serving and reconciling all people to you.[25]

---

20. *At the Lord's Table* (A Communion Service Book for Use by the Minister) (Nashville: Abingdon, 1981) 12–13.

21. Ibid., 14.

22. Ibid., 15.

23. Ibid., 17.

24. *Word/Bread/Cup* (Consultation on Church Union) (Cincinnati, Ohio: Forward Movement Publications, 1978) 25–27.

25. *At the Lord's Table*, 19.

This prayer asks for the pouring out of the Spirit that the gifts may be Christ's body and blood for the people, and the people may be Christ's body serving and reconciling the world. No explicit mention is made of receiving nor is there an eschatological dimension. This latter trait is characteristic of the first six epicleses in this set.

The epiclesis text in Great Thanksgiving 5 is:

> Send, we pray, your Holy Spirit on us, gathered here out of love for you, and on this offering. May your Spirit make real the signs that through breaking bread and drinking wine together we may know Christ present among us. By the Spirit make us one with the goodness of Christ, as you made him one with our sinfulness, that we may be one with each other and one in service to all you have created.[26]

The sending of the Spirit has for its purpose to "make real the signs" that the partakers may know Christ present among them (cf. G.T. 1, 7) and be one in serving the world.

Great Thanksgiving 6 parallels Eucharistic Prayer D in the *Book of Common Prayer* and Eucharistic Prayer IV in the *Roman Missal*. The epiclesis reads:

> Lord, we pray that in your goodness and mercy your Holy Spirit may descend upon us, and upon these gifts, sanctifying them and showing them to be the holy gifts for your holy people, the bread of life and the cup of salvation, the body and blood of your Son Jesus Christ. Grant that all who share this bread and cup may become one body and one spirit, a living sacrifice in Christ to the praise of your Name.[27]

This time the descent of the Holy Spirit is requested that the Spirit sanctify the gifts and show them to be Christ's body and blood. Those partaking will hopefully be united and become a living sacrifice of praise. Despite the similarities to Eucharistic Prayer IV of the *Roman Missal*, the epiclesis here, as in the Anglican Eucharistic Prayer D, *follows* the institution narrative.

The epiclesis in Great Thanksgiving 7 has become the prototype for those in Great Thanksgiving 8–22, which either repeat this one exactly or make minor alterations:

---

26. Ibid., 21.
27. Ibid., 23.

Send the power of your Holy Spirit on us and on these gifts, that in the breaking of this bread and the drinking of this wine we may know the presence of the living Christ; be one body in him, cleansed by his blood; faithfully serve him in the world; and look forward to his coming in final victory.[28]

As in Great Thanksgiving 1, the petition is for the sending of the *power* of the Holy Spirit on gifts and people. The desired effect is that in the partaking the people may know the presence of Christ, be one with him and find forgiveness. The service theme again appears and the eschatological dimension appears for the first time.

Finally, we have the Great Thanksgiving officially adopted by the General Conference of the United Methodist Church in May 1984. The epiclesis, which follows the institution narrative, reads:

Pour out your Holy Spirit on us, gathered here, and on these gifts of bread and wine. Make them be for us the body and blood of Christ, that we may be for the world the body of Christ, redeemed by his blood.

By your Spirit make us one with Christ, one with each other and one in ministry to all the world, until Christ comes in final victory and we feast at his heavenly banquet.[29]

This is perhaps the most complete of all the modern epicleses. While there is no explicit mention of partaking of the gifts, the appeal is for the pouring out of the Spirit on those gathered together and on the gifts. The transformation of the gifts is strongly stated—"Make them be for us . . . ." The prayer also spells out the purpose of this transformation, viz., that the people become Christ's body and blood for the world and united in their ministry to that world. The inclusion of Christ's final coming and the heavenly banquet makes clear the eschatological dimension.

---

28. Ibid., 24–25.

29. Cf. *The Book of Services: Containing the General Services of the Church Adopted by the 1984 General Conference* (Nashville: The United Methodist Publishing House, 1985) 24–25. This, together with the "prayer of consecration" in the old liturgies of the former Methodist and Evangelical United Brethren churches which united in 1968 to form the United Methodist Church, has official status. Other eucharistic prayers, such as those in *At the Lord's Table*, may be used but they are unofficial.

PRESBYTERIAN: *THE SERVICE FOR THE LORD'S DAY*

The epiclesis in Great Prayers of Thanksgiving A, B, C may be before or after the institution narrative, depending on whether or not they are said in relationship to the breaking of the bread.[30]

The epiclesis of Great Prayer of Thanksgiving A reads:

> Gracious God, pour out your Holy Spirit upon us, that this bread and this cup may be for us the body and blood of our Lord, and that we, and all who share this feast, may be one with Christ and he with us. Fill us with eternal life, that with joy we may be his faithful people until we feast with him in glory.[31]

The pouring out of the Holy Spirit on the *people* has for its desired effect that the bread and cup may be for them the body and blood of the Lord. Unity, joy, faithfulness, and eternal life are further objects of the prayer. The eschatological dimension is also evident.

The text of the epiclesis in Great Prayer of Thanksgiving B is:

> Gracious God, pour out your Holy Spirit on us, and on these your gifts of bread and wine, that in eating this bread and drinking this cup, we may know the presence of Christ and be made one with him, and one with all who come to this table.
>
> In union with your church in heaven and on earth, we pray that you will fulfill your eternal purpose in us and in all the world.[32]

Here the pouring out of the Spirit is on both gifts and people that the partaking may lead to recognizing the presence of Christ and to unity. Once again an eschatological note is present.

In Great Prayer of Thanksgiving C the epiclesis is shorter:

> Merciful God, by your Holy Spirit bless and make holy both us and these your gifts of bread and wine, that the bread we break may be the communion of the body of Christ, and the cup we bless may be the communion of the blood of Christ.[33]

---

30. *The Service for the Lord's Day: The Worship of God* (Supplemental Liturgical Resource 1) (Philadelphia: Westminster Press, 1984), 96.

31. Ibid., 97.

32. Ibid., 100.

33. Ibid., 105.

The request is simply for the Holy Spirit to bless and make holy people and gifts that the latter be "the communion of" the body and blood of Christ.

Great Prayer of Thanksgiving D reflects Hippolytus as does the epiclesis:

> We ask you to send your Holy Spirit upon the offering of the holy church, gathering into one all who share these holy mysteries, filling us with the Holy Spirit and confirming our faith in the truth, that together we may praise you and give you glory, through your Servant, Jesus Christ.[34]

The sending of the Spirit upon the offerings and the filling of the people with that same Holy Spirit has unity, confirmation of faith in truth and God's glory and praise as its object.

Great Prayer of Thanksgiving E parallels the Roman Catholic Eucharistic Prayer IV, the Methodist Great Thanksgiving 6, and the Anglican Eucharistic Prayer D. Here the epiclesis is *after* the institution narrative and reads:

> Lord, we pray that in your goodness and mercy your Holy Spirit may descend upon us, and upon these gifts, sanctifying them and showing them to be holy gifts for your holy people, the bread of life and the cup of salvation, the body and blood of your Son Jesus Christ.

> Grant that all who share this bread and cup may become one body and one spirit, a living sacrifice in Christ, to the praise of your name.[35]

Here the descent of the Holy Spirit upon gifts and people is to sanctify the gifts and show them to be the body and blood of Jesus Christ.

Great Prayer of Thanksgiving F has its parallel in the Methodist Great Thanksgiving 5 which is based on the Consultation on Church Union's Eucharistic Prayer II. The epiclesis reads:

> Loving God, pour out your Holy Spirit upon us and upon these gifts, that they may be for us the body and blood of our Savior Jesus Christ. Grant that we may be for the world the body of Christ, redeemed through his blood serving and reconciling all people to you.[36]

---

34. Ibid., 107.
35. Ibid., 110.
36. Ibid., 114.

As mentioned above, the desired effect of the outpouring of the Spirit on gifts and people is that the former "may be for us" Christ's body and blood while the latter may be Christ's body for the world. The service and reconciliation themes again emerge.

The epiclesis in Great Prayer of Thanksgiving G and H *precedes* the institution narrative which is said in relationship to the breaking of the bread.[37] The epiclesis is terse:

> Almighty God, pour out your Holy Spirit upon us, that as we receive bread and wine we may be assured that Christ's promise in these signs will be fulfilled.[38]

The request is simply that, through the outpouring of the Spirit upon the people, those receiving the bread and wine be assured of the fulfillment of Christ's promise in these signs. No mention is made of any transformation (although this may be implied) or of any further themes often connected with epiclesis.

Finally, the epiclesis in Great Prayer of Thanksgiving H is as follows:

> Send to us your Holy Spirit that this meal may be holy and your people may become one. Unite us in faith, inspire us to love, encourage us with hope, that we may receive Christ as he comes to us in this holy banquet.[39]

The request is for the sending of the Spirit that the "meal may be holy." The desired effects are unity, faith, hope, love, and receiving Christ as he comes in this meal.

ROMAN CATHOLIC EUCHARISTIC PRAYERS

The final set of eucharistic prayers for consideration are those contained in the *Roman Missal*, including the eucharistic prayers for Masses with Children and for Masses of Reconciliation.

Eucharistic Prayer I is really a translation, with slight modifications, of the old Roman Canon. There is no epiclesis, as we have defined it, since there is no mention of the Holy Spirit. There are, however, two prayers for acceptance, one before the institution narrative and one following it. The first reads:

---

37. Ibid., 117–18.
38. Ibid., 117.
39. Ibid., 118.

Bless and approve our offering;
make it acceptable to you,
an offering in spirit and in truth.
Let it become for us
the body and blood of Jesus Christ,
your only Son, our Lord.[40]

This does contain a typical epiclesis element, viz., a prayer
that the offering become for us Christ's body and blood. The appeal
to bless, approve, make acceptable is also similar to appeals found
in other fully developed epicleses.

The second prayer for acceptance reads:

Almighty God,
we pray that your angel may take this sacrifice
to your altar in heaven.
Then, as we receive from this altar
the sacred body and blood of your Son,
let us be filled with every grace and blessing.[41]

The image in this prayer is somewhat unique. Instead of
involving a descent it calls for an ascent to the heavenly altar at the hand
of God's angel. The benefits for those receiving are sweeping—every
grace and blessing.

The remaining eucharistic prayers also contain a relatively
unique element, viz., a "split epiclesis." Only in the ancient Alexandrian
type[42] and more recently in the Liturgy of Lima[43] does one, to my
knowledge, find this phenomenon. The laconic character of these
epicleses is also striking. The epiclesis (or epicleses) in Eucharistic
Prayer II, based on Hippolytus, reads:

a) Let your Spirit come upon these gifts to make them holy,
so that they may become for us
the body and blood of our Lord, Jesus Christ.

---

40. *The Roman Missal: The Sacramentary* (English Translation prepared by the International
Commission on English in the Liturgy) (New York: Catholic Book Publishing Company,
1985) 544.

41. Ibid., 546.

42. Cf. This volume, Chapter 1.

43. M. Thurian and G. Wainwright (eds.), *Baptism and Eucharist* (Ecumenical Convergence
in Celebration) (Grand Rapids: Wm. B. Eerdmans, 1983), 253.

b) May all of us who share in the body and blood of Christ
be brought together in unity by the Holy Spirit.[44]

The first part is much more explicit than the Hippolytan
text[45] in asking that the gifts "become for us" Christ's body and blood.
The second part is even more concise, asking only that the partakers
be "brought together in unity."

The epiclesis in Eucharistic Prayer III is only slightly more
developed:

a) We ask you to make them holy by the power of your Spirit,
that they may become the body and blood
of your Son, our Lord Jesus Christ,
at whose command we celebrate this eucharist.

b) Grant that we, who are nourished by his body and blood,
may be filled with his Holy Spirit,
and become one body, one spirit in Christ. [46]

It asks the Father to make the gifts holy, that they become
Christ's body and blood and that those receiving them be filled with
the Spirit and become one.

As we have noted above, Eucharistic Prayer IV parallels
Eucharistic Prayer D (Anglican), Great Thanksgiving 6 (Methodist)
and Great Prayer of Thanksgiving E (Presbyterian). Here, however,
the epiclesis is "split" and reads:

a) Father, may this Holy Spirit sanctify these offerings.
Let them become the body and blood of Jesus Christ our Lord
as we celebrate the great mystery
which he left us as an everlasting covenant.[47]

b) Lord, look upon this sacrifice which you have given to your Church;
and by your Holy Spirit, gather all who share this one bread and one cup
into one body of Christ, a living sacrifice of praise.[48]

---

44. *Roman Missal*, 549 and 550.

45. Cf. *Eucharistic Prayer of Hippolytus* (Text for Consultation) (Washington, D.C: International Commission on English in the Liturgy, 1983), 9.

46. *Roman Missal*, 552 and 554.

47. Ibid., 558.

48. Ibid., 559. Note that the second edition (1985) has changed "this bread and wine" to "this one bread and one cup." This is to bring out more clearly the link with 1 Corinthians 10:17 and

This epiclesis basically repeats the request of those in II and III to transform the gifts and achieve unity, simply adding the notion of a "living sacrifice of praise" as the eucharistic prayers which parallel it have done. Interestingly, for the Roman Catholic tradition, the second part of the epiclesis continues to refer to the transformed gifts as "bread" and "cup."

The text within Eucharistic Prayer for Masses with Children I is as follows:

a) We bring you bread and wine
and ask you to send your Holy Spirit to make these gifts
the body and blood of Jesus your Son.[49]

b) Father,
because you love us,
you invite us to come to your table.
Fill us with the joy of the Holy Spirit
as we receive the body and blood of your Son.[50]

Again the epiclesis is "split" and laconic. It asks simply that the sending of the Holy Spirit make the gifts the body and blood of Jesus that those receiving be filled with the joy of the Spirit.

The epiclesis in Eucharistic Prayer for Masses with Children II is similar:

a) God our Father,
we now ask you
to send your Holy Spirit
to change these gifts of bread and wine
into the body and blood
of Jesus Christ, our Lord.[51]

b) Lord our God,
listen to our prayer.
Send the Holy Spirit
to all of us who share in this meal.

---

the role of the Eucharist as sign and cause of unity. Cf. Bishops' Committee on the Liturgy's *Newsletter* 21 (January 1985) 1.

49. *Roman Missal*, 1104.

50. Ibid., 1106.

51. Ibid., 1110.

May this Spirit bring us closer together
in the family of the Church,
with N., our pope,
N., our bishop,
all other bishops,
and all who serve your people.[52]

Here the appeal is for the sending of the Spirit upon the gifts
to "change" them and upon the people sharing the meal to unite them.
The epiclesis of Children III is slightly different:

a) Father,
we ask you to bless these gifts of bread and wine
and make them holy.
Change them into the body and blood of
Jesus Christ, your Son.[53]

b) Father in heaven,
you have called us
to receive the body and blood of Christ at this table
and to be filled with the joy of the Holy Spirit.
Through this sacred meal
give us strength to please you more and more.[54]

The desired effect in the first part is similar to the others
(bless, make holy, change) but there is no mention of the Spirit. In the
second part the request is to fill those partaking with the joy of the
Holy Spirit and strengthen them to please God.

Eucharistic Prayer for Masses of Reconciliation I offers the
Roman Catholic pattern:

a) Look with kindness on your people
gathered here before you;
send forth the power of your Spirit
so that these gifts may become for us
the body and blood of your beloved Son, Jesus the Christ,
in whom we have become your sons and daughters.[55]

---

52. Ibid., 1112.
53. Ibid., 1116.
54. Ibid., 1118.
55. Ibid., 1123.

b) Father,
look with love
on those you have called
to share in the one sacrifice of Christ.
By the power of your Holy Spirit
make them one body,
healed of all division.[56]

The sending forth of the Spirit's power is to lead to the gifts becoming "for us" the body and blood of Christ. The sharing of the one sacrifice of Christ is to lead to unity, i.e., healing of all division.

Finally, we have the most concise of all epicleses in Reconciliation II:

a) We ask you to sanctify these gifts
by the power of your Spirit,
as we now fulfill your Son's command.[57]

b) Fill us with his Spirit
through our sharing in this meal.
May he take away all that divides us.[58]

This is the only time in a Roman Catholic prayer that there is no mention of Christ's body and blood. There is simply an appeal to sanctify the gifts and to fill those sharing the meal with the Holy Spirit so that divisions disappear.

Table 9.1 following this chapter should provide a helpful summary, with the ancient epicleses serving as a basis of comparison for the modern ones.

SUMMARY

The epicleses preserved for us in early Christian texts do not constitute an inflexible norm for current practice, but do offer a basis for comparison.

Some general characteristics of the epicleses seem evident. One is the reference to some change in the bread and wine in the

---

56. Ibid., 1126.
57. Ibid., 1129.
58. Ibid., 1131.

direction of Christ's body and blood. Another is the frequent appearance of the eschatological dimension and the rich variety of "other benefits." Finally, there is almost invariably a reference to partaking of the gifts

The epicleses in the *Book of Common Prayer* seem to exhibit no significant departures from this pattern. One might simply note that, had the term "word" been left as Cranmer intended it, as a reference to the institution narrative rather than the incarnate Word, we might have a compromise form which would draw us closer to the early Christian outlook. This emphasis viewed the eucharistic prayer in its entirety as "consecratory" with two highpoints—the institution narrative and the epiclesis.[59]

The Lutheran epiclesis reveal a significant variation. There is no reference to a change of the bread and wine into the body and blood of Christ, an absence of an element characteristic of most early epicleses. Is its absence due to an emphasis on the institution narrative as "consecratory" or a desire to avoid the implications of certain terms— or both? On the other hand, the Lutheran prayers show a strong sense of the eschatological dimension.

The Methodist epicleses reveal an emphasis on calling down the Spirit upon the people. The eschatological note is missing in the first six Great Thanksgivings but is present in the next sixteen— mainly because they use number seven as a prototype. The text made official in May 1984 has a strong eschatological emphasis and is probably the most complete resumé of elements traditionally associated with the epiclesis. It also forcefully underlines the transformation of the gifts as well as the assembly.

The Presbyterian prayers also show a great awareness of the calling down of the Spirit upon the people as well as the gifts. The eschatological dimension is lacking in most of the epicleses. The option to say the institution narrative with the breaking of the bread—thus placing the epiclesis before the institution narrative—is a significant variant from the ancient pattern.

The Roman Catholic pattern is perhaps the most complex when compared to the early Christian epicleses. Here we find the stress on the unity of those partaking, which is common to many of the modern epicleses and a good number of the ancient ones. The

---

59. This volume, Chapter 2.

"split" epiclesis, however, is found only in the Alexandrian type of earlier prayers and is an isolated phenomenon among more modern ones. Most probably this is a vestige of the old (but *not* ancient) "moment of consecration" question and the fear that mentioning a change in the gifts *after* the institution narrative would somehow rob the latter of its consecratory power.

Unfortunately, this pattern has several disadvantages. It neglects the stronger of the ancient traditions. It also interrupts the flow of the narration of the wonderful things God has accomplished in creation and in history. It fails to emphasize the basic helplessness or praying attitude of the assembly and thus fails to help avoid a "magical" notion of the institution narrative. Finally, this pattern could rob the epiclesis of one of its great strengths, viz., the ability to underline the unity between "consecration" and communion.[60]

The changing of the gifts into Christ's body and blood finds forceful emphasis in the Roman Catholic epicleses. There is, however, no trace of an eschatological dimension (which appears in the inter-cessions following the epiclesis). And, besides unity, other benefits to those partaking are scarcely mentioned.

Obviously, as I stated at the beginning of this chapter, the epiclesis is only one element in the eucharistic prayers and to isolate it, as we have done in this chapter, is to risk one-sidedness. Nevertheless, a comparison of the epiclesis in different traditions is revealing. At times, it shows contrasting mentalities, if not theological biases. At other times, it reveals the fruit of ecumenical dialogue and scholarship. One can only hope that this latter will yield further enrichment for all traditions and lead us closer to that day when Christ's final victory and the unity for which the epiclesis so often prays will become a reality.

---

60. This volume, Chapter 8.

Table 9.1 The Epiclesis in the Various Christian Churches and Contemporary Eucharistic Prayers

Anaphora	After instit. narrative	Father as Addressee	asked	For Holy Spirit	upon us	upon elements
Bk. of Common Prayer						
(E.P. I)	x	x	bless sanctify	w/Word & H. Sp.	—	x
Alternate Forms						
E.P. II	x	x	bless sanctify	w/Word & H. Sp.	—	x
E.P. A	x	x	sanctify by H. Sp.	x	x	x
E.P. B	x	x	send H. Sp.	x	x	x
E.P. C	before (?)	x	sanctify by H. Sp.	x	—	x
E.P. D	x	x	H. Sp. descend	x	x	x
Lutheran Bk. of Worship						
E.P. I	x	x	send H. Sp.	x	—	—
E.P. II	x	x	send H. Sp.	x	—	—
E. P. III	x	x	bless	w/Word & H. Sp.	x	x
E.P. IV	x	x	send H. Sp., fill us w/H. Sp.	x	x	x
At the Lord's Table (Methodist)						
G.T. 1	x	x	send power of H. Sp.	power of H. Sp.	x	x
G.T. 2						
(a)	before	x	hear us, grant	—	—	—
(b)	x	x	accept, grant	—	—	—
G.T. 3	x	x	bless & sanctify	x	x	x
G.T. 4	x	x	pour out your Spirit	x	x	x
G.T. 5	x	x	send H. Sp.	x	x	x
G.T. 6	x	x	H. Sp. descend	x	x	x
G.T. 7[1]	x	x	send power of H. Sp.	power of H. Sp.	x	x
G.T. (1984)	x	x	pour out H. Sp.	x	x	x
Service for the Lord's Day (Presbyterian)						
G.P.T. A	x or before[2]	x	pour out H. Sp.	x	x	—
G.P.T. B	x or before[2]	x	pour out H. Sp.	x	x.	x
G.P.T. C	x or before[2]	x	H. Sp. Bless make holy	x	x	x

1. Prototype for numbers 8–22.
2. Option to say institution narrative with breaking of bread.

So that bread, wine become Body, Blood	So that partakers benefit			other benefits
	unity	forgiveness	resurr. &/or eternal life (eschatological)	
—	—	—	—	partake of Body & Blood
". . . may be unto us"	—	—	—	—.
"to be for your people."	x	—	x	constancy peace
". . . may be Sacrament of"	x w/Xst	—	x	acceptable, sanctified
". . . to be . . ."	—	—	—	—
sanctify, showing to be holy gift...body & blood	x	—	—	living sacrifice of praise
—	—	—	x	may live to praise your glory
—	—	x	x	—
—	—	x	x	peace, joy, soul & body sanctified
—	x	—	—	establish faith in truth, that praise glorify you
—	x	—	—	know presence of Christ
—	—	—	—	partakers of divine nature
—	—	x	—	all other benefits of passion
"may be the . . . communion of body, blood"	—	—	—	—
"may be for us body & blood"	—	—	—	we body of Christ, serving, reconciling
"make real the signs"	x	—	—	may know Christ present
"sanctifying, showing them to be . . ."	x	—	—	living sacrifice of praise
—	x	x	x	may know presence of Christ , faithfully serve
"make them be for us"	x	—	x	we Body of Christ; ministering
"may be for us"	x	—	x	eternal life, joy, be faithful people
—	x	—	x	may know Christ's presence
"may be communion of body, blood"	—	—	—	—

G.P.T. D	x	x	send H. Sp.	x	x	x
G.P.T. E	x	x	H. Sp. Descend	x	x	x
G.P.T. F	x	x	pour out H. Sp.	x	x	x
G.P.T. G	before[3]	x	pour out H. Sp.	x	x	—
G.P.T. H	before[4]	x	send to us H. Sp.	x	x	—
Roman Catholic						
E.P. I						
(a)	before	x	bless, approve, make acceptable	—	x	—
(b)	x	x	take sacrifice to heaven	—	—	—
E.P II						
(a)	before	x	Spirit come upon	x		x
(b)	x	—	—	—		—
E.P. III						
(a)	before	x	make holy by power of H. Sp.	power of H. Sp.		x
(b)	x	x	—	—		—
E.P. IV						
(a)	before	x	H. Sp. Sanctify	x		x
(b)	x	x	look upon & by your H. Sp.	x		—
Children I						
(a)	before	x	send your H. Sp.	x		x
(b)	x	x	—	—		—
Children II						
(a)	before	x	send your H. Sp.	x		x
(b)	x	x	listen to our prayer, send H. Sp.	x	x	—
Children III						
(a)	before	x	bless these gifts	—		x
(b)	x	x	—	x		—
Reconciliation I						
(a)	before	x	look with kindness, send . . . power of H. Sp.	power of H. Sp.	___	x
(b)	x	x	look with love	x	___	—
Reconciliation II						
(a)	before	x	sanctify gifts by power of H. Sp.	power of H. Sp.	___	x
(b)	x	x	fill us with his Spirit	x	x	—

From J.H. McKenna, "The Eucharistic Epiclesis in twentieth century theology," *Ephemerides Liturgicae* 99 (Nos. 4–5,1985), 329–334. Used with permission.

---

3. Institution narrative with breaking of bread.
4. Institution narrative with breaking of bread.

—	x	—	—	confirm faith in truth; fill us w/H. Sp.; we praise, give glory
"sanctifying, showing them to be . . ."	—	—	—	
"may be for us"	—	—	—	we body of Christ, serving reconciling
—	—	—	—	assured Christ's promise in these signs fulfilled
"may be holy"	x	—	—	faith, hope, love; receive Christ in meal

"become for us"	—	—	—	—
—	—	—	—	filled with every grace & blessing
"may become us"	x			—
—	x			—
"may become"				—
—	x	—	—	filled with H. Sp.
"become"	x	—	—	living sacrifice of praise
"make these gifts . . ."	—	—	—	—
—	—	—	—	fill with joy of H. Sp.
"change . . . into"	x	=	=	—
make holy, change them for us	—	—	—	—
—	—	—	—	fill w/joy of H. Sp. give strength to please
become for us	—	—	—	—
—	x			healed of all division
—				—
—	x			—

Conclusion

By now it should be evident that with the epiclesis question, as with so many other questions in theology, it is not a question of an either/or. The epiclesis proper can be an expression of the faith *and* the divine intervention necessary for the realization of the sacrament. It can be an expression of the fact that the Eucharist is realized for the communicating assembly *and* also through the assembly. It can express the fact that it is only by praying and believing, i.e., as absolutely dependent on God's sovereign intervention that the *whole* assembly, not just the ordained minister, shares in the realization of the Eucharist. Finally, the epiclesis proper can underscore the unique role of the Holy Spirit in the Eucharist.

At the very beginning of our Introduction we cited what at first glance appeared to be a flat contradiction between the viewpoint of J. M. Tillard and that of E. Bishop, L. Vischer, and P. Evdokimov in regard to the epiclesis question. On the basis of our study we are now inclined to consider the contradiction as only apparent. Both viewpoints are correct.

Tillard is right in regarding the epiclesis question, seen in itself, as a very secondary one. He is also correct in saying that the epiclesis question can stifle theological reflection and limit us in our considerations of the Eucharist. This is especially so when one lets the moment of consecration question overshadow one's treatment of the epiclesis. Unfortunately this is just what has happened in a great deal of the writing done on the epiclesis in the modern period. To allow one's gaze to become fixed almost exclusively on one aspect of the epiclesis is to be indeed limited and to fail to do justice to the epiclesis' many-faceted nature.

On the other hand, it is precisely because of this many-faceted nature of the epiclesis that Bishop, Vischer, and Evdokimov are correct in considering the epiclesis question an extremely important one. Seen in itself it is secondary. When one realizes, however, that the various facets of the epiclesis make it a sort of microcosm of important theological issues, then this question takes on added dimensions. Any thorough treatment of the epiclesis forces one to confront theological issues such as the role of faith, of the praying assembly, of the ordained and universal priesthood, of the Holy Spirit in the realization of the Eucharist as well as the whole question of the eucharistic real presence. The epiclesis question thus involves one simultaneously in some of the basic issues of Christology, pneumatology, ecclesiology, and sacramental theology, and therein lies the importance of this question as well as its ecumenical significance.

Finally, this study of the eucharistic epiclesis has led to the conclusion that often there are no simple, either-or answers to the questions which the epiclesis raises. The epiclesis thus mirrors the tension in theology between the role of God and that of the assembly, between the role of the assembly and that of the ordained priesthood, between the activity of Christ and that of the Holy Spirit, etc. Some would seek to remove that tension by stressing one aspect at the expense, or even to the exclusion, of the other. It seems to us, on the other hand, that this tension will always be present. One must simply learn to live with it.

This tension would be eased greatly, however, if the various traditions share their characteristic and complementary insights with one another, instead of using these insights to deepen painful divisions. It is hoped this study has somehow been able to reflect such a sharing of insights. It is hoped, too, such a sharing will lead us closer to that day when we shall no longer discuss the *when* and the *how* of the Eucharist but shall simply celebrate together the wonder of *what* the Father has done for us through Jesus Christ and in his Holy Spirit.

Selected Bibliography

Abercrombie, Nigel. *The Life and Work of Edmund Bishop*. London, 1959

Afanassieff, N. "Le sacrament de l'assemblée."*Internationale Kirchliche Zeitschrift* 46 (1956), n.s. 200–13.

Von Allmen, Jean Jacques. *Essai sur le Repas du Seigneur.* Neuchâtel, 1966.

――――. *Prophétisme sacramentel.* Neuchâtel 1964.

――――. *Worship: It's Theology and Practice.* Translated by H. Knight & W. Fletcher Fleet, London, 1965.

Altaner, Berthold-Stuiber, Alfred. *Patrologie.* Freiburg i. Br., 1966[7].

Arndt, William F. and Gingrich, F. Wilbur. *A Greek-English Lexicon of the New Testamnet and Other Early Christian Literature.* (Chicago, 1952[4]).

Atchley, E.G.C.F. "The Epiclesis." *Theology 3* (1921), 90–98

――――. "The Epiclesis: A Criticism." *Theology 29* (1934), 28–35.

――――. *On the Epiclesis of the Eucharistic Liturgy and in the Consecration of the Font.* London, 1935.

Bartsch, E. *Die Sachbeschwörungen der römischen Liturgie* (= *Liturgie-wissenschaftliche Quellen und Forschungen* 46). Münster, 1967.

Batiffol, Pierre. *L'eucharistie* (La présence réelle et la transsubstantiation). Paris, 1930[9].

――――. "Nouvelles Etudes Dovumentaires sur la sainte Eucharistie." (1) *Revue du clergé français* 55 (1908), 513–548.

――――. "Nouvelles Etudes Documentaires sur la sainte Eucharistie." (2) *Revue du clergé français* 60 (1909), 513–40.

――――. "La question de l'épiclèse eucharistique" (à propos d'un essai de M. Bishop) *Revue du clergé français* 56 (1908), 641–62.

Baumstark, Anton. *Liturgie comparée.* Chevetogne, 1953[3].

――――. "Zu den Problemen der Epiklese und des römischen Messkanons." *Theologische Revue* 15 (1916), 337–50.

Betz, Johannes. *Die Eucharistie in der Zeit der griechisschen Väter.* 1/1: *Die Aktualpräsenz der Person und des Heilswerkes Jesu im Abendmahl nach der vorephesinischen griechischen Patristik.* Freiburg, 1955.

Biedermann, Hermengild M. "Das Konzil von Florenz und die Einheit der Kirchen." OC 48 (1964), 23–43

Bishop, Edmund. "The Moument of Consecration." *Texts and Studies* 8/1 (1909), 126–63.

――――. "Notes and Studies" Liturgical Comments and Memoranda II." JTS 10 (1909), 592–603.

――――. "Notes and Studies: Liturgical Comments and Memoranda VIII." JTS 14 (1912), 23–29.

――――. "Notes and Studies: Liturgical Comments and Memoranda IX." JTS 14 (1912), 39–61.

Bishop, W. C. "The Primitive Form of Consecration of the Holy Eucharist." *The Church Quarterly Review* 66 (1908), 385–404.

Blaise, Albert. *Dictionnaire Latin-Francais des Auteurs Chrétiens.* Turnhout, 1954.

Bobrinskoy, Boris. "Liturgie et ecclésiologie trinitaire de sainte Basil." *Verbum Caro* 23 (1969), 1–32.

———. "Présence réelle et communion eucharistique." RSPT 53 (1969), 402–20.

———. "Le Saint-Esprit dans la Liturgie." *Studia Liturgica* 1 (1962) 47–60.

———. "Le Saint-Esprit, vie de l'église." *Contacts* 18 (1966), 179–97.

———. "Worship and the Ascension of Christ." *Studia Liturgica* 2 (1963), 108–23.

Bornet, René. *Les Commentaires byzantines de la divine liturgie du VIIe au XVe siècle.* Paris, 1966.

Botte, Bernard. "L'Anaphore Chaldéenne des Apôtres." O. Chr. P. 15 (1949), 259–76.

———. "A propos de le 'Tradition Apostolique.'" RTAM 33 (19966), 177–86.

———. *Le Canon de la Messe romaine*, Louvain, 1935.

———. "L'épiclèse dans les liturgies syriennes orientales." SE 6 (1954), 48–72.

———. "L'Epiclèse de l'Anaphore d'Hippolyte." RTAM 14 (1947), 241–51.

———. "L'Eucologe de Sérapion est-il authentique?" OC 48 (1964). 50–56.

———. "Les plus anciennes collections canoniques." OS 5 (1960), 331–50.

———. "Problèmes de l'anaphore syrienne des apôtres Addai et Mari." OS 10 (1965), 89–105.

———. (Review of Bouyer's *Eucharistie* [Paris, 1966¹]). QLP 48 (1967), 173.

———. (Review of Jugie's *De forma eucharistiae. De epiclesibus eucharisticis.* Rome, 1947). BTAM 5 (1947), 245–46.

———. (Review of Salaville's "L'épiclèse africaine"). BTAM 5 (1947), 200.

———. *La Tradition Apostolique de saint Hippolyte* (essai de reconstitution). Münster, 1963.

———. And Mohrmann, Christine. *L'ordinaire de la messe* (Texte critique, traduction et études). Paris, 1953.

Boularand, E. "L'épiclèse au concile de Florence." BLE 60 (1959), 241–73.

Bouyer, Louis. "The Different Forms of the Eucharistic Prayer and Their Genealogy." *Studia Patristica* 8 (= *Texte und Untersuchungen* 93). Edited by F. Cross. Berlin, 1966, 156–70.

———. *Eucharistie* (Theologie et Spiritualité de la prière eucharistique). Paris, 1966, 1968². Appeared in English as *Eucharist.* Translated by C. U. Quinn from the second French edition. Notre Dame, Ind., 1968. Unless otherwise noted we shall cite the page numbers from the 1966 edition together with the page numbers from the English edition which we shall place in parentheses.

Brightman, F. E. (Correspondence: Invocation in the Holy Spirit). *Theology* 9 (1924), 33–40.

Brinktrine, Johannes. "De epiclesi eucharistica." EL 37 (1923), 9–18; 49–57; 111–16; 155–64.

———. "Enthielt die alte römische Liturgie eine Epiklese?" *Römische Quartalschrift für christliche—Altertumskunde und für Kirchengeschichte* 31 (1923), 21–28.

———. "Zur Entstehung der morgenländischen Epiklese." ZKT 42 (1918), 301–26; 483–518.

———. "Neue Beiträge zur Epiklesenfrage." *Theologie und Glaube* 21 (1929), 434–51.

Brunner, Peter. "Zur Lehre vom Gottesdienst der im Namen Jesu versammelten Gemeinde." *Leiturgia* 1 (1954), 84–364. In *Leiturgia: Handbuch des evangelischen Gottesdienstes.* Edited by K. F. Müller and J. Blankenburg. Kassel, 1952 ff.

Buchwald, Rudolf. "Die Epiklese in der römischen Messe." *Weidenauer Studien* 1 (1906), 21–56.

Bulgakov, Sergius. "Das eucharistische Dogma." *Kyrios* 3 (1963), 32–57; 78–96.

Burmester, O.H.E. "The Epiklesis in the Eastern Church and the 'Heavenly Altar' of the Roman Canon." In *Tome Commémoratif du millénaire de la Bibliothèque Patriarcale d"Alexandrie.* Alexandria, 1953.

Cabasilas, Nicholas. *A Commentary on the Divine Liturgy.* Translated by J. M. Hussey & P.A. McNulty. London, 1960.

Cabrol, F. "Amen." DACL 1/1 (1924), 1554–73.

———. "Anamnèse." DACL 1/2 (1924), 1880–96.

———. "Anaphore." DACL 1/2 (1924), 1898–1918.

———. "Le canon romain et la messe." RSPT 3 (1909), 490–524.

———. "Epiclèse." DACL 5/1 (1922), 142–84.

Cagin, Paul. *L'Anaphore apostolique.* Paris, 1919.

L'Eucharistia. Paris, 1912.

Capelle, B. "L'Anaphore de Sérapion. Essai d'exégèse." *Le Muséon* 59 (1946), 425–43.

Casel, Odo. *Das christliche Opfermysterium* (Zur Morphologie und Theologie des eucharistischen Hochgebetes). Edited by Viktor Warnach. Graz, 1968.

———. "Ein orientalisches Kultwort in abendländischer Umschmelzung." JLW 11 (1931), 1–19.

———. "Die Eucharistielehre des h1. Justinus Martyr." *Katholik* 13 (1914), 153–76; 243–63; 331–55; 414–36.

———. "Die Λογικὴ Οὐσία der antiken Mystik in christlich-Liturgischer Umdeutung." *JLW* 4 (1924), 34–37.

———. "Neue Beiträge zur Epiklesenfrage." JLW 4 (1924), 169–78.

———. "Die ostchristliche Opferfeier als Mysteriengeschehen." In J. Tyciak *et al., Der christliche Osten: Geist und Gestalt.* Regensburg, 1939, 59–75.

———. (Review of Atchley's *On the epiclesis of the Eucharistic Liturgy and in the Consecration of the Font). JLW* 15 (1941), 445–447.

———. (Review of Brinktrine's "De epiclesi eucharistica"). JLW 3 (1923), 136–37.

———. (Review of H. Elfers' *Die Kirchenordnung Hippolytus von Rom).* ALW 2 (1952), 115–30, esp. 118–20;123–26; 128–29.

———. (Review of W. H. Frere's *The Anaphora of Great Eucharistic Prayer).* ALW 2 (1952), 160–64.

———. (Review of W. H. Frere's *The Primitive Consecration Prayer).* JLW 3 (1923), 173–175.

———. (Review of H. Lietzmann's, *Messe und Herrenmahl).* JLW 6 (1926), 209–17, esp. 209–14.

———. "Zur Epiklese." JLW 3 (1923), 100–102.

Chavasse, A. "L'épiclèse eucharistique dans les anciennes liturgies orientales." MSR 3 (1946), 197–206.

Clément, Olivier. "Après Vatican II: Vers un dialogue théologique entre catholiques et orthodoxes." *La Pensée Orthodoxe* 2 (1968), 39–52.

Clerici, Luigi. *Einsammlung der Zerstruten* (Liturgiegeschichtliche Untersuchung zur Vor- und Nachgeschichte der Fürbitte für die Kirche in Didache 9, 4 und 10,5) (= *Liturgiewissenschaftliche Quellen und Forschungen 44*) Münster, 1966.

Connolly, R. Hugh. "The Eucharistic Prayer of Hippolytus." JTS 39 (1938), 350–69.

———. "The Meaning of ἐπίκλησις: A Reply." JTS 25 (1923/24), 337–64.

———. "On the Meaning of 'Epiclesis.'" *Downside Review* 41 (1923), 28–43.

————. (Review of W.H. Frere's *The Primitive Consecration Prayer*). JTS 24 (1923), 457–60.

Cooper, James and MacLean, Arthur J. (eds.). *The Testament of Our Lord*. (Translated into English from the Syriac with Introduction and Notes.) Edinburgh, 1902.

Craig, R.N.S. "Nicholas Cabasilas: *An Exposition of the Divine Liturgy.*" In *Studia Patristica* 2 (= *Texte und Untersuchungen 64*). Edited by K. Aland & F. L. Cross. Berlin, 1957, 21–28.

Crehan, J. H. "Epiklesis." *A Catholic Dictionary of Theology* 2 (1967), 223–26.

Davies, J. G. *The Spirit, the Church and the Sacraments*. London, 1954.

Davis, Charles. "Understanding the Real Presence." In *The Word in History: The St. Xavier Symposium*. Edited by T. Patrick Burke. New York, 1966, 154–78.

Diekamp, Franz – Jüssen, Klaudius. *Katholische Dogmatik III: Die Lehre von den Sakramenten – Die Lehre von den letzten Dingen*. Münster, 1962¹³.

Dinesen, P. "Die Epiklese in Rahmen altkirchlicher Liturgien (Eine Studie über die Eucharistische Epiklese)." *Studia Theologica* 16 (1962), 42–107.

Dix, Gregory. "The Epiclesis: Some Considerations." *Theology* 29 (1934), 287–94.

————. "The Origins of the Epiclesis." *Theology* 28 (1934), 125–37; 187–202.

————. *The Shape of the Liturgy*. Westminster, 1945². (ed.) *The Treatise on the Apostolic Tradition of St. Hippolytus of Rome*. Reissued with corrections preface and bibliography by Henry Chadwick. London, 1968².

Dölger, Franz Joseph. *Das Fischsymbol in frühchristlicher Zeit I: Religionsgeschichtliche und epigraphische Untersuchungen*. Münster, 1928².

ΙΧΘΥΣ II: *Der heilige Fisch in den Antiken Religionen und im Christentum*. Münster, 1922.

Doresse, J. and Lanne, E. *Un Témoin archaique de la liturgie copte de S. Basile* (with Appendix by B. Capelle "Les liturgies basiliennes et saint Basile") (= *Bibliotheque de Muséon 47*).Louvain, 1960.

Drews, Paul. *Zur Entstehungsgeschichte des Kanons*. Tübingen, 1902.

Emery, P.Y. "La Cène, une liturgie ou un sacrament?" *Verbum Caro* 18 (1964), 93–107.

Engberding, Hieronymus. "Neues Licht über die Geschichte des Textes der ägyptischen Markusliturgie." OC 40 (1956), 40–68, esp. 57–68.

Evdokimov, Paul. "Eucharistie – Mystère de L'Eglise." *La Pensée Orthodoxe* 2 (1968), 53–69.

————. *L'Orthodoxie*. Neuchâtel, 1959.

————. *Faith and Order Studies* 1964–1967. (Reprinted from Faith and Order Paper No. 50: New Directions in Faith and Order. World Council of Churches, Geneva). Lausanne, 1968.

Fischer, Balthasar. "Das Gebet der Kirche, als Wesenselement des Weihsakramentes." *Liturgisches Jahrbuch* 20 (1970).

Fortescue, Adrian. *The Mass*. London, 1913².

Fransen, P.F. *Faith and the Sacraments*. London, 1958.

Frere, Walter Howard. *The Anaphora of Great Eucharistic Prayer*. London, 1938.

————. *The Primitive Consecration Prayer*. London, 1922.

Gallagher, J.F. *Significando Causant* (A Study of Sacramental Efficiency). Fribourg, 1965.

Gamber, K. "Die Christus-Epiklese in der altgallischen Liturgie." ALW 9/2 (1966), 375–82.

Geiselmann, Josef R. *Die Abendmahlslehre an der Wende der christlichen Spätantike zum Frühmittelalter*. München, 1933.

256   *Eucharistic Epiclesis*

Gill, Joseph. *The Council of Florence.* Cambridge, 1959.

Goldammer, Kurt. *Die eucharistische Epiklese in der mittelalterlichen abendländischen Frömmigkeit.* Marburg, 1941.

Gore, Charles. *The Body of Christ.* London, 1901.

Gutberlet, Konstantin. *Das heilige Sakrament des Altares.* Regensburg, 1919.

Hahn, Wilhelm. *Worhsip and Congregation.* Tranlsated by G. Buswell. London, 1963.

Harvey, W. W. (ed.) *Sancti Irenaei op. Lugdunensis libros quinque adversus haereses.* 2 vols. Cambridge, 1857.

Havet, J. "Les sacrements et le role de l'Esprit-Saint d'après Isidore de Séville." ETL 16 (1939), 32–93.

Hebert, A. Gabriel. "The Meaning of the Epiclesis." *Theology* 27 (1933), 198–210.

Höller, Joseph. *Die Epiklese der griechischorientalischen Liturgien.* Vienna, 1912.

———. "Die Epiklese in den griechischen und orientalischen Liturgien." *Historisches Jahrbuch* 35 (1914), 110–26.

Johanny, Raymond. *L'Eucharistie Centre de l'histoire du Salut chez Saint Ambroise de Milan.* Paris, 1968.

Jong, Johannes Petrus de. "Epiklese." LThK 3 (1959²), 935–37.

———. "La Connexion entre le rite de la Consignation et l'"epiclèse dans Saint Ephrem." In *Studia Patristica 2* (= *Texte und Untersuchungen 64).* Edited by K. Aland and F. L. Cross. Berlin, 1957, 29–34.

———. "Le rite de la commixtion dans la messe romaine dans ses rapports avec les liturgies syriennes." ALW 4/2 (1956), 245–78; 5/1 (1957), 33–79.

———. "Der ursprüngliche Sinn von Epiklese und Mischungsritus nach der Eucharistielehre des heiligen Irenäus." ALW 9/1 (1965), 28–47.

Jugie, Martin. "Considérations générales sur la question de l'épiclèse." EO 35 (1936), 324–30.

———. "L'épiclèse et le mot antitype de la messe de saint Basile." EO 9 (1906), 193–98.

———. "De epiclesi eucharistica secundum Basilium Magnum." *Acta Academiae Velehradensis* 19 (1948), 202–207.

———. "La forme du Sacrement de l'Eucharistie d'après Saint Irénée." *Bibliotheque de la Faculté cath. de Theol. de Lyon V: Memorial J. Chaine.* Lyon, 1950, 223–33.

———. *De forma eucharistiae. De epiclesibus eucharisticis.* Rome, 1943.

———. "Le 'Liber ad baptizandos' de Théodore de Mopsueste." EO 38 (1935), 257–71.

———. *Theologia Dogmatica Christianorum Orientalum ab Ecclesia Dissidentium III: De Sacramentis.* Paris, 1930; V: *De Theologia dogmatica Nestorianorum et Monophysitorum.* Paris, 1935

Jungmann, Jos. *Liturgie der christlichen Frühzeit* (bis auf Gregor den Grossen). Freiburg, 1967.

———. *Missarum Sollemnia.* 2 vols. Vienna, 1962⁵.

———. (Review of L. Bouyer's *Eucharisitie* [1966¹]). ZKT 89 (1967), 460–66.

Kavanagh, Aidan. "Thoughts on the New Eucharistic Prayers." *Worship* 43 (1969), 2–12

———. "Thoughts on the Roman Anaphora." *Worship* 39 (1965), 515–29; 40 (1966), 2–16.

Kern, Cyprien. "En marge de l'"Epiclèse." *Irénikon* 24 (1951), 166–94.

Kretschmar, Georg. *Studien zur frühchristlichen Trinitätstheologie* (= *Beiträge zur historischen Theologie 21*) Tübingen, 1956.

Laager, J. "Epiklesis." RAC 5 (1962), 577–99.

Lampe, G.W.H. (ed.). *A Patristic Greek Lexicon.* Oxford, 1961–68.

La Taille, Maurice de. *The Mystery of Faith.* Vol. II Translated by J. Carroll and
    P.J. Dalton. London, 1950.
Lebau, Paul. *Le vin nouveau du Royaume.* Paris, 1966.
Lebreton, Jules. "Chronique de Théologie." *Revue prat. d'apologétique* 4 (1907),
    427–37.
Lécuyer, Joseph. "La Théologie de l'anaphore selon les Pères de l'école d'Antioche."
    OS 6 (1961), 385–412. Appeared in German as "Die Theologie der Anaphore
    nach der Schule von Antiochien." LJ 11 (1961), 81–92.
Ledogar, Robert, "The Eucharistic Prayer and the Gifts over Which It Is Spoken."
    Worship 41 (1967), 578–96.
———. "Faith, Feeling, Music and the Spirit." *Worship* 43 (1969), 13–23.
Leenhardt, F.J. *et al. Le Saint-Esprit,* Geneva, 1963.
L'Huillier, Pierre. "La théologie de l'épiclèse." *Verbum Caro* 14 (1960), 307–27.
Liddell, Henry G. And Scott, Robert (eds.) *A Greek English Lexicon.* (Reprint of 1940⁹
    edition revised and augmented by H. S. Jones with assistance from R.
    McKenzie). Oxford, 1953.
Lietzmann, Hans. *Messe und Herrenmahl.* Bonn, 1926. Appearing in English as *Mass
    and Lord's Supper.* Translated by D. Reeve. Leiden, 1953 ff.
Ligier, Louis. "De la Cène de Jesus à l'Anaphore de l'Eglise." MD 87 (1966), 7–51.
———. *Magnae orationis eucharisticae seu anaphorae origo et significatio.* Rome, 1964.
Lossky, Vladimir. *The Mystical Theology of the Eastern Church.* Translated by members
    of the Fellowship of St. Alban and St. Sergius. London, 1957.
Lubac, Henri de. *Catholicisme.* Paris, 1938⁴.
MacLean, A.J. "Invocation (liturgical)." ERE 7 (1914), 407a–413a.
Macomber, W. "The Oldest Known Text of the Anaphora of the Apostles Addai and
    Mari," OCP 32 (1966), 335–71.
Maltzew, Alexios von. *Liturgikon.* Berlin, 1902.
Mascall, E.L. *Corpus Christi.* London, 1965².
Mateos, Juan. "L'action du Saint-Esprit dans la liturgie dite de S. Jean Chrysostome."
    Proche-Orient Chrétien 9 (1959), 193–208.
Maximilian of Saxony. "Pensées sur la question de l'union des Eglises." *Roma e l'Oriente*
    1 (1910), 13–29.
Merk, K.J. "Die Epiklese: Ein neuer Lösungsversuch." TQS 96 (1914), 367–400.
———. *Der Konsekrationstext der römischen Messe.* Rottenburg a. N., 1915. Pp. 103–147
    are an almost unchanged version of the preceding article.
Meyendorff, John. "Notes on the Orthodox Understanding of the Eucharist."
    Concilium 4/3 (Burns and Oates edition) (1967), 27–30.
Mingana, A. *Commentary of Theodore of Mopsuestia on the Lord's Prayer and on the
    Sacraments of Baptism and the Eucharist* (= *Woodbrooke Studies* 6). Cambridge,
    1933.
Moreau, Josaphat. *Les anaphores des liturgies de saint Jean Chrysostome et de saint Basile
    comparées aux Canons Romain et Callican.* Paris, 1927.
Nissiotis, Nikos. "Pneumatological Christology as a Presupposition of Ecclesiology."
    Oecumenica 2 (1967), 235–52.
———. "Pneumatologie orthodoxe." In F.J. Leenhardt *et al. Le Saint-Esprit.* Geneva,
    1963, 85–106.
———. "Worship, Eucharist and Intercommunion: An orthodox reflection." *Studia
    Liturgica* 2 (1963), 193–222.

Nötscher, F. "Epiklesis in biblischer Beleuchtung." *Biblica* 30 (1949), 401–404.

Oesterley, W.O.E. *The Jewish Background of the Liturgy.* Oxford, 1925.

Paquier, Richard. *Traité de Liturgie.* Neuchâtel, 1954.

Pascher, Joseph, *Eucharistia* Münster, 1953⁷.

———. *Form und Formenwandel sakramentaler Feier.* Münster, 1949.

Perler, O. "Logos und Eucharistie nach Justinus I Apol. c. 66." DT 18 (1940), 296–316.

Peterson, Erik. "Die Bedeutung von *anadeiknumi* in den griechischen Liturgien," In *Festgabe für Adolf Deissmann.* Tübingen, 1927, 302–26.

Pièdagnel, Auguste and Paris, Pierre (eds.). *Cyrille de Jérusalem: Catéechèses Mystagogiques* (= SC 126). Paris, 1966.

Pohle, Joseph—Gummersbach, J. *Lehrbuch der Dogmatik III: Sakramentenlehre und Eschatologie.* Paderborn, 1960¹⁰). *N.B.* In citing this work we shall either list it as Pohle-Gummersbach in which case we are referring to the 1960, 10th edition (an unchanged reprint of the 1937⁹ edition), or as Pohle, with the year and the number of the edition when it is a question of an earlier edition.

Porter, W.S. "The Mozarbic *Post Pridie.*" JTS 44 (1943), 182–94.

Pourrat, Pierre. *La Théologie Sacramentaire.* Paris, 1908³.

Powers, Joseph M. *Eucharistic Theology.* New York, 1967.

Quasten, Johannes. *Patrology.* 3 vols. Westminster, Md,. 1950–1960.

Rabau, J. "L'Invocation du Saint-Esprit dans la Messe." *Collectanea Mechliniensis* 33 (1948). 29–43.

Raes, A. "L'Authenticité de la Liturgie Byzantine de S. Jean Chrysostome." O.Chr.P. 24 (1958), 5–16.

———. "Un nouveau document de la Liturgie de S. Basile." O.Chr.P. 26 (1960), 401–11.

Rahner, K. "Die Gegenwart Christi im Sakrament des Herrenmahles." In *Schriften zur Theologie IV.* Einsiedeln, 1960, 357–85. Appeared in English as "The Presence of Christ in the Sacrament of the Lord's Supper." *Theological Investigations IV.* Translated by K. Smyth. London, 1966, 287–311.

———. "Über die Dauer der Gegenwart Christi nach der Kommunion." In *Schriften zur Theologie IV.* Einsiedeln, 1960, 387–97. Appeared in English as, "On the Duration of the Presence of Christ after Communion." *Theological Investigations IV.* Translated by K. Smyth. London, 1966, 312–320.

———. "Wort und Eucharistie." In *Schriften zur Theologie IV.* Einsiedeln, 1960, 313–55. Appeared in English as, "The Word and the Eucharist." *Theological Investigations IV.* Translated by K. Smyth. London, 1966, 253–86.

———. "Zur Theologie des Symbols." In *Schriften zur Theologie IV.* Einsiedeln, 1960, 275–311. Appeared in English as, "The Theology of the Symbol." *Theological Investigations IV.* Translated by K. Smyth. London, 1966, 221–52.

Ratcliff, Edward. "The original form of the anaphora of Addai and Mari." JTS 30 (1929), 23–32.

Rauschen, Gerhard. *Eucharistie und Bussakrament in den ersten sechs Jahrhunderten der Kirche.* Freibourg i. Br., 1910².

Reine, Francis. *The Eucharistic Doctrine and Liturgy of the Mystagogical Catecheses of Theodore of Mopsuestia.* Washington, D.C., 1942.

Renz, Franz S. *Die Geschichte des Messopfer-Begriffs I: Altertum u. Mittelalter.* Freising, 1901.

Richardson, Cyril C. "A Note on the Epicleses in Hippolytus and the Testamentum Domini." RTAM 15 (1948), 357–59.

———. "The Origin of the Epiclesis." *Anglican Theological Review* 28 (1946), 148–53.

———. "The So-Called Epiclesis in Hippolytus." HTR 40 (1947), 101–108.

Ritter, Karl Bernhard. "Bemerkungen zur eucharistischen Epiklese." In *Kosmos und Ekklesia.* (*Festschrift* for W. Stählin). Edited by H.D. Wendland. Kassel, 1953, 163–73.

Robinson, J. Armitage. "Invocation in the Holy Eucharist." *Theology* 8 (1924), 89–100.

Roguet, A.M. *L'Eucharistie I* (Translation into French of S.T. III, qq. 73–78 with doctrinal notes in an appendix). Paris, 1960.

Rupprecht, Placidus. "Zum Vollbegriff der eucharistischen Konsekration." DT 15 (1937), 371–414.

Sage, A. "Saint Augustin et le prière du canon "Supplices quaesumus." REB 11 (1953), 252–65.

Salaville, Sévérien. "A propos de l'épiclèse." *Revue augustinienne* 14 (1909), 547–68.

"Consécration et épiclèse d'après Chosrov le Grand." EO 14 (1911), 10–16.

———. "La consécration eucharistique d'après quelques auteurs grecs et syriens." EO 3 (1910), 321–324.

———. "La double épiclèse des anaphors égyptiennes." EO 13 (1910), 133–34.

———. "L' épiclèse africaine." EO 39 (1941/42), 268–82.

———. "L' épiclèse d'après sain Jean Chrysostome et la tradition occidentale." EO 11 (1908), 101–12.

———. "L'épiclèse dans le canon romain de la messe." *Revue augustinienne* 14 (1909), 303–18.

———. "Epiclèse eucharistique." DThC 5/1 (1913), 194–300. This article has appeared in the numerous reprints of the DThC but, as far as we can determine, without any revision.

———. "Epiclèse eucharistique." *Catholicisme* 4 (1956), 302–307. *N.B.* This article will always be cited fully to avoid confusion with the article bearing the same title which appeared in DThC 5/1 (1913) and which we have cited often.

———. "Les fondements scripturaires de l'épiclèse." EO 12 (1909), 5–14.

———. "La Liturgie décrite par saint Justin et l'épiclèse." EO 12, (1909), 129–36; 222–27.

———. "Le nouveau fragment d'anaphore égyptienne de Deir-Balyzeh." EO 12 (1909), 329–35.

———. "Spiritus liturgiae orientalis et doctrina de epiclesis in theologia orientali." *Acta V. Vonventus Congressus Velehradensis.* Olmütz, 1927, 131–39.

———. *Studia Orientalia Liturgico-Theologica.* Rome, 1940

Schillebeeckx, E.H. *Christ the Sacrament of the Encounter with God.* Stagbook edition. Translated by P. Barrett and N.D. Smith. London, 1963.

———. *The Eucharist.* Stagbook edition. Translated by N.D. Smith. London, 1968.

———. *De Sacramentele Heilseconomie,* Antwerp, 1952.

Schmaus, M. *Katholische Dogmatik IV/1: Die Lehre von den Sakramenten.* Munich, 1964[6].

Schmidt-Lauber, Hand-Christoph. *Die Eucharistie als Entfaltung der Verba Testamenti.* Kassel, 1957.

Schoonenberg, Piet. "The Real Presence in Contemporary Discussion." *Theology Digest* 15 (1967), 3–11.

Schultze, Bernhard. "Zum Problem der Epiklese anlässlich der Veröffentlichung eines russinschen Theologen" (Cyprian Kern). O.Chr.P. 15 (1949), 368–404.

Semmelroth, Otto. "Personalismus und Sakramentalismus." In *Theologie in Geschichte und Gegenwart.* Editied by J. Auer and II. Volk. Munich, 1957, 199–218.

Smit, G.C. "Epiclèse et Théologie des Sacrements." MSR 15 (1958), 95–136.

Spacil, Theophilus. "Doctrina theologiae Orientis separati de ss. Eucharistia." *Orientalia Christiana* 13 (1928), 189–280; 14 (1929), 5–173.

———. "Lis de epiclesi." (A review of G. Kosteljnik's book entitled *Lis de epiclesis inter orientem et occidentem*). Or.Chr.A. 16 (1929), 99–114.

Srawley, James H. *The Early History of the Liturgy.* Cambridge, 1947².

Stählin, Rudolf. "Der Herr ist Geist." In *Kosmos und Ekklesia (Festschrift* for W. Stählin). Edited by H.D. Wendland. Kassel, 1953, 40–54.

Stolz, Anselmo, *Manuale Theologiae Dogmaticae VI: De Sacramentis.* Freiburg i. Br., 1943.

Struckmann, Adolf. *Die Gegenwart Christi in der heiligen Eucharistie* (Nach den schriftlichen Quellen der Vornizänischen Zeit). Vienna, 1905.

Thurian, Max. *L'Eucharistie, Mémorial du Seigneur, Sacrifice d'action de grace et d'intercession.* Lausanne, 1963².

———. *Le pain unique.* Taizé, 1967.

Tillard, J.M.R. "L'Eucharistie et le Saint-Esprit." NRT 90 (April, 1968), 362–87.

———. *The Eucharist: Pasch of God's People.* Translated by D. Wienk. New York, 1967.

Tonneau, Raymond—DeVreesse, Robert. *Les Homélies Catéchétiques de Théodore de Mopsueste* (= *Studi e Testi* 145). Vatican City, 1949.

Trembelas, Panagiotis. *Dogmatique de l'eglise orthodoxe catholique III: Les Sacrements— Eschatologie.* Translated by P. Dumont, Paris, 1968.

Tyrer, J.W. *The Eucharistic Epiclesis.* London, 1917.

———. "The meaning of Epiklesis." JTS 25 (1923/24), 139–50.

Vagaggini, Cipriano. *The Canon of the Mass and Liturgical Reform.* Translation editor, Peter Coughlan. Staten Island, N.J., 1967.

Varaine, Francisque. *L'épiclèse eucharistique* (étude de théologie positive et de l'histoire liturgique). Lyon, 1910.

———. "L'épiclèse eucharistique." QLP 1 (1911), 119–31.

Verheul, A. *Introduction to the Liturgy* (Towards a Theology of Worship). Translated by M. Clark. London, 1967.

Vischer, Lukas. "Epiklese, Zeichen der Einheit, der Erneuerung und des Aufbruchs." *Oecumenica* 2 (1967), 302–12. Appeared in English as, "The Epiclesis: Sign of Unity and Renewal," *Studia Liturgica* 6 (1969), 30–39.

Ware, Timothy. *Eustratios Argenti* (A study of the Greek Church under Turkish Rule). Oxford, 1964.

Wetter, Gillis P. *Altchristliche Liturgien I: Das christliche Mysterium.* Göttingen, 1921

Woolley, Reginald W. *The Liturgy of the Primitive Church.* Cambridge, 1910.

Index

About the Liturgical Institute

The Liturgical Institute, founded in 2000 by His Eminence Francis Cardinal George of Chicago, offers a variety of options for education in Liturgical Studies. A unified, rites-based core curriculum constitutes the foundation of the program, providing integrated and balanced studies toward the advancement of the renewal promoted by the Second Vatican Council. The musical, artistic, and architectural dimensions of worship are given particular emphasis in the curriculum. Institute students are encouraged to participate in its "liturgical heart" of daily Mass and Morning and Evening Prayer. The academic program of the Institute serves a diverse, international student population — laity, religious, and clergy — who are preparing for service in parishes, dioceses, and religious communities. Personalized mentoring is provided in view of each student's ministerial and professional goals. The Institute is housed on the campus of the University of St. Mary of the Lake/Mundelein Seminary, which offers the largest priestly formation program in the United States and is the center of the permanent diaconate and lay ministry training programs of the Archdiocese of Chicago. In addition, the University has the distinction of being the first chartered institution of higher learning in Chicago (1844), and one of only seven pontifical faculties in North America.

For more information about the Liturgical Institute and its programs, contact: usml.edu/liturgicalinstitute. Phone: 847-837-4542. E-mail: litinst@usml.edu.

Msgr. Reynold Hillenbrand
1904-1979

Monsignor Reynold Hillenbrand, ordained a priest by Cardinal George Mundelein in 1929, was Rector of St. Mary of the Lake Seminary from 1936 to 1944.

He was a leading figure in the liturgical and social action movement in the United States during the 1930s and worked to promote active, intelligent, and informed participation in the Church's liturgy.

He believed that a reconstruction of society would occur as a result of the renewal of the Christian spirit, whose source and center is the liturgy.

Hillenbrand taught that, since the ultimate purpose of Catholic action is to Christianize society, the renewal of the liturgy must undoubtedly play the key role in achieving this goal.

Hillenbrand Books strives to reflect the spirit of Monsignor Reynold Hillenbrand's pioneering work by making available innovative and scholarly resources that advance the liturgical and sacramental life of the Church.